SAP PRESS e-books

Print or e-book, Kindle or iPad, workplace or airplane: Choose where and how to read your SAP PRESS books! You can now get all our titles as e-books, too:

- ▶ By download and online access
- ▶ For all popular devices
- ▶ And, of course, DRM-free

Convinced? Then go to **www.sap-press.com** and get your e-book today.

Self-Services with SAP® ERP HCM

 **PRESS**

SAP PRESS is a joint initiative of SAP and Galileo Press. The know-how offered by SAP specialists combined with the expertise of the Galileo Press publishing house offers the reader expert books in the field. SAP PRESS features first-hand information and expert advice, and provides useful skills for professional decision-making.

SAP PRESS offers a variety of books on technical and business-related topics for the SAP user. For further information, please visit our website: *www.sap-press.com*.

Martin Gillet
Configuring and Customizing Employee and
Manager Self-Services in SAP ERP HCM
2011, 580 pp., hardcover
ISBN 978-1-59229-356-8

Justin Morgalis, Brandon Toombs
SAP ERP HCM Processes and Forms
2013, 344 pp., hardcover
ISBN 978-1-59229-425-1

Amy Grubb, Luke Marson
SuccessFactors with SAP ERP HCM:
Business Processes and Use (2nd Edition)
2015, 644 pp., hardcover
ISBN 978-1-4932-1173-9

Manuel Gallardo, Martin Gillet
SAP CATS: Configuration, Use, and Processes
2014, 464 pp., hardcover
ISBN 978-1-59229-978-2

Jeremy Masters, Brandon Toombs, Kris Bland, Justin Morgalis

Self-Services with SAP® ERP HCM

ESS, MSS, and HR Renewal

Galileo Press

Bonn • Boston

Galileo Press is named after the Italian physicist, mathematician, and philosopher Galileo Galilei (1564 – 1642). He is known as one of the founders of modern science and an advocate of our contemporary, heliocentric worldview. His words *Eppur si muove* (And yet it moves) have become legendary. The Galileo Press logo depicts Jupiter orbited by the four Galilean moons, which were discovered by Galileo in 1610.

Editor Emily Nicholls
Copyeditor Melinda Rankin
Cover Design Graham Geary
Photo Credit Shutterstock.com/167347892/© Gajus
Layout Design Vera Brauner
Production Graham Geary
Typesetting SatzPro, Krefeld (Germany)
Printed and bound in the United States of America, on paper from sustainable sources

ISBN 978-1-59229-984-3
© 2015 by Galileo Press Inc., Boston (MA)
1st edition 2015

Library of Congress Cataloging-in-Publication Data
Bland, Kris.
Self-services with SAP ERP HCM : ESS, MSS, and HR renewal / Kris Bland, Jeremy Masters, Justin Morgalis,
Brandon Toombs. -- 1st edition.
pages cm
Includes index.
ISBN 978-1-59229-984-3 (print : alk. paper) -- ISBN 1-59229-984-9 (print : alk. paper) -- ISBN 978-1-59229-985-0 (ebook)
-- ISBN 978-1-59229-986-7 (print and ebook : alk. paper) 1. SAP ERP. 2. Personnel management--Data processing.
3. Personnel management--Computer programs. 4. Web services. 5. Service-oriented architecture (Computer science)
6. Management information systems. I. Title.
HF5549.5.D37B425 2014
658.300285'53--dc23
2014040400

Contents at a Glance

Dear Reader,

As with new products or paradigms like HR Renewal, new books are met with a mix of excitement and intrigue from their readers. *What's really new here?* you may be asking. *What's the connection with everything I already know? Will it really change my work, or is it just marketing hype?*

So please bear with me, dear reader, as I shamelessly borrow a few key design principles from SAP's new UX strategy and apply them loosely to this book to show you what's ahead. *Self-Services with SAP ERP HCM* is the following:

▶ Role-based: Provides you with the information about the state of ESS, MSS, and HR Professional self-services that you need.

▶ Responsive: Offers you targeted insight based on existing self-services arrangements.

▶ Simple: Outlines the essential features and functions enabled by HR Renewal.

▶ Coherent: Teaches you the changing language of self-services in an increasingly mobile HCM landscape, and applies those ideas throughout.

▶ Delightful: Explains with playful irreverence how SAP is updating its longstanding self-services offering.

So tell us what you think! We at SAP PRESS would be interested to hear your opinion of *Self-Services with SAP ERP HCM*. How could it be improved? Your comments and suggestions are the most useful tools to help us make our books the best they can be, so we encourage you to share your feedback. Thank you for purchasing a book from SAP PRESS!

Emily Nicholls
Editor, SAP PRESS

Galileo Press
Boston, MA

emily.nicholls@galileo-press.com
www.sap-press.com

Contents

9   Best Practices and Additional Resources 297

10   Summary 319

Appendices 325

Foreword: The New Age of Self-Service

As we jump into the digital age, we increasingly expect information to be readily available at our fingertips, on demand. Gone are the days in which people guarded their data and held personal information behind lock and key. A new generation has arisen that challenges those mindsets and demands more in terms of self-service capabilities. The challenge for conventional HR systems is to respond.

How does HR move forward? Can an organization engage and empower employees in clever, adaptive ways? A self-service strategy has to be at the heart of it.

At Comcast, we implemented SAP ERP HCM Employee Self-Service in late 2007. We dipped our toes into these waters of enabling basic features of address changes, direct deposits, and updating emergency contacts—and were surprised by our immediate success. One month in, we had eliminated over 30,000 manual transactions that once would have been faxed to headquarters and keyed into our legacy systems. One year and new features later, we'd executed over 150,000 automated transactions, giving employees and managers robust self-service capabilities.

From the beginnings of that journey, we have added features for managers to see more information on their teams, approve time, make merit and bonus decisions, and approve and initiate transactions that impact employees. With our latest implementation of SuccessFactors, our team leaders can directly participate in the annual talent assessment program, making their role even more critical in talent development programs.

For employees, we introduced new features, such as the ability to enter time and view pay statements, which has also driven high volumes of activity. On average, our self-service portal sees between 30,000 and 40,000 unique logins a day. On a busy day tied to the release of our quarterly bonus payouts (which link performance and customer satisfaction to impact employee pay), we see over 50,000 unique people entering the portal.

A robust learning catalog and course library puts employees into the driver's seat of both their learning development and their careers, with the added capability to complete the online employee talent profile. Managers can now recommend training that aligns with employee goals and development areas. Enhanced visibility for employees and managers has driven high levels of engagement for our organization, as evidenced in our approximately 90% or higher completion rates of key compliance activity and annual performance processes.

As we look forward at Comcast, we will continue to evolve our self-service tools to meet the needs of a company that dwells at the intersection of media and technology. We will drive more self-service features to our customers *and* to our employees: rich user interfaces that attract and simplify the user experience for employees and new features and capabilities that allow employees and managers access to data and tasks from anywhere. We will seek to implement a modified version of the Xfinity Olympic Experience to transform our self-service capabilities in order to scale "Every Minute, OnDemand" on a variety of desktop and mobile-enabled platforms.

We hear the challenge for conventional HR systems and are responding—and wish you good luck on your journey as you do the same.

Sissy Abraham
Vice President, HR Systems and Technology, Comcast

Leo Gampa
Director SAP HR Systems, Comcast

Preface

Even 15 years after the first self-services for employees and managers were available in SAP, deploying them has still been a challenge. Let's set the stage by looking at the concept of self-service within a service delivery model and then preview the book's target audience, layout, and release coverage to address this topic.

At its most basic level, self-service is a mechanism for empowering end users to own and manage their data. Driving ownership and responsibility to the right person helps ensure that there is data integrity. Within an HR context, self-service is particularly important because a lot of HR data is classified as private, and some data have payroll and compensation implications if incorrect.

Thinking more broadly, self-service is part of a larger service delivery model that many organizations today struggle to manage. Delivery of service is sometimes thought of in terms of tiers or layers. In a tiered model, such as the one shown in Figure 1, the premise is to ensure that you are pushing as many transactions as possible down to lowest level possible. In HR's case, this means using Employee and Manager Self-Services (ESS and MSS).

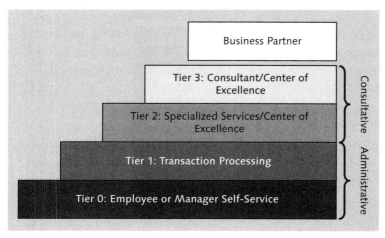

Figure 1 Service Delivery Tiers

Tiers within an HR service delivery model can be grouped as follows:

▶ Tier 0 is Employee and Manager Self-Service. The objective is to achieve over 80% of user transactions being performed by employees and managers themselves, typically online through a portal or on a mobile device. An example activity for this tier is an employee updating his or her address on the portal.

▶ Tier 1 is for transaction processing, in which an agent from a service center or an HR professional handles a request from an employee or manager by phone, email, or fax and performs the transaction on behalf of the caller. This should be about 16% of transactions. An example activity for this tier is an employee calling in to a service center (or to his or her local HR professional) to obtain employment verification.

▶ Tiers 2 and 3 are specialized and consultative services that involve a center of excellence (or its equivalent) in your organization; these tiers handle 3% and 1% of transactions, respectively. Questions that go to these tiers are those for which HR specialists in functional areas can counsel on HR policies that are not clear to the employee or manager (for example, a compensation specialist answering a question posed by an HR professional on a compensation policy, such as the lump sum payment process during the annual merit increase cycle).

▶ The topmost layer is for the HR business partner, whose role now becomes more strategic. "Strategic HR" is a wider topic in and of itself well beyond the scope of this book, but an easy example is a senior HR business partner rethinking how his or her organization can provide more robust analytics to its managers and executives through dashboards and other tools.

Although it's great to have a perspective on the delivery of HR services, implementing these solutions doesn't ensure that they will be automatically adopted by our user community if we follow this service model. Since the beginning of self-service, user adoption has been the earmark for success, because if self-service—the bottom tier of the delivery pyramid—is not adopted, then your users will ultimately reject the solution.

Now that we have a framework for understanding HR service delivery, let's step back and look at the history of self-service within SAP ERP HCM. This will bring added perspective when we start introducing the latest innovations around SAP ERP HCM self-services. Many readers may have already implemented at least some scope of self-service functionality for HR at their companies. Some of them probably still struggle with keeping up with the latest innovations (for a variety of reasons). To understand where we are and where we want to go, it helps to know where we have been.

In the beginning, there was the Internet Transaction Server (ITS), which was the basis for SAP's first web applications. Back in 1997, the first ESS functionality was available from SAP. The focus was on employee personal data, such as employee addresses available in straightforward services, such as an employee directory. ITS provided one of the first multitiered platforms on an SAP ERP system. For all its ugliness by today's UI standards, it was a fairly dependable platform (and is still around in the form of an internal ITS). Although the screens look quaint today, at the time they were a big deal, and they paved the way for future innovation in HR Professional Self-Services within SAP.

After another iteration of web technology (including a design SAP called "frog-design"), HTML Business (HTMLB) was developed. HTMLB consisted of a library of screen elements based on the familiar HTML languages to ensure consistent usage and look and feel across all SAP web applications. Additional services for HR were created using HTMLB and the EnjoySAP theme, which some readers probably remember.

A turning point came in 2001, when SAP acquired TopTier for $400 million. Its CEO, Shai Agassi, became the president of SAP Portals, and the TopTier Portal became the SAP Portal, version 5.0. This SAP Portal team wrapped the new portal around the existing ITS framework and provided single sign-on (SSO) between the two for a seamless authentication experience.

The introduction of the business package (BP) in 2004 was an important step to provide a cohesive set of web applications in various roles. The practical idea behind these BPs was to provide an accelerated way to deploy self-services using the SAP NetWeaver Portal framework, now called the SAP Enterprise Portal. Pre-packaged roles, worksets, pages, and iViews were made available for customers to enable a quicker time to value by reducing the time to implement.

All across HR, functional areas were expanded to cover most employee and manager services, including benefits and payment, working time, career and job, employee search, personal data, travel management, corporate information, and life and work events services. Managers could initiate and approve so-called personnel change requests (PCRs); this functionality was the forerunner of our current HCM Processes and Forms functionality.

Around 2006, a catalog of BPs made available in the SAP NetWeaver Portal for customers was expanded to include the following elements:

▸ BP for Employee Self-Service

▸ BP for Manager Self-Service

▸ BP for HR Administrator

▸ BP for Compensation Specialists

▸ BP for Learning

▸ BP for Instructor/Tutor

▸ BP for Talent Development Specialist

▸ BP for Talent Management Specialist

▸ BP for HR Executive Analytics

▸ BP for Employee Interaction Center

▸ BP for Recruiting Administrator

As part of the SAP ERP 5.0 release in 2007, the introduction of the Homepage framework provided a way to manage Employee and Manager Self-Services from the SAP backend—that is, from the SAP GUI. Configuration in the Homepage framework (Figure 2) influenced the navigation and services offered on the SAP Enterprise Portal.

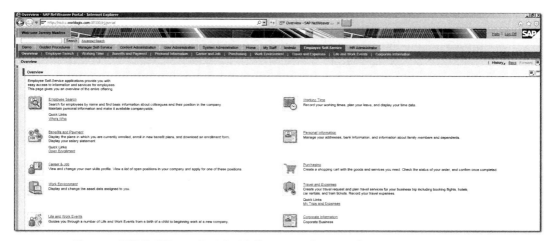

Figure 2 SAP NetWeaver Portal with Homepage Framework

BP innovations continued from 2008 to 2012, even as SAP changed technologies and converted most of Web Dynpro for Java to Web Dynpro for ABAP. Despite this massive overhaul, most customers still have a mix of ITS, JSP, BSP, Web Dynpro for Java, and Web Dynpro for ABAP services. This makes for a complicated landscape that's been a challenge to maintain for many customers.

In 2013, at its annual conference, SAPPHIRE, SAP introduced a new vision of web applications: SAP Fiori and its underlying technology, SAPUI5.

> **Additional Information**
>
> For detailed information on prior versions of SAP's Employee and Manager Self-Services, refer to the SAP PRESS book *Implementing Employee and Manager Self-Services in SAP ERP HCM*, by Jeremy Masters and Christos Kotsakis (SAP PRESS, 2008). The book is now available only on Amazon.
>
> For an implementation guide of less dated ESS and MSS, refer to *Configuring and Customizing Employee and Manager Self-Services in SAP ERP HCM* by Martin Gillet (SAP PRESS, 2011).

Our current state of self-services lies squarely in the SAPUI5 technology. Whether it is consumed within the SAP Enterprise Portal, SAP NetWeaver Business Client, or SAP Fiori Launchpad, accessing SAPUI5 applications will be the go-forward state of self-services within SAP for the foreseeable future. The abundance and use of mobile devices in the workplace (and at home) have been the major influences on this set of next-generation services for employees, managers, and HR professionals. In response, SAPUI5 and SAP Fiori are SAP's answer to simplification and "anytime, anywhere" access.

As important as knowing where we have been is imagining where we are going. What's ahead for empowering our workforce using smarter and more intuitive technology? What will employee and manager solutions look like in 10, 20, or even 30 years? Certainly, wearable devices (including glasses, watches, and jackets) have already been invented and even implemented in some scenarios. Some employers have already begun pilot programs to monitor employee health via a bracelet that tracks fitness data. Despite the exciting opportunities associated with wearable technology, privacy issues will be the biggest impediment for these types of forward-thinking scenarios in the future. Time will tell whether these types of innovations will be widely adopted.

As with wearable tech, the proliferation of the *Internet of Things* (IoT) also provides some unique opportunities for HR technology. Forecasters say that by 2016 there will be over 19 billion connected things—from personal computers, to tablets, to smartphones, and beyond. But how will an even more interconnected world provide opportunities for a more connected and productive workforce? Again, time will tell.

So, where does this book fit in?

Target Audience

This book is written for HR and IT professionals and SAP ERP HCM consultants interested in understanding the steps needed to deliver and operationally support a successful self-service implementation using the latest SAP versions.

Project and program managers of self-service implementations and upgrades will also find this book helpful. We expect that the information in this book will resonate with both project leaders and team members; the lessons illustrated here can provide immediate value, especially for those implementing self-services technology for the first time. For those customers already using an older version of self-service in SAP ERP HCM, we also believe this book provides significant value, because we review the latest technologies and services available in recent feature packs and enhancement packages. We also round out the book by providing an overview of SAP's self-service roadmap for HCM.

Book Layout

We have organized the book both to help you explore the components of a self-service project and to assist you such a project's implementation. The book begins with an introduction to the changing landscape of self-service and then covers more technical topics, including user interface technologies, deployment options, and mobility. We review a wide range of functional and technical subjects, including configuration, portal, search, security, and integration. The book concludes with a resources chapter that contains useful information for your project team to reference.

Let's take a quick look at what will be covered in each chapter.

▶ **Chapter 1** covers the new landscape, configurations, and deployment options in today's self-service implementations, including hybrid and mobility.

▶ In **Chapter 2**, we explore the options available for customers from a deployment perspective. With the emergence of new technologies (such as SAP NetWeaver Business Client and SAP HANA Cloud Portal) and third-party portals, it's important to ground the reader in these topics before stepping further into the book.

▶ **Chapter 3** explains the new user interface (UI) technologies available using SAP. Topic areas include the latest functional areas (including HR Renewal and SAP Fiori), which serve as the best examples of how to leverage the new SAPUI5 framework.

▶ In **Chapter 4**, **Chapter 5**, and **Chapter 6**, we cover the features and functions of the ESS, MSS, and HR Professional platforms using SAP ERP HCM and offer a full description of each work area.

▶ **Chapter 7** explores connecting on-premise and cloud self-service functionality with mobile devices. It focuses on the mobility offerings from SAP, including those via the SAP Mobile Platform and SAP Fiori. Alternative third-party solutions will also be discussed so that customers and consultants understand some additional options for extending self-service applications to a mobile device.

▶ **Chapter 8** covers SAP Fiori. In this chapter, we review the functionality provided within the SAP Fiori framework for employees and managers and the associated launchpad. We also explore the reasons that SAP Fiori came to be and dig into why SAP has seemingly provided two separate (competing?) self-service solutions.

▶ **Chapter 9** will provide you with best practices and valuable resources for additional help on self-service, including key resources from the SAP Community Network (SCN), SAP Help, SAP Service Marketplace, SAP PRESS, and SAPInsider and a discussion of conferences you can attend.

▶ A summary is provided in **Chapter 10**, in which we look back at the ground we've covered.

Product Releases

Although many of the concepts and configuration elements apply to all versions of SAP, this book is based on the latest version of SAP ERP, which at the time of writing is SAP ERP 6.0 EHP 7.

Using EHP 7 as a baseline will keep this book relevant for years to come, because SAPUI5 technology will be the de facto standard for some time. We'll also cover the latest versions of the popular portals to access self-services within SAP ERP HCM: SAP Enterprise Portal 7.4, SAP NetWeaver Business Client 4.0, and SAP Fiori Launchpad.

Conclusion

This book serves as a comprehensive guide for understanding and implementing self-service solutions in your SAP ERP HCM system for employees, managers, and/or HR professionals. It highlights important process constructs, explains key implementation components, and provides best practices for implementation. We hope you enjoy reading the book as much as we enjoyed writing it.

Acknowledgments

This project draws inspiration from the efforts and support of many individuals. Without these friends and colleagues, this book would not have been possible.

Thank you first to our friends at SAP PRESS for their guidance, patience, and support. We would especially like to thank Emily Nicholls, who made this book possible and encouraged us to get the words onto the printed page. A special thanks to Florian Zimniak and the SAP PRESS editorial board for their patience throughout this project.

We would also like to thank our friends at SAP for their support during this project, including Carrie Lande, Simone Roth, Gertrud Beisel, and Parvathy Sankar.

We owe the utmost gratitude to our families, who supported us during the writing of this book. Thank you for your love and patience throughout this project.

We hope you find this book informative and easy to read. We are hopeful that we will provide you with new perspectives and food for thought as you embark on your self-service implementations.

Jeremy Masters, **Brandon Toombs**, **Kris Bland**, and **Justin Morgalis**
January 2015

A lot of changes are occurring right now in SAP ERP HCM. This chapter describes the application technologies that SAP is investing in and why.

1 The Changing Landscape of Self-Service with SAP ERP HCM

When you work with technology, you are confronted with change on a regular basis. In fact, change is the name of the game: newer technologies enable better processes and higher adoption, driving everything forward.

In the world of HR at SAP, change has happened almost constantly since SAP ERP HCM came into being. However, because of market forces and technical innovations in the past three to four years, the rate of change has accelerated to a level unprecedented in the history of SAP ERP HCM.

In this chapter, we will first discuss the drivers behind the changes. We will take some time to discuss the application technologies that SAP is using to build the next generation of its user interfaces for SAP ERP HCM, which are part of SAP's go-forward strategy, and will mention those technologies that are *not* part of the go-forward strategy.

1.1 Why Are Things Changing?

Before we talk about the "what," it's important to that we talk about the "why" of important shifts in HR. Two key trends that are impacting the SAP ERP HCM applications are the cloud and mobility.

Any application can be loosely defined as being *cloud based* if it is managed by a third party and is delivered over the Internet rather than being housed on a server that the customer owns. Almost all leading cloud applications are also *multitenant*, which means that everyone is running the same set of code. A good analogy is an apartment building: occupants may have their own décor but they all share the same plumbing, electrical, foundation, and roof. From an application standpoint, the key benefit of a multitenant architecture is that a change only needs to be made in one place. Contrast this with the software world, in which a company like SAP must maintain numerous versions of its software because customers upgrade their software at their own pace. It is much easier to evolve and innovate on a cloud platform.

Two impacts have been felt from the cloud trend—one general and one specific. The general impact is that because cloud applications are able to constantly innovate, a competitive pressure has developed around SAP's on-premise HR solution, SAP ERP HCM, and its aging user interface (UI). To respond to this pressure, SAP has invested significantly in revamping its core SAP ERP HCM. SAP has even gone so far as to adopt a quarterly release cycle for some of its SAP ERP HCM products in order to accelerate the benefits to its customers.

The specific impact of the cloud came in the form of an acquisition. In 2012, SAP acquired one of the leaders in the talent management marketplace, SuccessFactors. From the day that the merger was made official, SAP has made it clear that the go-forward technology for talent management solutions was going to be SuccessFactors. Therefore, if an SAP ERP HCM customer wants to align with SAP's future direction, that customer will be moving to a hybrid landscape—that is, the customer would keep core SAP ERP HCM on-premise (or "in house") and move talent functions for performance, recruiting, and succession, for example, to the cloud with SuccessFactors.

Hybrid Integration

Because the focus of this book is core SAP ERP HCM technologies rather than talent management, we will only briefly touch on hybrid integration. For a closer look at hybrid integration, we recommend the SAP PRESS book *SuccessFactors with SAP ERP HCM: Business Processes and Use* by Amy Grubb and Luke Marson (2nd edition, 2015).

It is not hyperbole to state that the advent of smartphones and tablets has fundamentally changed expectations of how users can interact with the technology in their lives. It is no longer acceptable to expect users to only interact thorough a laptop. In fact, more and more of us are using our laptops less and less; instead, we now demand mobile access to the tools we need to do our jobs.

As we will discuss later in this chapter, SAP recognized this trend and has responded by investing in new programming technologies that are mobile capable.

It has also learned the primary lesson of mobile development: develop simplified, focused applications that serve one purpose and serve it well.

In this way, marketplace pressures play a key role in the decisions that SAP has made about which technologies to invest in and which to deemphasize. In this chapter, we'll walk through the technologies that are part of SAP's go-forward strategy (Section 1.2) and then those technologies that, although still supported by SAP, are most likely not the source of future investments from an SAP ERP HCM perspective (Section 1.3).

1.2   Go-Forward Technologies

In this section, our objective is to introduce the key go-forward SAP ERP HCM technologies so that you have a better sense of what the technologies do and SAP's current intentions for their use. We will also highlight which technologies we will discuss in greater detail in subsequent chapters in this book.

1.2.1   HR Renewal

If you think of SAP ERP HCM as a house, that house currently has a nice 1980s look. It's probably time to get rid of the shag carpet and possibly update the countertops.

HR Renewal is an initiative within SAP to remodel the look and feel of core SAP ERP HCM and to revamp the way that users interact with the foundational aspects of SAP ERP HCM: Personnel Administration and Organizational Management. The end result of HR Renewal is to remake the core HCM UI in order to provide a "consumer-grade" user experience.

To accomplish this task, HR Renewal is built on two key technologies: SAPUI5 and Web Dynpro for ABAP.

SAPUI5

SAPUI5 is SAP's latest application technology. It is written to take advantage of the next generation of web tools, known as HTML5. HTML5 was created by the internet community at large to take advantage of multimedia and mobile applications without requiring extra plug-ins. SAPUI5 has a special library to make it easier to develop SAP applications for HTML5 with the following benefits:

▶ **Mobile-responsive design**
Probably the most important aspect of SAPUI5 is that it is capable of mobile-responsive design, which means that the application can detect the type of device that is currently accessing it and can display its screen appropriately. This means that an application can look "right" regardless of whether its user is on a laptop, tablet, or smartphone.

▶ **More advanced look and feel**
SAPUI5 applications look advanced and are more on par with the leading-edge applications that employees are using on their own devices. The user interactions and scrollbars are smoother and more in line with what users experience on best-of-breed smartphone and tablet applications. As you can see in Figure 1.1, the SAPUI5 look and feel is clean and colorful.

▶ **Faster performance**
SAPUI5 uses OData, which is a protocol that handles the back-and-forth communication between the UI and the backend database in an efficient manner that speeds up the user experience.

Figure 1.1 SAP UI5 Example

To tap into these benefits, SAP has started rebuilding Employee Self-Service (ESS), Manager Self-Service (MSS), and HR administrator functionality based on SAPUI5. As of the time of this writing, many of the ESS view-only services and the MSS Team Viewer have been rebuilt on this new technology. It can be assumed that SAP will be heavily biased toward using SAPUI5 for any new interface development required for SAP ERP HCM in the near future.

If there is a primary downside to SAPUI5, it is that it requires a separate server process, called SAP Gateway, in order to render. We will talk more about SAP Gateway in Chapter 3.

Because SAPUI5 has been used recently to create new home screens for the ESS, MSS, and HR Professional roles, much of the new functionality we will be discussing in this book is written in SAPUI5.

Web Dynpro for ABAP

SAPUI5 is the sleek new thoroughbred for web-based user design, but let's not forget the current workhorse, Web Dynpro for ABAP.

Over the past few years, SAP has consolidated almost all HR web development into Web Dynpro for ABAP. Web Dynpro for ABAP's biggest strength lies in the fact that it is based on ABAP. Considering that the entire SAP ecosystem is quite familiar with ABAP, barriers to its adoption were very low. In addition, unlike many of the other technologies on this list, Web Dynpro for ABAP can run directly from an SAP ERP environment—no additional server is required. Fewer servers mean fewer points of failure.

SAP has streamlined the Web Dynpro development process even further with the advent of its Floorplan Manager (FPM) framework, which programmers use to build modular components that can communicate with one another. This speeds up the development process and results in a consistent UI, which in turns speeds user adoption. You'll see this modular design through the book. The personal profile contains several subcomponents that are tied to the overall application using configuration.

Web Dynpro for ABAP has two key limitations. First, and most critically, it is not capable of mobile-responsive design, which is pretty devastating in a mobile-enabled world. Second, Web Dynpro for ABAP does not allow client-side scripting. Client-side scripting is a piece of code that runs on the browser without having to talk to the backend server. Its absence means that almost every user interaction with the application requires a communication with the backend server. This slows the response time on user commands.

Still, let the record show that for applications that do *not* need to be mobile enabled and *don't* require a "cutting-edge" look and feel, Web Dynpro for ABAP is a prudent choice. Although SAP is certainly rewriting some applications to use SAPUI5 and moving away from Web Dynpro for ABAP, the sheer number of Web Dynpro for ABAP applications for SAP ERP HCM means that Web Dynpro for ABAP will remain the backbone for SAP ERP HCM web enablement for the fore-seeable future.

The next tool doesn't necessarily fall under the HR Renewal umbrella, but it is still important to consider.

1.2.2   SAP Fiori

As we'll discuss in more detail in Chapter 8, SAP Fiori is an initiative across SAP to provide simple, consumer-grade, mobile-ready applications that customers can use out of the box. SAP Fiori is meant to serve as the flagship for future UI devel-opment across all of SAP, so a great deal of time has been spent on the UI controls so that the applications follow a few key design principles:

▶ Role-based experience, meaning that tasks are organized by whoever performs them

▶ Responsive design to enable presentation on a desktop, smartphone, or tablet

▶ 1-1-3 (one user, one use case, and three screens) paradigm

▶ Apps that speak the same language

▶ Low barriers to adoption

Like many of the ESS, MSS, and HR Professional applications we will be review-ing in depth later in the book, SAP Fiori applications are written in SAPUI5, so they inherit SAPUI5's positive characteristics: mobile responsiveness, modern look and feel, and so on. Think of SAP Fiori as a tightly controlled subset of SAPUI5. As a consequence, applications are not intended to be adjusted signifi-cantly by customers.

Of the bundle of applications that come with SAP Fiori, several are HR based: My Leave Requests (ESS), Leave Request Approval (MSS), My Timesheet (ESS),

Timesheet Approval (MSS), My Paystubs (ESS), and My Benefits (ESS). You'll notice that there is overlap between SAP Fiori applications for HR and SAPUI5 HR Renewal applications. For example, the SAPUI5 version of ESS that we will discuss in this book has an SAPUI5 pay statement, and SAP Fiori also has the My Paystubs application. Why is this?

The simple answer is that SAP Fiori is an initiative that began with the idea of packaging many company applications in several functional areas: Cash Management, Sales Order, Materials Management, Human Resources, and so on. These applications were to be sold by SAP (at one point, additional license fees were to be required) to provide instant, across-the-business value. Thus, the SAP Fiori group within SAP had cherry-picked a few HR applications for the bundle; meanwhile, the core SAP ERP HCM design team had continued with their work of using SAPUI5 to rebuild the ESS, MSS, and HR Professional roles.

The result is parallel solutions in select situations in SAP ERP HCM. Because the ESS, MSS, and HR Professional SAPUI5 solutions were comprehensive in nature—and were already available to them, instead of purchasable by them—many customers had chosen to focus on the applications delivered by the core SAP ERP HCM design team.

The situation became more interesting in May of 2014 when SAP announced at SAPPHIRE that SAP Fiori applications would no longer carry an additional license fee, effectively leaving customers free to choose between SAP Fiori applications and non-SAP Fiori applications without worrying about the costs involved.

What's a customer to do? HR Renewal, or SAP Fiori? SAP will undoubtedly move to a unified set of HR applications over time; we expect SAP to adopt the look and feel of SAP Fiori as the UI for HR Renewal. However, organizations can feel comfortable that the underlying application logic will not be rewritten. Therefore, even if, for example, the HR Professional main page is altered to be more like SAP Fiori, organizations should not have to make major configuration changes.

1.2.3 SAP GUI

Considering that the Windows GUI has been around for more than two decades, the idea of referring to it as a go-forward area and a source of future investment may seem like a stretch. Indeed, SAP clearly intends for casual users to move away from accessing the GUI on an ongoing basis and instead use HR Renewal and/or SAP Fiori applications.

However, it needs to be noted here that SAP GUI has been and will continue to remain the primary point of access for power users. It is feature rich and surprisingly responsive. The reality is that "/oSE16N" will continue to be typed into countless keyboards for the foreseeable future.

However, SAP also has a few surprises in store for the GUI, in the form of Screen Personas. SAP Screen Personas is the product of SAP Imagineering, a unit that co-innovates with SAP customers and partners. It is a toolset that companies can use to quickly build streamlined, attractive UIs within the GUI itself. Business users with limited training can even create forms with it. SAP Screen Personas can hide unnecessary fields and automate keystrokes. End users who accomplish specialized, repeated tasks can use SAP Screen Personas to build their own screens that focus on only those fields that they need to interact with.

As with SAP Fiori, SAP additional license fees were previously charged for SAP Screen Personas, producing an impediment to its adoption. However, these additional costs were also eliminated in May of 2014. Because SAP has already invested in other technologies to build streamlined UIs for ESS, MSS, and now HR Professional users, the use of SAP Screen Personas has not been as high in HR as in other SAP modules. Accordingly, SAP Screen Personas will not be covered in this book. However, if your organization relies heavily on Windows GUI, you may want to give some thought to using SAP Screen Personas.

Where does that leave us with the technologies on SAP's plate? Table 1.1 outlines the pros and cons of each to give you a brief snapshot of their characteristics.

Technology	Description	Pros	Cons
SAPUI5	New look and feel employed by HR Renewal for landing pages.	Mobile-responsive and advanced look and feel.	Requires SAP Gateway server.
Web Dynpro for ABAP	Main technology used today to enable HCM content for the web.	No additional costs or servers required.	Not mobile responsive.

Table 1.1 Go-Forward Technologies

Technology	Description	Pros	Cons
SAP Fiori	Cutting-edge applications delivered by SAP.	Mobile-enabled versions of key HCM applications.	Requires SAP Gateway server; only partial HCM coverage.
GUI/SAP Screen Personas	Toolset to create streamlined GUI HCM transactions.	Easy creation of streamlined screens for GUI.	Toolset only; requires build by customer to get value. Also, Windows GUI based rather than web based.

Table 1.1 Go-Forward Technologies (Cont.)

1.3   Legacy Technologies

Having previewed the path forward, we are going to briefly look at some of the previous technologies that we can now state fairly conclusively are no longer in SAP ERP HCM's go-forward strategy. We do not present these in order to depress any reader whose company is currently using these tools. Instead, we present these in order to emphasize that further investment in these areas is probably not the wisest long-term decision.

That's not to say that these tools are unsupported or that these technologies are not the current status quo in other SAP modules. What we *are* saying is that, from our perspective, these are the tools that are being deemphasized in the area of SAP ERP HCM going forward.

Without further ado let's take a moment to consider the technologies we have lost over the past decade:

▶ **Internet Transaction Server ESS**
The ITS was developed to faithfully render SAP Windows GUI in a web page. Although this served a necessary purpose—presenting Windows GUI–based pages to "plug holes" in self-service offerings—SAP took the effort a step further and made ITS the basis for all ESS services. Needless to say, this did not result in the most attractive frontend, so it was discontinued.

▶ **SAP Web Dynpro for Java ESS**
SAP's next generation of ESS was based on Web Dynpro for Java. Web Dynpro

for Java ran on a Java server, with function calls going back to SAP ERP HCM. It was light years ahead of ITS-based ESS in performance and look and feel, but its Achilles heel was the development infrastructure that had to be installed in order to make any changes to its functionality. Many developers have reported spending months getting the infrastructure up and running in order to make a few hours' worth of changes.

- **Manager's Desktop**
  SAP's first foray in to Manager Self-Service was useful, but it had one small flaw: it was not web enabled. Considering that Manager's Desktop was developed almost 20 years ago, if your company is still using this tool you should probably turn in your pagers and consider an upgrade.

- **Manager Self-Service 1.0**
  Manager Self-Service 1.0, the first version of MSS to be completely web enabled, was largely successful. It introduced the personnel change requests (PCRs), which were the precursor of the present-day HCM Processes and Forms. If users had a complaint with this version of MSS, it was the performance issues, particularly for higher-level managers.

- **Manager Self-Service (Adobe Flash based)**
  The Adobe Flash MSS frontend has the distinction of being the shortest-lived of all of the discarded technologies on this list. The downfall for this UI is that it relied upon Adobe Flash Islands, which is not mobile friendly.

- **Adobe Interactive Forms**
  Adobe Interactive Forms served as the first frontend for HCM Processes and Forms, and we can now consider it on life support. Three challenges limited its adoption by the SAP ERP HCM install base: companies had to pay an additional license cost for its use; they had to maintain an additional plug-in on individual users' desktops, creating support headaches; and many people found the UI to be a step backward with its paper-like look and feel.

Because Adobe Interactive Forms is technically still in use in HR Renewal, we cannot explicitly state that it is not part of SAP's go-forward strategy. However, it has been made clear in recent releases of HR Renewal that the Adobe Interactive Forms UI is being deemphasized. It's our opinion that companies rolling out new forms should not use the Adobe Interactive Forms framework.

1.4 Summary

In this chapter, we have spent some time talking about the drivers behind the upheaval in SAP ERP HCM and reviewed the application technologies that are integral parts of SAP's go-forward strategy. In the next chapter, we will discuss the deployment options available for accessing those technologies.

This chapter covers all of the options available for customers from a deployment perspective. With the emergence of new technologies, such as SAP NetWeaver Business Client, SAP HANA Cloud Portal, and third-party portals, it is important to cover these topics before proceeding further into the book.

2   Deployment Options

In the previous chapter, we painted SAP's change initiative in the SAP ERP HCM self-services space in broad strokes. We introduced terms such as SAPUI5 and cloud. We also covered some technologies that have slipped into obsolescence now that SAP has decided to party like it's no longer 1999.

In this chapter, we'll focus on how you can bring these newer technologies to bear on your organization. In terms of UI technology, the introduction of all of these new options has also led to a number of new deployment possibilities for these new technologies. Before we dive deeper into self-services, we need to define the deployment options. The purpose of this chapter to introduce and describe SAP's current deployment options, portal or otherwise, for delivering self-services.

First up, in the interests of thoroughness, is the SAP GUI and its ability to act as a deployment option for the latest updates of SAP ERP HCM self-services.

2.1   SAP GUI

The venerable SAP GUI is still a vital part of any customer's implementation of SAP ERP HCM. It is not going away anytime soon. That said, it was a marginal player in the self-services game *before* the latest innovations—meaning that attempting to use it as a full-featured self-service deployment option is no longer only a fool's errand but also, in fact, impossible.

In the past, by using tools such as the Manager's Desktop and some creative use of transactions it was possible to approve items and take some remedial actions in self-services from the SAP GUI. Now, because HCM Processes and Forms (to show just one example) cannot use the workflow inbox from the SAP GUI to approve items, attempting to leverage the SAP GUI as your primary option for self-services is akin to trying to use an abacus to do payroll.

However, the SAP GUI space is not entirely without innovation; clearly new updates and new functionalities, such as the introduction of SAP Screen Personas, occur regularly. In terms of implementing SAP ERP HCM self-services, however, SAP GUI won't offer enough firepower.

That's where SAP Enterprise Portal comes into play.

2.2 SAP Enterprise Portal

The SAP Enterprise Portal (formerly the SAP NetWeaver Portal) has been the standard method of deploying and accessing SAP ERP HCM self-services for the last decade, and, in the face of all of this new innovation from SAP, it is thriving. As they say, rumors of its demise have been greatly exaggerated.

In fact, the SAP Enterprise Portal has been consistently and constantly updated with new features, technologies, and themes, to the point that the latest releases bear very little resemblance to the portal of five years ago. As of the time of writing (fall 2014), the latest release of SAP Enterprise Portal is SAP Enterprise Portal 7.4 SP 5; it is SAP HANA enabled for the modern user experience platform, integrating with SAP Fiori. It is also integrated with the latest technologies from SAP—that is, SAPUI5 and SAP Gateway—which allows it to serve up both the latest SAPUI5-based applications and the traditional Web Dynpro for ABAP Floorplan Manager applications. SAP Enterprise Portal 7.4 also includes a new UI Theme Designer, which allows fine-tuning of several new themes introduced to the portal. These new features and innovations mean that the SAP Enterprise Portal is ready and able to be accessed via any mobile device or traditional desktop, as shown in Figure 2.1.

Figure 2.1 SAP Enterprise Portal on Various Platforms

Innovations and new technologies have come fast and heavy for the SAP Enterprise Portal in recent years. However, SAP's commitment to the platform seems unchanged for the foreseeable future. The introduction of an SAP HANA-enabled version of the portal complete with SAPUI5 support means that the SAP Enterprise Portal is still the primary source of self-services and will be for some time to come.

Ajax (which stands for "Asynchronous JavaScript and XML") is a group of interrelated web development techniques that are used to create web applications, primarily on the client-side. Introduced in SAP NetWeaver 7.0 EHP 2 as an alternative to the traditional SAP Enterprise Portal default framework page, the Ajax Framework Page (AFP) provides an enhanced user experience, enhanced functionality, and an Ajax-based development infrastructure. AFP takes a lot of the page's functionality and moves it to the client side, allowing for increased usability. By caching elements such as navigation hierarchies on the client side, AFP circumvents the need to go to the server to refresh the page, effectively reducing data load, increasing performance, and allowing for a "flicker-free" experience for the user. Figure 2.2 shows the default AFP in action.

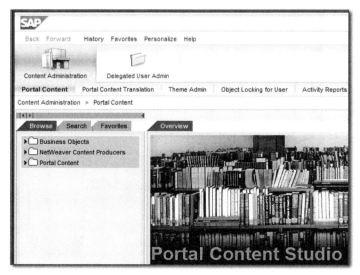

Figure 2.2 Ajax Framework Page Look and Feel

This new development infrastructure gives portal developers and administrators more freedom to customize the look and feel of the SAP Enterprise Portal. The move to Ajax allows for the use of more client-side scripting, opening up a world of new possibilities to those with the skillset to take advantage of it, but therein lies one of the drawbacks of the Ajax Framework Page: more options and power are usually accompanied by more work. Customizing a portal using the AFP takes more time and requires more development than the traditional framework page. Don't be too afraid of rolling up your sleeves, though; after all, as of SAP NetWeaver 7.3, the AFP is the default framework page of SAP Enterprise Portal.

Portal Look and Feel

In our experience with many clients and many implementations, one of the most over-looked aspects of a customer's implementation of SAP ERP HCM self-services is the portal look and feel. Too often, responsibility for such portal customization falls outside the domain of most existing client resources, and the project plan has not adequately accounted for this need.

The standard SAP Enterprise Portal look and feel works for delivering self-service functionality, but what it lacks is everything that is unique to *your* company: your brand, your theme, and your personality. Because self-services are often the face of HR to your employees, it's usually worth the (relatively small) expenditure in time and money to bring it up to par with your company's intranet presence.

One of the main issues with the AFP, or the SAP Enterprise Portal as a whole, is the issue of mobile access. If your organization is ready and willing to go to SAPUI5 landing pages for your self-service needs, then the solution to this mobility issue within the SAP Enterprise Portal is...wait for it...SAP Enterprise Portal mobile edition, which we talk about next.

2.3   SAP Enterprise Portal Mobile Edition

There is no escape from mobility affecting how we work. Sometimes, it seems to take strenuous effort *not* to act like your mobile device is surgically attached to your body—or maybe that's just us. SAP has not ignored this new business reality (even if it took them a bit of time to catch up to it). Over the past couple of years, SAP has introduced the SAP Enterprise Portal mobile edition to help bring some of your favorite portal content to your smartphone and tablet devices.

There have been attempts by SAP to provide some mobile services in the past, such as the mobile universal worklist (UWL) on Java, but with the change from Web Dynpro for Java to Web Dynpro for ABAP a shift needed to be made to stay consistent while still providing mobile capability on the new platform. Hence, SAP Enterprise Portal mobile edition was introduced.

SAP Enterprise Portal mobile edition leverages existing SAP Enterprise Portal installations by sitting on top of the SAP Enterprise Portal and providing alias rules based on device type; it routes users to the normal SAP Enterprise Portal if they are using a desktop and to the mobile portal if they are using a smartphone or tablet, as shown in Figure 2.3. This is called the *multichannel approach*, in which the same content can be provided through multiple channels on multiple devices while using one infrastructure.

SAP Enterprise Portal mobile edition has several similarities to the traditional SAP Enterprise Portal. First, it provides role-based content, meaning that content is served based on the roles that a user has (i.e., employees get ESS, managers get MSS, and so on). Second, it supports personalization. However, unlike the traditional SAP Enterprise Portal, the mobile edition can be consumed on any mobile device, because it delivers predefined templates (analogous to apps) for common portal content, such as My Paystub, My Spend, and various approvals. The SAP Enterprise Portal mobile edition also serves up reports and administrative functions, such as Portal Content Management, Portal Site Management, and Web Page Composer.

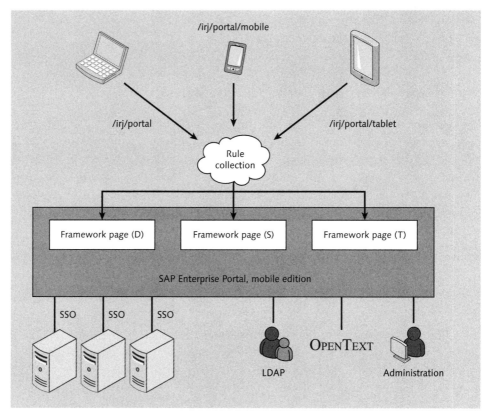

Figure 2.3 SAP Enterprise Portal Mobile Edition

In the world of SAP ERP HCM, the primary driver for mobility is usually approvals. The SAP Enterprise Portal mobile edition replaces the traditional Java-based UWL with a newer, mobile-friendly, HTML5-based mobile UWL (Figure 2.4).

In keeping with the multichannel approach espoused by the SAP Enterprise Portal mobile edition, requests originating from desktop computers would still use the traditional, Java-based UWL, whereas tablets and smartphones would be directed to the new mobile UWL.

Figure 2.4 Mobile Universal Worklist

One final note on the SAP Enterprise Portal mobile edition: although SAP's mobile portal may seem like an alternative to SAP Fiori, which we will talk about in more depth in Chapter 8, SAP Fiori has been designed to be more of a complementary component rather than a competitor.

SAP Fiori is just one set of "apps" available to the end user, with the SAP Enterprise Portal mobile edition potentially serving up SAP-delivered or even third-party apps as well as reports and administrative content.

Although SAP makes a great portal, as we have seen, not all customers choose to use SAP Enterprise Portal or its mobile edition. Some customers choose to use other, third-party portals for their self-service needs.

2.4 Third-Party Portals

Back in the day—say, five years ago—if you wanted an SAP online presence, for most people the only good option was SAP Enterprise Portal. With the vast majority of online applications running on the Web Dynpro for Java platform, the SAP Enterprise Portal and its Java stack were a necessity. However, thanks to the conversion of self-service applications from Web Dynpro for Java to Web

Dynpro for ABAP and now to SAPUI5, the SAP Enterprise Portal's Java stack is not the primary method of serving these applications to the user.

This conversion has opened the door for third-party portals, making them actual, reasonable alternatives to the SAP Enterprise Portal. Although they were feasible before, they required much in the way of connectors to be built in order to run Web Dynpro for Java applications. On the other hand, Web Dynpro for ABAP applications are simply served by calling a URL and are much easier to call into a third-party portal.

Many robust third-party portals can work with SAP self-services applications— including Microsoft's SharePoint, IBM's WebSphere, and RedHat's JBoss—and even Oracle's WebLogic application servers can work with a portal that can consume and deliver SAP applications. This means that more customers with mature portals can add SAP self-services without deploying SAP Enterprise Portal for the sole purpose of delivering ESS and MSS.

2.5   SAP NetWeaver Business Client

Third-party portals are definitely an option for customers looking for SAP self-services without using SAP Enterprise Portal, but they are not the only option. Recent innovations and content releases in the SAP NetWeaver Business Client have now made it a viable option to deliver SAP ERP HCM self-services to customers with certain requirements.

The SAP NetWeaver Business Client is a role-based single point of access for SAP Business Suite applications. It embeds both SAP GUI for Windows and Web Dynpro for ABAP applications, giving a consistent user experience. The goal is to use this consistent experience to increase productivity.

SAP NetWeaver Business Client comes in two different flavors: SAP NetWeaver Business Client for Desktop and SAP NetWeaver Business Client for HTML, which is browser based. Further complicating—that is, enhancing—our options is that SAP NetWeaver Business Client for HTML also comes either for Web Dynpro for ABAP or SAPUI5. Figure 2.5 through Figure 2.8 show different types of content rendered in SAP NetWeaver Business Client: Web Dynpro transactions, Web Dynpro for ABAP applications, SAPUI5 content, and web content, respectively.

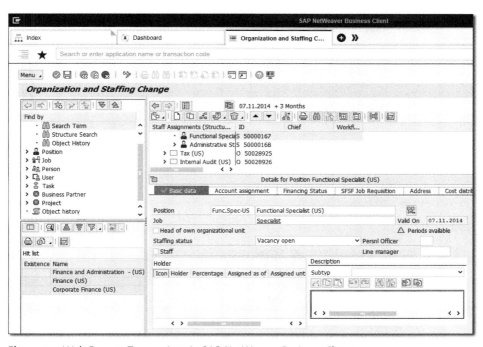

Figure 2.5 Web Dynpro Transactions in SAP NetWeaver Business Client

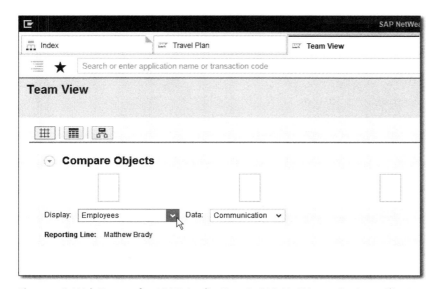

Figure 2.6 Web Dynpro for ABAP Applications in SAP NetWeaver Business Client

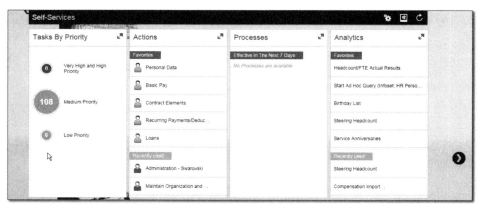

Figure 2.7 SAPUI5 Content in SAP NetWeaver Business Client

Figure 2.8 Web Content in SAP NetWeaver Business Client

From an end user perspective, there is little difference between SAP NetWeaver Business Client for Desktop and SAP NetWeaver Business Client for HTML. The user either starts the SAP NetWeaver Business Client from his or her desktop or opens a browser window and then navigates to the SAP NetWeaver Business Client landing page. Once accessed, SAP NetWeaver Business Client will behave similarly across all platforms. However, for deciding which route to choose for SAP NetWeaver Business Client, Table 2.1 provides some comparison criteria that can be helpful when assessing which direction to go.

Characteristic	SAP NetWeaver Business Client for Desktop	SAP NetWeaver Business Client for HTML
User type	Power users	Casual users
Installation type	Installed on desktop	Zero installation; accessible from anywhere
Type of GUI	Embeds SAP GUI for Windows	Integrated in web browser (uses SAP GUI for HTML)
Role of SAP Enterprise Portal	Can use SAP Enterprise Portal, including role content	Doesn't use SAP Enterprise Portal
Platform	Runs only on Windows	Runs on any platform

Table 2.1 Comparing SAP NetWeaver Business Client for Desktop and for HTML

Alongside SAP Enterprise Portal, SAP NetWeaver Business Client is considered part of the SAP User Experience as one of its UI clients. When deciding between the SAP Enterprise Portal and SAP NetWeaver Business Client, consider the factors listed in Table 2.2.

Characteristic	SAP NetWeaver Business Client	SAP Enterprise Portal
User access	Windows and browser	Browser only
Purpose	Successor to SAPLogon/SAP GUI standalone	Portal demand for intranet/externet (on-premise, on demand)
Environment	Mainly ABAP environment	Heterogeneous environment
UI technologies	Integration of web UI technologies (Web Dynpro, side panel), SAPUI5	Integration of web UI technologies (Web Dynpro, side panel), SAPUI5
System access	Access to one main system with casual access to other systems	Focus on portal-like scenarios with access to a large set of systems
Additional features	Configurable entry pages	

Table 2.2 Comparing SAP NetWeaver Business Client to SAP Enterprise Portal

SAP NetWeaver Business Client is a viable option for delivering self-services. If SAP NetWeaver Business Client is in use for certain segments of the user population, such as HR professionals or other power users, and you want to augment their SAP NetWeaver Business Client with self-services, that is absolutely an option. If there is no other portal requirement, then SAP NetWeaver Business Client might prove to be an economical option. However, in many cases, businesses use their portals for many things other than simply self-services, so using SAP NetWeaver Business Client as the primary means of self-service delivery would make little sense.

2.6   SAP HANA Cloud Portal

According to SAP:

> *SAP HANA Cloud Portal is SAP's new cloud-based solution for easy site creation and consumption with a consumer-grade user experience. It is designed for mobile consumption and is based on SAPUI5. Using SAP HANA Cloud Portal, customers can connect SAP applications, reports, and social content. It is powered by SAP HANA via SAP HANA Cloud.*

That is the official definition of SAP HANA Cloud Portal—but what does it really mean, underneath the jargon?

SAP HANA Cloud Portal is a type of *platform as a service*, or PaaS. Platform as a service is a category of cloud computing services that provides a platform and a solution stack as a service. In this model, the consumer creates applications or services by using tools from the provider. The consumer also controls the deployment and configuration of these applications. The provider provides the networks, servers, storage, and any other service required to host the application.

SAP takes this concept to the next level with SAP HANA Cloud Portal, creating a *portal platform as a service*, or portal PaaS. SAP HANA Cloud Portal provides an on-demand portal with a lean, flexible portal PaaS and with fast time to value due to regular updates. SAP HANA Cloud Portal also has easy integration with any on-premise solution currently being run via the SAP Cloud Connector. SAP HANA Cloud Portal is a scalable, public cloud, which means lower total cost of ownership as well. It is also standards based and on an open platform. Figure 2.9 shows the high level architecture of SAP HANA Cloud Portal, with the SAP HANA Cloud Portal running on top of the SAP HANA Cloud Platform and using SAP Gateway and SAP Cloud Connector to integrate with SAP Business Suite where needed.

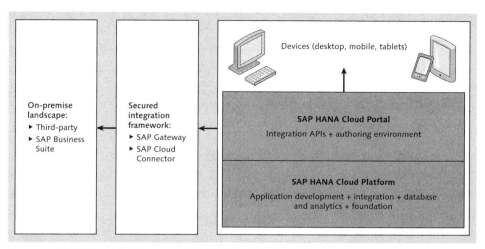

Figure 2.9 High-Level Architecture of SAP HANA Cloud Portal

Currently, the SAP HANA Cloud Portal is designed to have a consumer-grade user experience, designed for mobility and access via any device. It has a SuccessFactors extensions UI framework and integration with SAP Jam. SAP Fiori and SAP Lumira integration are also on the short-term roadmap. Extensions of this platform as a service are possible using the Metadata Framework (MDF). And, to repeat, because it is such an important feature, SAP Cloud Connector allows customers to leverage their existing on-premise investments.

How does this relate to self-services? Why would you care about SAP HANA Cloud Portal in your quest to provide online self-services to employees and managers? SAP HANA Cloud Portal is not an avenue by which to deliver traditional self-service applications, nor is it meant as a replacement for the SAP Enterprise Portal.

Instead, it is meant to provide a platform for cloud applications to run, whether they are custom or prepackaged. Custom SAPUI5 applications running in the SAP HANA Cloud Portal and providing self-services is a real business case, but that is not to be confused with hosting and delivering traditional SAP business packages, such as ESS and MSS. SAP HANA Cloud Portal's true destiny lies in that it will be the future integration hub for on-premise and cloud applications. The new SAPUI5 self-service applications can be consumed by the SAP HANA Cloud Portal and delivered to various devices alongside any custom cloud applications that you would choose to develop.

The bottom line for SAP HANA Cloud Portal for SAP ERP HCM and self-services is that it is something to be aware of. SAP HANA is a powerful technology that, to date, has not shown to be hugely important in the SAP ERP HCM space. Real-time access to data has not been a big driver for SAP ERP HCM applications, so it is rarely HR that makes the business case to move to SAP HANA. If your organization *does* move to SAP HANA, then it does make sense to attempt to utilize the tools at your disposal—in that case, SAP HANA Cloud Portal—for delivering new, cloud-based applications to your user base. These applications can be homegrown or can use the available integration with SAP business applications side by side in an on-demand architecture. SAP HANA Cloud Portal provides an opportunity to extend SAP's cloud offerings in a seamless way, which is not something that the traditional SAP Enterprise Portal can do.

2.7 Summary

In this chapter, we set out to discuss all the various deployment options available to a customer looking to implement SAP ERP HCM self-services in the current environment. We'll move from infrastructure that can deliver the content to applications in subsequent chapters; when we get into the meat of ESS, MSS, and the HR Professional role, that content will be able to be served via multiple channels. We talked about those channels in this chapter.

First, we took a look at the venerable SAP GUI and how its usefulness for self-services has passed. We then spent some time talking about the SAP Enterprise Portal's most recent innovations and the fact that, as a deployment option, it is as relevant as ever. We briefly talked about the Ajax Framework Page as a part of our SAP Enterprise Portal discussion. We moved on to talk about the SAP Enterprise Portal mobile edition and its ability to stand alongside the SAP Enterprise Portal and serve content to mobile devices. Next, we talked about the capabilities of SAP to support third-party portals as a deployment option.

Then, we talked about the SAP NetWeaver Business Client and its various flavors and strengths. We wrapped up by talking about the SAP HANA Cloud Portal and about how it allows you to extend SAP's cloud offerings in a seamless way. In our next chapter, we will talk about how SAP has undertaken a large effort to "consumerize" its user interface technologies in order to provide a more robust and intuitive user experience.

This chapter explains the new UI technologies that are available when using HR Renewal in SAP. It will cover the latest functional releases as well as supporting technologies.

3   Refreshing the UI

What's in a name? In the case of SAP's HR Renewal program, the answer is a lot. HR Renewal is SAP's effort to modernize its SAP ERP HCM user interface and functionality to the point of delivering not only a user interface but also a user experience of the quality now expected by consumers. Contemporary consumers of technology now demand more than an artless collection of data, controls, and words on a screen or a simple user interface. A user experience is deeper than merely using the software to accomplish a task. It involves reaching the user emotionally as well.

Although it may sound strange to be talking about self-services software reaching us emotionally, all consumer-grade software does this at some innate level. For example, our interaction with our desktops, our smartphones, or even our DVRs immerses us subconsciously to a degree. The design goal of consumer-grade software has moved from "functional" to "enjoyable." In fact, "functional" has almost become a sort of backhanded compliment in this context.

It is in this new market that SAP finds itself. HR Renewal is SAP's program to move SAP ERP HCM from a user interface (UI) to a user experience (UX).

3.1   From UI to UX

We have reached an interesting point in the field of personal technology.

For the first time, an enterprise's employees have better technology in their pockets than they have at their desks at work—and this fact has not gone unnoticed by either the employees or their enterprises. The "consumerization" of IT has become a real push, both by enterprises for internal usage and by enterprise software vendors. The renewed focus on the user and his or her experience has set clear expectations for a more consumer-driven and simplified user experience. This evolution of user expectations is at the heart of SAP's drive to move from a traditional UI to a UX.

Consumer-grade software has started to become an enormous influence over enterprise software, primarily because of the stark contrasts that could be drawn between them. In self-services more than any other area in SAP, this has been a drawn-out issue. Many of SAP's criticisms in the self-service space had been centered on the idea that something may work well enough but it is ugly and ungainly. Many customers we have encountered offer a highly designed and customized corporate intranet experience but then rely on standard SAP self-services in the standard theme and on a standard portal for its employees. The contrast is notable, and it can send several messages, none of them particularly good:

▸ This is how my company regards its employees and the services that are important to them.

▸ This is how critical my company thinks HR is to its overall mission.

▸ My HR department is very behind the times.

The new push into the UX space allows enterprises to avoid this pitfall either through the use of an SAP Rapid Deployment solution or by providing the toolset needed to create a custom UX for your employees. Given that the typical release of an SAP implementation at a customer usually takes the better part of a year and that that window of time can often span an entire generation of consumer software, clearly something needed to change. Before we go into the tools available, it is important that we understand SAP's overall UX strategy.

In the interests of simplicity, let's just start this section with the main question: why a UX, SAP? Simply stated, the answer is *value*. And by "value" we mean money, in all sorts of direct and indirect forms. SAP's UX strategy delivers value by enabling enterprises to achieve the following goals:

▸ **Gain productivity**
Simpler and mobile software means more and more efficient usage anywhere a user goes.

▸ **Increase user adoption**
User-centric design leads to a more personalized experience that is more likely to be used early and often to get the job done.

▶ **Decrease errors**
Simpler, role-based software reduces the risk of data entry errors. Fewer mistakes means lower cost of potential rework.

▶ **Decrease training costs**
Simpler, more intuitive software means a reduced need for large training staffs and classes, lowering training costs as a result.

Once we know *why*, let's talk about *how*, which is arguably more important anyway. SAP's UX strategy focuses on the three key words: *New*, *Renew*, and *Enable*. These ideas describe how SAP wants its customers to approach their options going forward with their UX-to-be.

3.1.1 New

The concept behind New is that SAP wants to provide a consumer-grade UX for all new applications, or applications that will be brand-new for a customer. These are not upgrades but new functionality.

SAP has started this process, using SAP HANA and SAPUI5 as core technologies. This effort will continue for cloud-based, mobile, SAP HANA, and on-premise software. What's key here is that SAP isn't simply releasing new versions of this software; it's changing its thinking on how to deliver it.

For new applications, SAP wants customers using its latest and greatest technologies: SAPUI5 on SAP Gateway (or SAP Fiori with SAP Fiori Launchpad), preferably on SAP HANA.

SAP HANA

SAP HANA is definitely a big buzzword and, according to SAP, a foundation for SAP's future technology base. Its in-memory capability is a boon for industries that need that real-time data and feedback as a crucial component of their core business.

To date, however, we have not seen a use case in the SAP ERP HCM space that would require that level of real-time data. For the purposes of the self-service space, we will choose to be SAP HANA agnostic, in the sense that our discussions are not going to be impacted by whether or not you, as a customer, choose to use SAP HANA. It is not typically HCM that drives the decision for SAP HANA, but if your enterprise is using SAP HANA, then that's great. If it's not, then this book will still work for you.

So, New is great for brand new functionalities and installations. There is, of course, a substantial install base of existing applications. This is where Renew comes into play.

3.1.2 Renew

SAP analyzed its application usage and found that a limited number of business scenarios were used by a large number of users. It was these business functions that SAP focused on with the Renew portion of its UX strategy, which involves using SAP's newest technologies to refresh the look and function of the most widely used scenarios.

The technological foundation of SAP's Renew effort is SAPUI5, accessing the backend via SAP Gateway; we will discuss these technologies in more detail later in the chapter. The goal of Renew is to simplify the UIs for key applications and roles. SAP Fiori is used as the basis for simpler applications, whereas more complex current applications are being renovated via Web Dynpro for ABAP with the Floorplan Manager (FPM). These key technologies and how they relate are shown in Figure 3.1.

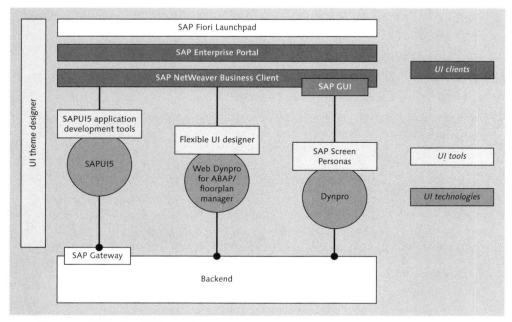

Figure 3.1 SAP's Key UX Technologies

SAP Enterprise Portal, SAP NetWeaver Business Client, and SAP Fiori Launchpad are all viable UI clients that primarily use SAPUI5 on SAP Gateway or Web Dynpro for ABAP with Floorplan Manager for applications and content. Web Dynpro for ABAP/Floorplan Manager is generally preferred for applications with broad functional scope or with complex functionality, because it offers easy support for function-rich scenarios that need deep integration with the backend. Web Dynpro for ABAP/Floorplan Manager is also generally preferred for data entry use cases or pure desktop usage. SAPUI5 with SAP Gateway encompasses both the HR Renewal landing pages and SAP Fiori, because both are built on the same technological backbone.

3.1.3   Enable

Simply put, the Enable portion of SAP's UX strategy is for all the do-it-yourselfers out there. Whereas New and Renew are focused on renovating applications that SAP is delivering to the customer, Enable is about the applications that customers are building for themselves. The idea here is to provide customers with the tools to create their own custom applications with a consumer-grade UX. These customer-specific value scenarios happen in just about every implementation to fill business needs not quite envisaged in SAP's standard offerings.

SAP provides tools such as the following to enable customers to build consumer-grade UXs for their custom applications:

▶ **SAP Screen Personas**
As shown in Figure 3.2 (before) and Figure 3.3 (after), SAP Screen Personas is a way to give the traditional SAP GUI and its functionalities a modern look and feel.

▶ **Floorplan Manager/Web Dynpro for ABAP**
More traditional technology still can be optimized for data entry and high-complexity applications.

▶ **SAPUI5**
This is a newer technology based on current Internet standards, used as a base for SAP Fiori and other HR Renewal UIs.

▶ **SAP NetWeaver Business Client and side panel**
This UI client option comes with the capability to add additional content, such as business graphics, to a page in a side panel.

▶ **UI Theme Designer**
This tool allows a customer to develop custom themes to adapt the appearance of applications.

In addition to these existing tools, SAP has just released its web integrated development environment (IDE), which will allow the extension and construction of SAPUI5 and SAP Fiori apps. SAP Web IDE is a browser-based web development tool, available as of the time of writing (fall 2014). It is discussed in more detail later in this chapter.

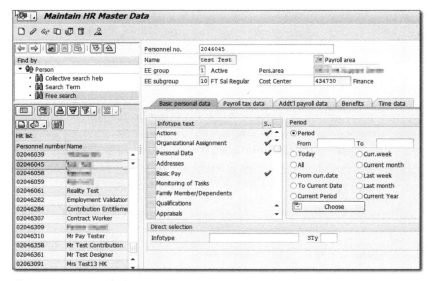

Figure 3.2 SAP GUI before SAP Screen Personas

Figure 3.3 SAP GUI after SAP Screen Personas

Where is SAP's UX strategy taking us? By following New, Renew, and Enable, where does SAP expect us to end up? The vision is the "unified shell." Shown in Figure 3.4, the unified shell concept shows a web-based entry point for all business applications on any platform or any device. SAP Fiori Launchpad, discussed in more detail later, is the first implementation of this concept.

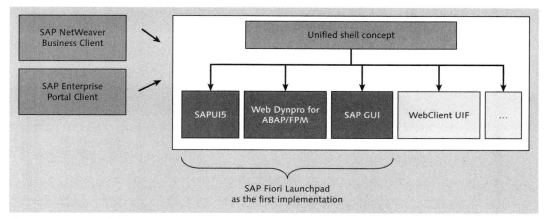

Figure 3.4 Unified Shell Concept

SAP's drive to move from its traditional and, frankly, lackluster UIs to a more consumer-grade UX is at the heart of HR Renewal. Next, we talk about the UX for all SAP applications going forward: SAP Fiori.

3.2 SAP Fiori

SAP Fiori, simply speaking, is the new UX for SAP software. It represents SAP's intent to deliver a consumer-grade UX for the most broadly and frequently used business transactions. Rather than collecting transactions, SAP Fiori delivers apps that can be accessed and experienced by users across multiple interaction channels, such as desktop, mobile, and tablet. Each app follows a simple and intuitive pattern that enables users to accomplish their tasks quickly and efficiently. These apps were so well received in their initial offering that SAP decided to expand the concept into the new standard.

SAP Fiori and HR Renewal

SAP Fiori is not part of the HR Renewal program in a technical sense. It is not packaged as a part of that component stack, but it is a part of the movement to renew HR applications with a consumer-grade UX, which is the driver of the HR Renewal program. It is for this reason that we spend so much time in this chapter and in Chapter 8 discussing SAP Fiori.

It is vital to understand that SAP Fiori is centered on apps, rather than on more traditional transactions as is typically the case in enterprise software. Transactions read and write from an underlying database and are optimized based on the underlying data structure. Unfortunately, this type of traditional design tends to suffer from a couple of flaws over time. Transaction-based software tends to accumulate more data per transaction than is typically needed by the most common user of the transaction, meaning that the user has to sift through a very crowded screen of data to get the data that he or she needs. Transactions become less simple as time goes by; each incremental use case gets added to an already crowded screen. Another problem with the transaction model is that transactions can also suffer from being broken up according to system or functional limitations. The result is that a single logical unit of work gets spread across multiple transactions, requiring manual integration between transactions or toggling back and forth to gather the required data to complete a task.

SAP Fiori breaks from this traditional architecture by offering simple, narrowly focused apps based upon frequently used business cases and organizes these apps by role. This organization by role is one of the key features and tenets of SAP Fiori, and it stems from one of the SAP Fiori design principles. For example, for managers, the SAP Fiori apps might be My Spend, Approve Requests, Approve Timesheets, Approve Shopping Carts, and Contracts. For employees, the apps might be My Leave Requests, My Timesheet, Track Shopping Cart, and My Paystub.

It seems clear that SAP has heavily invested in SAP Fiori, to the point of declaring it *the* UX for SAP business applications going forward. Why is it so special? What makes SAP Fiori so unique for SAP is not its technology. SAP Fiori's technical base is no different than the HR Renewal swim lane style landing pages. Both are built with SAPUI5 on top of SAP Gateway and use OData to speak to the backend server.

The key differentiator for SAP Fiori is not the technology it uses but the principles upon which it was created. SAPUI5 was created to be more mobile friendly, and the UI5 swim lanes flowed naturally from that mobile-friendly concept. With SAP Fiori, SAP took a step back and reevaluated its entire design approach, focusing on the larger UX. The result was a new community—the SAP User Experience community at *http://experience.sap.com*—that focuses on helping the user base understand and embrace the movement toward a UX. The SAP User Experience community embodies SAP Fiori's design principles and is built upon with SAP and customer interaction and contribution.

SAP claims that all new development will strictly adhere to SAP Fiori's design principles, and it's fair to say that these principles constitute a major departure from SAP's traditional application design. This shift toward the following five principles is the major component in the move from a UI to a UX:

► **Role-based**

SAP Fiori apps are designed with who you are and what you do in mind. How you work is important to SAP Fiori. All SAP Fiori software is designed to understand the tasks that a user needs to perform and to help each user accomplish tasks more easily.

In comparison to transaction-based software, role-based software is more concerned with bringing together all the information *necessary* for a particular user doing a task rather than all the information *possible* for a particular transaction. This streamlines the task for the user, seeming to design it with the user in mind. All SAP Fiori apps, therefore, are decomposed to their lowest levels as task-based experiences.

► **Responsive**

SAP Fiori supports where you work or, in other words, adapts to whatever device you are using to access its applications. No matter the device, be it a tablet, desktop, or smartphone, SAP Fiori apps will react appropriately without the need for separate apps for each device type.

► **Simple**

SAP Fiori focuses on what's important and nothing else. This kind of streamlining makes essential functions obvious and easy to use. Similar to the idea that the iPhone needs no instruction manual, SAP Fiori apps strive for a simplicity that makes the software intuitive to use. Within the Simple principle, SAP Fiori apps, whenever possible, try to stick to the 1-1-3 rule. This means that for each application the scope is limited to one task, able to be performed by one person, and takes three screens or fewer to complete.

SAP Fiori apps also try to automate everything possible, but nothing beyond what is needed. The user needs to feel in control of the task at hand. This facilitates intuitive usage but also increases adoption.

▸ **Coherent**
SAP Fiori strives to deliver one fluid, intuitive experience from start to finish, meaning that from app to app every SAP Fiori app will speak the same language and use the same terms. Familiarity and comfort are important to a UX. Coherence is an important part of providing familiarity and comfort.

▸ **Delightful**
Admittedly, this is not a term you'd normally expect to see in reference to enterprise software. Traditionally, SAP software has been anything but delightful. Robust? Reliable? Certainly. Delightful? Hardly.

But SAP Fiori is all about turning traditional software design on its head, and this is the design principle that most typifies that. SAP Fiori apps seek to make an emotional connection with the user. They're designed to make a user better at his or her job, letting him or her feel like an expert. The impact of the user's contribution is made plain, again reinforcing the user's positive experience.

The creation of SAP Fiori design principles and, indeed, the creation of an entire SAP User Experience community speak to the lofty goals SAP has for SAP Fiori. SAP Fiori is SAP's powerful vision for the future. In fact, as referenced earlier in Figure 3.4, SAP Fiori is intended to be the backbone of the unified UX for SAP. An example of SAP Fiori Launchpad, the single point of entry into SAP content, can be seen in Figure 3.5. SAP Fiori serves up applications and analytics side by side, fed by SAP HANA in the backend.

SAP Fiori is set to play a major role in the future of SAP self-services and beyond. It is neither static nor magic. SAP Fiori is created on a technical backbone of SAPUI5 and SAP Gateway, speaking through OData to the SAP backend. We will get into more detail with SAP Fiori in Chapter 8.

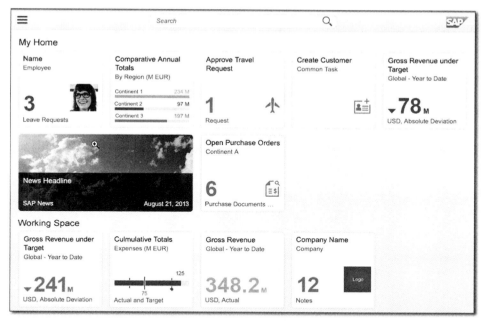

Figure 3.5 SAP Fiori Launchpad

3.3 SAPUI5

SAPUI5 is a client-side HTML5 and JavaScript-based rendering library and pro-gramming model that is optimized for consumption of SAP data. It combines new qualities, such as openness and flexibility, with known SAP strengths, such as enterprise readiness and product standard support. SAPUI5 is well suited to flex-ibly build UIs across different devices (mobile and desktop) on top of SAP Gate-way. SAPUI5 is the first half of the technical backbone of the newest HR Renewal landing pages and SAP Fiori.

Jargon aside, SAPUI5 is SAP's answer to the rising tide of mobile devices in the marketplace. Web Dynpro for Java and Web Dynpro for ABAP were, quite frankly, ill-equipped to handle these devices in the way that users expected. A solution had to be found, and the answer was SAPUI5.

SAPUI5 brings the following features to the table:

- A rich control set, including charts for all devices
- An application development environment for all platforms
- OData integration in line with the latest standards
- Extensibility concepts for custom controls
- Modern theming and branding concepts
- Inclusion of open source framework(s) and web standards
- Targets developers with web development skills (HTML5, CSS3, JavaScript)

The benefits of SAPUI5 are enormous: it provides business agility through availability on any device and on any platform, effectively increasing user productivity and satisfaction through flexibility, openness, and design.

Why SAPUI5?

Why was SAPUI5 the choice to fill this new mobile-friendly, device-agnostic technological need? The answer is quite simple: standards.

SAPUI5 is built on the latest Internet standards instead of on SAP's proprietary technology. Technologies such as HTML5, CSS3, JavaScript, and jQuery are used to build the libraries that make up SAPUI5, but they are much bigger than SAPUI5. These technologies are agreed-upon standards in the international web development community, and SAP's decision to build upon them rather than on its own technology underscores how committed it is to making its solutions within the mobile and cloud areas more compatible with today's devices.

Development for SAPUI5 has typically been handled in Eclipse, as shown in Figure 3.6. This will look very familiar to those customers who have worked in Web Dynpro for Java. For a while, it seemed that SAP was going to recycle its Java backbone with an "everything's that old is new again" mantra.

Instead, SAP recently introduced SAP Web IDE, a browser-based development environment specifically designed for creating new SAPUI5 or SAP Fiori apps or for extending existing SAPUI5 or SAP Fiori apps. SAP Web IDE can be seen in Figure 3.7.

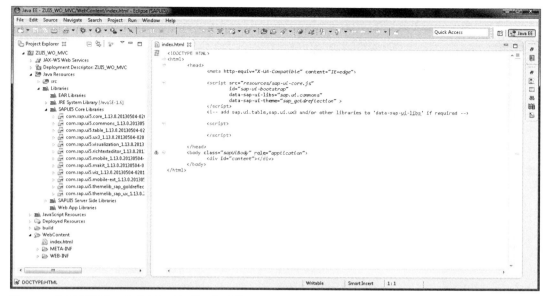

Figure 3.6 SAPUI5 JavaScript Application in Eclipse

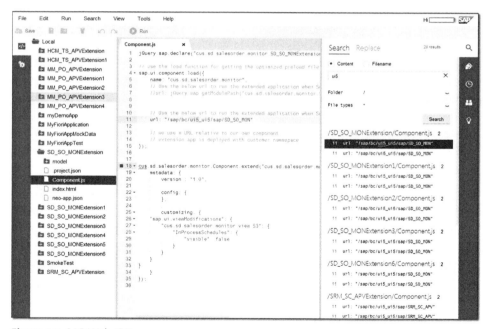

Figure 3.7 SAP Web IDE

SAP Web IDE provides a template library to aid the developer, allowing the developer to choose the type of project and have the template do much of the setup. Through the use of templated projects and assisted development, testing, and deployment, SAP Web IDE provides end-to-end application lifecycle support with zero installation.

SAP Web IDE allows developers to rapidly build SAPUI5 and SAP Fiori apps. These apps still need a communication backbone in order to interface with the SAP backend, however, and that is where SAP Gateway and OData come in.

3.4   SAP Gateway and OData

The other half of the technical backbone of HR Renewal and SAP Fiori consists of SAP Gateway and the OData protocol. SAP Gateway and OData have a broader application than only self-services or even SAP ERP HCM. SAP Gateway is a technology that provides a simple way to connect devices, environments, and platforms to SAP software based on market standards. It is technically an SAP NetWeaver Application Server add-on.

SAP Gateway's main purpose is to make any type of application viable for accessing and using SAP data. Therefore, it offers connectivity to SAP applications using any programming language or model without the need for SAP knowledge by leveraging Representational State Transfer (REST) services and Open Data Protocol (OData). REST and OData are Internet standards, thus explaining their usage as a part of SAP's inclusive UX strategy. This is another example of SAP making its data and technology more accessible to a broader range of applications rather than enforcing the use of proprietary technology with a narrow range of functionality.

REST is a style of software architecture for distributed systems, such as the World Wide Web. In fact, thanks to its simpler style, REST has increasingly displaced other design models, such as SOAP and WSDL. It uses the standard GET, PUT, POST, and DELETE methods and other existing features of the HTTP protocol. Key goals of REST include scalability of component interactions, generality of interfaces, independent deployment of components, and the use of intermediary components to reduce latency, enforce security, and encapsulate legacy systems.

OData is an open web protocol for querying and updating data. The protocol allows for a consumer to query a datasource over the HTTP protocol and get the result back in formats such as Atom, JSON, or plain XML, including pagination, ordering, or filtering of the data. It provides database-like access to business data, somewhat like an ODBC for the web. You can make OData calls even if you don't have any prior knowledge of SAP.

What makes SAP Gateway so valuable? It has several key benefits:

▶ REST enables your SAP system; no special knowledge of an SAP system is required before SAP business data and functionality can be consumed.

▶ It hides the technical complexities of your SAP system landscape behind a single interface that is easy to use and nonproprietary.

▶ It makes your SAP business data and functionality accessible to any external device or system that can do two things:

  ▶ Communicate using the HTTP(S) protocol

  ▶ Understand OData messages

Because just about any web application can meet the previously listed standards, just about any web application can consume SAP data via SAP Gateway. For our purposes, this means that any delivered SAPUI5 application—SAP Fiori or otherwise—already uses SAP Gateway and OData as standard.

Additional Resources

In the interest of staying focused, we've only touched on this topic, but if you're looking to dig into every possible detail of installing, using, and developing with these new tools, we recommend the SAP PRESS book *OData and SAP NetWeaver Gateway* by Carsten Bönnen, Volker Drees, André Fischer, Ludwig Heinz, and Karsten Strothmann (2014), which has much to offer anyone looking to install SAP Gateway—to the tune of 666 pages of nerdy goodness.

3.5 Summary

In this chapter, we looked at SAP's effort to renovate its self-service landscape. In fact, this effort is broader than merely the HCM space. By being responsive to technology and the marketplace, SAP is moving its software from a typical user interface (UI), such as we are used to at work, to a user experience (UX), which we see much more frequently in our consumer-based technology.

We talked about SAP's UX strategy and how it has affected the development of the new landscape, both from a design and a technical standpoint. We then talked about some of the technologies chosen on which to build SAP's UX, starting with SAP Fiori, the new SAP UX. We talked about SAP Fiori's design principles and its available offerings, and about how to develop custom apps at a very high level.

We introduced SAPUI5 and looked at what it is and how it benefits both SAP and SAP's customers. We then wrapped up our chapter by talking about SAP Gateway and OData, the backend building blocks of the new SAP UX. Next, we will see some of this refreshed software in action in our ESS chapter.

Implementing ESS has many perks, chief among them reduction of administrative times and costs and a greater sense of ownership in the HR process. This chapter discusses ESS functionality available in SAP's latest ESS delivery and will focus on those services affected by HR Renewal.

4   Employee Self-Service in SAP ERP HCM

For several years, SAP has been working toward harmonization of its UIs—the SAP backend, SAP NetWeaver Business Client, and SAP Enterprise Portal—and has made significant improvements to the function and feel of core SAP ERP HCM. The product of that focus on strategic innovation and enhancements to the core HR processes is HR Renewal, and SAP has placed added emphasis on providing the user with a more "consumer-grade" experience, more on par with what you'd experience while browsing or shopping online.

HR Renewal and Employee Self-Service (ESS) with HR Renewal reflects SAP's continued commitment to improving the user experience while expanding the availability of new services yet continuing to support the vast array of existing ESS services. In this chapter, we explore the latest version of ESS based on the SAPUI5 framework as part of HR Renewal 2.0.

4.1   ESS Highlights

In this section, we will explore a few of the new features for ESS delivered with the most recent version(s) of HR Renewal 2.0 Feature Pack (FP) 1 and HR Renewal 1.0 FP 4. In later sections, we will dig deeper into the functionality delivered and also review some configuration steps.

Starting with HR Renewal 1.0 FP 4, SAP introduced the *lanes* concept for ESS and MSS. If you're a current customer who has already implemented ESS and MSS, especially older versions, you'll notice that the landing page represents a marked difference not only in the look and feel, but also in navigation. The landing page represents a "command central" approach that provides a central entrance into ESS, MSS, and the HR Professional role. Based on roles assigned to the user, you can mix and match lanes to display information that is relevant to the user, such as an employee or a manager who needs to perform a task for someone on his or her team. Starting with HR Renewal 1.0 FP 4, SAP began to also convert some of the existing services to SAPUI5, and HR Renewal 2.0 continues that conversion.

Let's look at some of the ESS services that have been converted to SAPUI5:

▶ **Landing page**
The new landing page is now a one-stop shop for all your self-service needs. It provides a clean, modern feel for the homepage concept. If you've only been assigned the ESS role, then you will only see service options related to ESS. If, however, you've also been assigned the MSS role, then you also have the option to display MSS service lanes side by side with ESS content. The lanes can be shifted or moved on the landing page based on user preference, and you can customize the background image of the landing page, as shown in Figure 4.1.

Figure 4.1 ESS (HR Self-Services) Landing Page

▶ **New Timesheet lane and refreshed timesheet appearance**
One of the newly refreshed components in HR Renewal 2.0 FP 1 is the ESS timesheet. If you are an existing customer with ESS, then you'll be familiar with the previous incarnations of this ESS service. Since the conversion of the ESS

timesheet to SAPUI5, there are changes to the look and feel and minor changes to functionality (we'll discuss this in greater detail in Section 4.6). As shown in Figure 4.2 and Figure 4.3, a new lane is available on the ESS landing page for a quick calendar view, with buttons that let you either view the full timesheet or print the timesheet.

Figure 4.2 Timesheet Lane (Closeup)

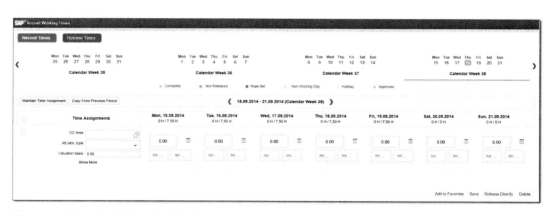

Figure 4.3 Timesheet (Expanded View)

▶ **Leave request revamp**

As of HR Renewal 1.0 FP 4, the leave request and leave request approval are two areas in which you can see the conversion to SAPUI5. In keeping with the trend found within the SAPUI5 services, the new look for the leave request is clean and modern. There are two tabs available in the service that allow the user to complete his or her request (PLANNING) or view his or her leave history (LEAVE HISTORY). The LEAVE HISTORY tab displays a summary of leave taken in the refreshed card view (see Figure 4.4).

Figure 4.4 Leave Request

▶ **ESS pay statement conversion**

Another service in HR Renewal 1.0 FP 4 that was converted to SAPUI5 is the ESS pay statement. The users are presented with an initial card view of available pay statements, and each card has two new icons: the printer icon allows the user to print (provided batch printing has been set up), and the PDF icon allows the user to display his or her full timesheet in the familiar PDF form. Another new feature since the SAPUI5 update is a horizontal sliding bar to determine the number of pay statements available to the user, as shown in Figure 4.5.

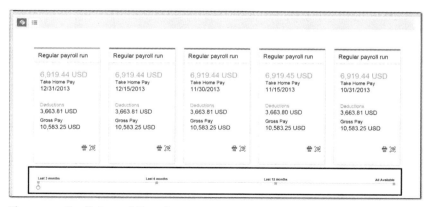

Figure 4.5 Pay Statement Overview

Now that we've reviewed some of the new and updated services that we'll cover at greater length later in the chapter, let's look into the enhanced functionality of ESS. Remember, the primary focus of the chapter will be on the updated services in HR Renewal, specifically the SAPUI5 services and how you can leverage your existing configuration to take advantage of the new updates.

4.2   Getting Started

Let's get started with a basic laundry list of information and tasks that are needed to get up and running with the newest version of ESS.

4.2.1   Application Area

The application area for Employee Self-Service covers all of the supported technologies used in ESS. The application area can be used for searching for SAP Notes and is particularly relevant to the activation of business function sets in the SAP backend switch framework. For the SAPUI5 ESS content, the application area is PA-ESS-XX, but a few other application areas are also available for Employee Self-Service, including the following:

▸ **PA-ESS — Employee Self-Service Application**
Generally, related to ESS content in EHP 4 and below.

▸ **PA-ESS-WDA — Employee Self-Service Web Dynpro for ABAP**
Related to content available in EHP 5 and above.

4.2.2 Software Components

At the time of writing (fall 2014), HR Renewal 2.0 FP 1 is currently in general availability (GA) release. The software components listed in Table 4.1 are those that are delivered with HR Renewal 2.0 FP 1 and used by the latest version of Employee Self-Service, Manager Self Service, and HR Professional self-service.

Software Component	Release	Required for
EA-HR (Enterprise extension for HR)	608 SP 4	All features
SAP_HR	608 SP 4	All features
SAP NetWeaver (with SAP UI 740 SP 8 & SAP GWFND SP 6)	7.40 SPS 5	All features
SAP Gateway	2.0 SP 7	All features
XI Content EA-HR	608 SP 4	
XI Content HR	608 SP 4	

Table 4.1 Software Component Requirements for HR Renewal 2.0 FP 1

Before you install HR Renewal on your system, remember to check the Administrative Guide for the latest patch and stack releases. The installation guides found in SAP Service Marketplace will always contain the most current information.

4.2.3 Deployment Options

Chapter 3 details the options available to you when deciding how to provide access to self-services for your users. When deciding which deployment options work best for your organization, there are a few points to consider:

- **Usability**
  Is supporting information readily available to the users as they perform their specific tasks, or do users have to refer to various document areas to access required information?

- **Hardware**
  Is existing hardware sufficient to deploy your self-service options, or will you need to purchase new hardware?

- **Gateway deployment options**
  Should you set up an external gateway or an internal gateway on your backend system?

▶ **Timing**

Are there required components that can be implemented independently to help defer implementation costs?

▶ **Browser requirements**

What version of what browser version is used as your company standard? When deploying new SAPUI5 functionality found in HR Renewal 2.0 (or HR Renewal 1.0 FP 4 if on a lower version), note that Internet Explorer 8 and below is not supported for HTML5, which is the basis for SAPUI5. For more information, please reference SAP Note 1900896 (Browser: IE Restrictions for Portal and NWBC Content).

The next sections will detail the additional steps you'll need to take when implementing the newest version of ESS.

Business Functions and Applications

Please reference Appendix A for a thorough list of key business functions and applications for ESS, MSS, and the HR Professional role.

Business Functions

Business functions are individual components within the larger enhancement pack that allow customers to determine which features they would like to use in a selective fashion. The business functions can be accessed in Transaction SFW5 (Switch Framework).

Before you activate any business functions, one best practice is to review the release notes for that business function. The good news is that in the most *recent* enhancement pack releases SAP is making more business functions reversible, so if you decide that you don't want to use a particular piece of functionality after it's been activated, you can deactivate it without a negative impact. However, the majority of business functions are still a one-shot activation (i.e., they can't be deactivated once activated), so it's wise to work closely with your SAP Basis team and business SMEs to review what's new with each enhancement pack update.

Another suggestion: if there is a sandbox environment available, then activate the business functions there first and use the sandbox as your initial evaluation area.

In this chapter, we have assumed that the business functions in Table 4.2 have been switched on (see Figure 4.6) as part of an EHP 7, HR Renewal 2.0 Add-On implementation. You will be prompted for input when activating business functions that have dependencies.

Business Function	Name	Business Function Prerequisites	Release
HCM_ESS_CE	SAP ERP HCM, ESS for Concurrent and Global Employment	None	603
HCM_ESS_CI_1	SAP ERP HCM, ESS for Personal Information	None	603
HCM_ESS_UI5_2	SAP ERP HCM, Employee Self-service on SAPUI5 (Reversible)	None	609
HCM_ESS_UI5_1	SAP ERP HCM, Employee self-service on SAPUI5 (Reversible)	None	607
HCM_ESS_WDA_1	Employee Self-Service on Web Dynpro for ABAP	None	605
HCM_ESS_WDA_2	SAP ERP HCM, ESS on Web Dynpro for ABAP 2	None	606
HCM_ESS_WDA_3	SAP ERP HCM, Employee Self-Services on Web Dynpro for ABAP 3	None	607

Table 4.2 Business Functions Relevant to EHP 7, HR Renewal 2.0 Add-On Implementation

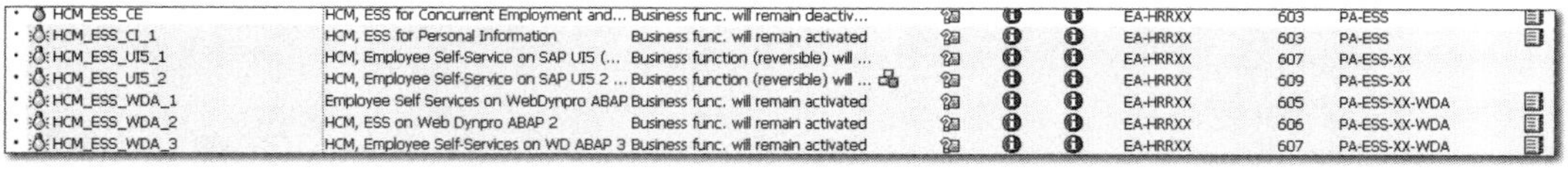

Figure 4.6 Switch Framework Activation for ESS Business Functions

Activation of Services

In the IMG, go to the activity under SAP NETWEAVER • GATEWAY • ODATA CHANNEL • ADMINISTRATION • GENERAL SETTINGS • ACTIVATE AND MAINTAIN SERVICES or use Transaction /IWFND/MAINT_SERVICE. The following OData services need to be activated for Employee Self-Services:

▶ HRESS_CATS_G

▶ HRESS_EMPMENU_G

▶ HRESS_EMP_PRO_G

▶ HRESS_ICONS

- ► HRESS_LEAVREQ_G

- ► HRESS_LRNSOLN_G

- ► HRESS_MYINFO_G

- ► HRMSS_MYSRV_G

- ► HRESS_PAYSLIP_G

- ► HRESS_TEAMCDR_G

- ► HRESS_WRKFEED_G

- ► HRGEN_QUICKVIEW

These services are specific to the SAPUI5 services available as of HR Renewal 2.0 FP 1 and HR Renewal 1.0 FP 4. For additional Web Dynpro for ABAP ESS service activation, you should use the following service path: DEFAULT_HOST · SAP · BC · WEBDYNPRO · SAP.

SAP Gateway Basic Setup and OData Service Activation

In this section, we will cover briefly some areas of set up required for the SAPUI5 OData services. For our purposes, we'll assume that you have set up SAP Gateway externally, which is the most common deployment option for the SAP Gateway server.

> **Service Activation**
>
> We'll examine the most basic steps that are required for initial setup and used by the ESS launch page and the SAPUI5 services, as shown in Figure 4.7. Although the focus of this section is on ESS, the same steps would be required to set up MSS and HR Professional SAPUI5 services.

Following the IMG path Transaction SPRO · SAP NetWeaver · Gateway · OData Channel · Configuration · Connection Settings leads you to four subitems, but we'll cover the three that are most relevant for initial setup:

- ► Manage RFC Destinations
  These are RFC connections that will be used to "talk" to the SAP ERP system.

- ► Define Trust for SAP Business Systems
  These are configuration settings for enabling single sign-on (SSO) for uni- or bidirectional trust between the SAP Gateway system and the SAP business system.

▶ MANAGE SYSTEM ALIAS

This is the setup of logical RFC destinations to SAP business systems. The aliases defined in this step will also be used when assigning activated OData services to a system alias for data retrieval.

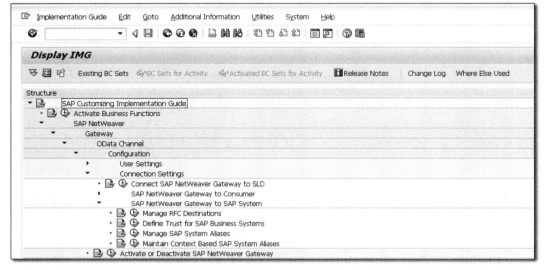

Figure 4.7 IMG Path for Initial SAP Gateway 2.0 Setup

Follow the IMG path Transaction SPRO • SAP NETWEAVER • GATEWAY • ODATA CHANNEL • ADMINISTRATION • GENERAL SETTINGS • ACTIVATE AND MAINTAIN SERVICES to activate the following OData services for Employee Self-Service (see Figure 4.8):

▶ HROVIS_ORGCHART_SERVICE

▶ HRESS_CATS_RECORDING

▶ HRESS_EMP_LANE_PROF_SERVICE

▶ HRESS_EMP_LSO_SERVICE

▶ HRESS_EMP_PROFILE_SERVICE

▶ HRESS_EMP_WORK_FEEDS_SERVICE

▶ HRESS_LEAVE_REQUEST_SERVICE

▶ HRESS_PAYSLIP_SERVICE

- ► HRESS_TEAM_CALENDAR_SERVICE

- ► HRESS_TIME_ACCOUNTS_SERVICE

- ► HRXSS_PERNR_MEMID_SERVICE

- ► HRXSS_PERS_KEY

- ► HRESS_TEAM_CALENDAR_SERVICE

- ► HRGEN_QUICK_VIEW_SERVICE

- ► HROVIS_ORGCHART_SERVICE

- ► LAUNCHPAD

- ► QUICKVIEW

- ► PAGE_BUILDER_CONF (for Suite Page Builder)

- ► PAGE_BUILDER_CUST (for Suite Page Builder)

- ► PAGE_BUILDER_PERS (for Suite Page Builder)

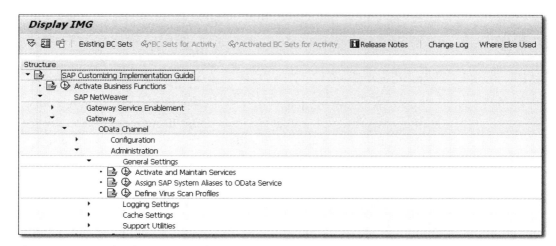

Figure 4.8 IMG Path Administration of OData Services

If you are using an external SAP Gateway server, you'll need to set up the OData service activation there instead on your SAP ERP system, as is the case for the internal SAP Gateway server. You can also reach the configuration table for service activation by running Transaction /IWFND/MAINT_SERVICE (see Figure 4.9).

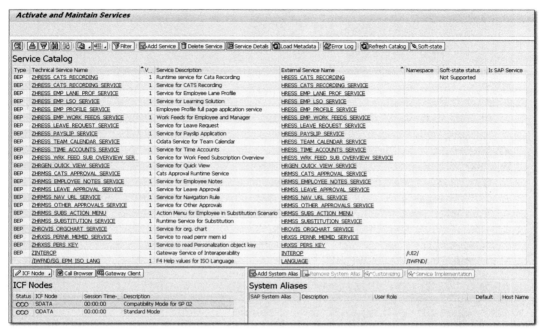

Figure 4.9 Initial View of Service Activation Table

Based on the deployment option chosen for your SAP Gateway setup, these SAPUI5 services might not be available at this point; if the required ESS services are not available, then you will need to add them to your SAP ERP system service catalog via remote call by following these steps:

1. Click the ADD SERVICE button (see Figure 4.10), and in the following screen enter the system alias for the SAP ERP system that had been previously defined in the initial configuration steps.

2. Select the binoculars icon for GET SERVICES (see Figure 4.11) to retrieve the available services.

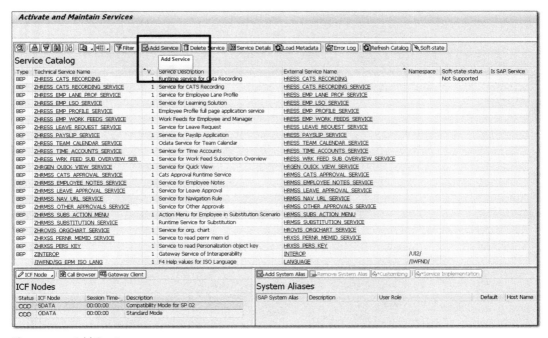

Figure 4.10 Add Service

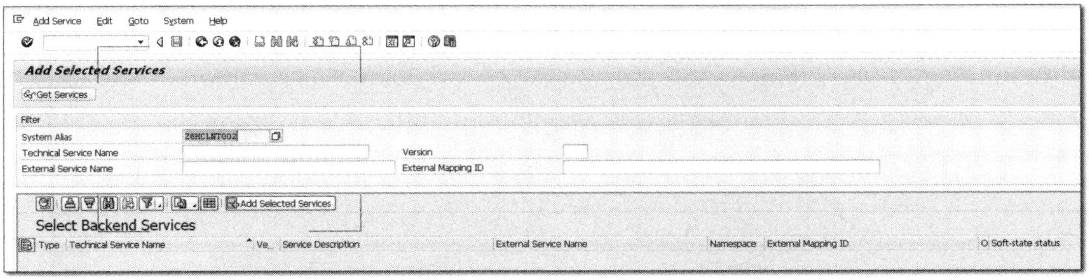

Figure 4.11 Remote Call of Available Services

3. Highlight the required service, and click the ADD SELECTED SERVICES button (see Figure 4.12). You will be prompted to create a transport, and a "Z" copy will be created, as shown in Figure 4.13.

4. After saving the transport, you will be returned to the initial service catalog, and the newly added service will be displayed in the list (see Figure 4.14).

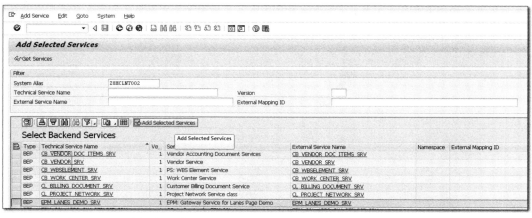

Figure 4.12 Add Selected Services Button

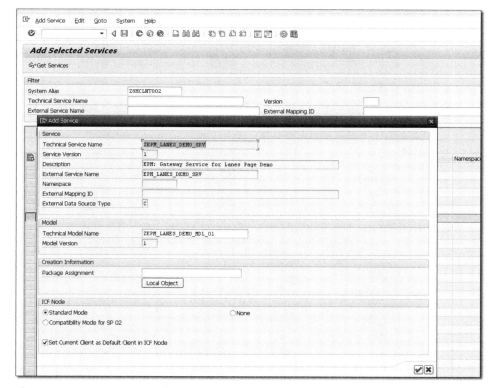

Figure 4.13 Transport Prompt for OData Service Addition

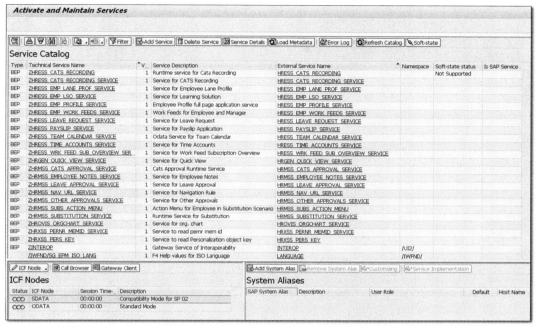

Figure 4.14 SAP Gateway Service Catalog Overview

5. Next, you need to assign the previously set up system alias to the activated services. In the IMG, go to the activity under SAP NetWeaver • Gateway • OData Channel • Administration • General Settings • Assign SAP System Aliases to OData Service.

All activated OData services should be listed within the configuration table, but you can also add any required entries for your ESS services. Figure 4.15 illustrates how ESS services will be assigned. If you created system aliases for your services, then you can select the required system(s) in the SAP System Alias column.

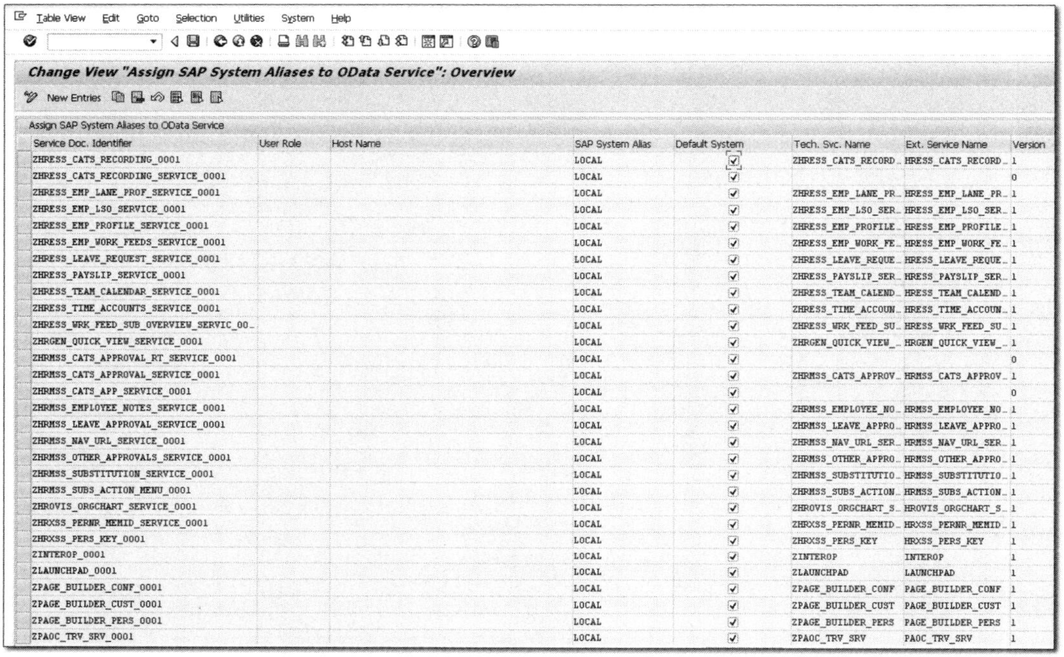

Service Doc. Identifier	User Role	Host Name	SAP System Alias	Default System	Tech. Svc. Name	Ext. Service Name	Version
ZHRESS_CATS_RECORDING_0001			LOCAL	✓	ZHRESS_CATS_RECORD…	HRESS_CATS_RECORD…	1
ZHRESS_CATS_RECORDING_SERVICE_0001			LOCAL	✓			0
ZHRESS_EMP_LANE_PROF_SERVICE_0001			LOCAL	✓	ZHRESS_EMP_LANE_PR…	HRESS_EMP_LANE_PR…	1
ZHRESS_EMP_LSO_SERVICE_0001			LOCAL	✓	ZHRESS_EMP_LSO_SER…	HRESS_EMP_LSO_SER…	1
ZHRESS_EMP_PROFILE_SERVICE_0001			LOCAL	✓	ZHRESS_EMP_PROFILE…	HRESS_EMP_PROFILE…	1
ZHRESS_EMP_WORK_FEEDS_SERVICE_0001			LOCAL	✓	ZHRESS_EMP_WORK_FE…	HRESS_EMP_WORK_FE…	1
ZHRESS_LEAVE_REQUEST_SERVICE_0001			LOCAL	✓	ZHRESS_LEAVE_REQUE…	HRESS_LEAVE_REQUE…	1
ZHRESS_PAYSLIP_SERVICE_0001			LOCAL	✓	ZHRESS_PAYSLIP_SER…	HRESS_PAYSLIP_SER…	1
ZHRESS_TEAM_CALENDAR_SERVICE_0001			LOCAL	✓	ZHRESS_TEAM_CALEND…	HRESS_TEAM_CALEND…	1
ZHRESS_TIME_ACCOUNTS_SERVICE_0001			LOCAL	✓	ZHRESS_TIME_ACCOUN…	HRESS_TIME_ACCOUN…	1
ZHRESS_WRK_FEED_SUB_OVERVIEW_SERVIC_00…			LOCAL	✓	ZHRESS_WRK_FEED_SU…	HRESS_WRK_FEED_SU…	1
ZHRGEN_QUICK_VIEW_SERVICE_0001			LOCAL	✓	ZHRGEN_QUICK_VIEW_…	HRGEN_QUICK_VIEW_…	1
ZHRMSS_CATS_APPROVAL_RT_SERVICE_0001			LOCAL	✓			0
ZHRMSS_CATS_APPROVAL_SERVICE_0001			LOCAL	✓	ZHRMSS_CATS_APPROV…	HRMSS_CATS_APPROV…	1
ZHRMSS_CATS_APP_SERVICE_0001			LOCAL	✓			0
ZHRMSS_EMPLOYEE_NOTES_SERVICE_0001			LOCAL	✓	ZHRMSS_EMPLOYEE_NO…	HRMSS_EMPLOYEE_NO…	1
ZHRMSS_LEAVE_APPROVAL_SERVICE_0001			LOCAL	✓	ZHRMSS_LEAVE_APPRO…	HRMSS_LEAVE_APPRO…	1
ZHRMSS_NAV_URL_SERVICE_0001			LOCAL	✓	ZHRMSS_NAV_URL_SER…	HRMSS_NAV_URL_SER…	1
ZHRMSS_OTHER_APPROVALS_SERVICE_0001			LOCAL	✓	ZHRMSS_OTHER_APPRO…	HRMSS_OTHER_APPRO…	1
ZHRMSS_SUBSTITUTION_SERVICE_0001			LOCAL	✓	ZHRMSS_SUBSTITUTIO…	HRMSS_SUBSTITUTIO…	1
ZHRMSS_SUBS_ACTION_MENU_0001			LOCAL	✓	ZHRMSS_SUBS_ACTION…	HRMSS_SUBS_ACTION…	1
ZHROVIS_ORGCHART_SERVICE_0001			LOCAL	✓	ZHROVIS_ORGCHART_S…	HROVIS_ORGCHART_S…	1
ZHRXSS_PERNR_MEMID_SERVICE_0001			LOCAL	✓	ZHRXSS_PERNR_MEMID…	HRXSS_PERNR_MEMID…	1
ZHRXSS_PERS_KEY_0001			LOCAL	✓	ZHRXSS_PERS_KEY	HRXSS_PERS_KEY	1
ZINTEROP_0001			LOCAL	✓	ZINTEROP	INTEROP	1
ZLAUNCHPAD_0001			LOCAL	✓	ZLAUNCHPAD	LAUNCHPAD	1
ZPAGE_BUILDER_CONF_0001			LOCAL	✓	ZPAGE_BUILDER_CONF	PAGE_BUILDER_CONF	1
ZPAGE_BUILDER_CUST_0001			LOCAL	✓	ZPAGE_BUILDER_CUST	PAGE_BUILDER_CUST	1
ZPAGE_BUILDER_PERS_0001			LOCAL	✓	ZPAGE_BUILDER_PERS	PAGE_BUILDER_PERS	1
ZPAOC_TRV_SRV_0001			LOCAL	✓	ZPAOC_TRV_SRV	PAOC_TRV_SRV	1

Figure 4.15 System Alias Mapping for OData Services

Remember to work with your SAP Basis or developer resource for the setup required for base SAP Gateway configuration, especially because there are additional settings that can be made and OData modeling discussions to take place that won't be discussed in this book.

If you've made it this far, congratulations! You've completed the basic setup steps for the new SAPUI5 ESS services and landing page. You'll see lots of overlap in the MSS and HR Professional chapters (Chapter 5 and Chapter 6, respectively).

4.3 ESS Landing Page and Suite Page Builder

In this section, we will take a deeper look at the new landing page for the Employee Self-Services. Remember that the objective of the landing page is to act as a "command central" for the user to perform various tasks based on roles that have been assigned to him or her. The user has the option to personalize his or her workspace and decide what content he or she wants to have displayed. The content that is available to users is assigned to "catalogs," and those catalogs are then assigned to the various backend self-service roles.

For example, with ESS the following lanes are delivered with the HREMPLOYEE catalog:

- ▶ My Info
- ▶ My Services
- ▶ My Timesheet
- ▶ My Learnings
- ▶ Work Feeds
- ▶ Search

What if you decide not to use one of these lanes that are delivered with the ESS? Your admin can easily use the Suite Page Builder to adjust the content that is presented to the user. Suite Page Builder uses a browser-based frontend to allow an administrator to create or adjust catalogs and catalog content. We will take a broader look at that administrative content in Section 4.3.3. In the meantime, let's take a look at the delivered landing page personalization options.

4.3.1 Functions and Personalization Options

When ESS users initially log into ESS via the SAP Enterprise Portal or SAP NetWeaver Business Client, they are presented with the screen shown in Figure 4.16, which is an opaque grey.

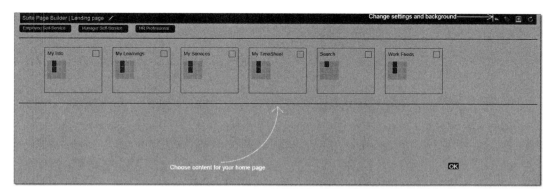

Figure 4.16 Initial Personalization Screen for the ESS Landing Page

The first step for the user is to select the content he or she wants to have available, including both the lanes and the personalized background image. Figure 4.17 shows the base view, without a background image or any selected services. The user is presented with the available services within the ESS catalog and can select each box for the desired service, populating it into the landing page "work space" (see Figure 4.18).

Figure 4.17 Landing Page without Service Selection

Figure 4.18 Landing Page with Added Services

Next, the user can add some additional personality to his or her landing page by adding a background image (see Figure 4.19 and Figure 4.20).

Figure 4.19 Toggle Panel with Background Images

Figure 4.20 Landing Page after Applying Background Image

Table 4.3 lists the four icons that are displayed in the upper-right corner of the landing page and used for the personalization options.

Icon	Description
	REMOVE PERSONALIZATION: Removes all services displayed in the ESS workspace and the selected background image.
	TOGGLE SETTING: Displays a panel with available services based on role selection if multiple roles are assigned. Users can also select this icon to collapse the service or role panel for maximum workspace.
	WALLPAPER: Displays available images for selection.
	REFRESH: Refreshes the landing page and collapses the selection pane.

Table 4.3 Landing Page Personalization Option Icons

If ESS users have also been assigned additional roles, such as Manager Self-Service and/or HR Professional, these additional roles will be presented as buttons for the user to click, and clicking these buttons displays the available content for a specific role. If the user would like to remove a lane from the landing page, he or she can select the "X" icon in the upper right corner of the lane to remove the lane from the user's workspace but not from the catalog of available services (see Figure 4.21 and Figure 4.22).

Figure 4.21 Toggle Selection Panel in Expanded Position

Figure 4.22 Landing Page with ESS, MSS, and HR Professional Lanes

4.3.2 Landing Page Image Setup

SAP delivers a series of wallpaper images for the landing page background out of the box. Although these provided images are beautiful and graphic, they aren't specific to your organization, so you may want to use configuration options to replace the delivered images with images selected by your organization.

You have a couple of options for substituting images for the landing page. You can use the Suite Page Builder admin to upload background images in either CUST or CONF mode or you can use the Mime Repository (Transaction SE80) in your backend SAP ERP system. Navigate to SAP • BC • BSP • SAP • ARSRVC_SUITE_PB • THEMES • IMAGES • BGIMAGES.

SAP delivers two sizes of the same available image, and both are saved as JPG files with different extensions (i.e., _thumbnail_ and _uxga_), as shown in Figure 4.23 and Figure 4.24. Your replacement images ideally should be sized to the same pixel ratio as the standard images.

Once you download the delivered images to a secure location, right-click on the bgimages folder to get a set of options. You can import mime images from another stored location, and then save to create a transport.

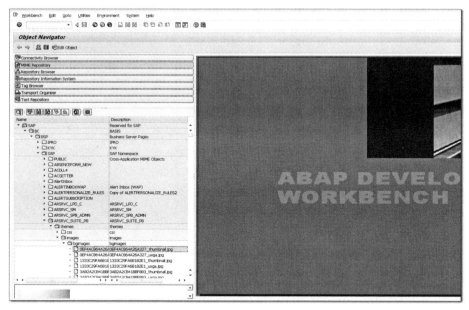

Figure 4.23 Landing Page Mime Repository

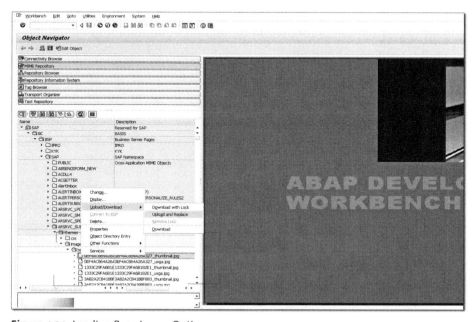

Figure 4.24 Landing Page Image Options

4.3.3 Suite Page Builder Administration

Suite Page Builder is part of the UI development toolkit for SAPUI5 applications and acts as an administration frontend for maintaining the collaborative human interface parts (CHIPs) that display the ESS services within the lanes. The administration page for Suite Page Builder is available via a browser-based user interface, but you'll need to meet the following prerequisites to use the administrative functions:

▶ **Use of the Suite Page Builder URL**
http://<webdispatcher_host>:<webdispatcher_port>/sap/bc/ui5_ui5/sap/arsrvc_spb_admn/main.html or *<webdispatcher_host >:<webdispatcher_port>/sap/bc/ui5_ui5/sap/ARSRVC_SUITE_PB/main.html?page=HREMPLOYEE&scope=CUST*

▶ **Ensure you have the Suite Page Builder administration roles**
SAP_UI2_ADMIN_700 administration role for OData services with backend systems on SAP NetWeaver 7.0 and higher contains authorizations for the following object:

   ▶ /UI2/LAUNCHPAD

   SAP_UI2_ADMIN_731 administration role for OData services with backend systems on SAP NetWeaver 7.3 and higher contains authorizations for the following objects:

   ▶ /UI2/PAGE_BUILDER_CONF (configuration)

   ▶ /UI2/PAGE_BUILDER_CUST (customization)

   ▶ /UI2/PAGE_BUILDER_PERS

▶ **Save to transports**
Changes made within Suite Page Builder administrative view can be transported. The administrator should maintain the following parameters in "own data." If an administrator creates or maintains any page builder contents, then the contents are saved to the transport.

   ▶ /UI2/WDC_DEVCLASS

   ▶ /UI2/WD_TRKORR_CONF

   ▶ /UI2/WD_TRKORR_CUST

The Suite Page Builder administrative view allows the administrator the following rights:

▸ Perform page administration (Figure 4.25)

▸ Upload and maintain background images for the landing page (Figure 4.26)

▸ Assign content to specific catalogs (Figure 4.27)

▸ Perform CHIP and page administration (Figure 4.28)

▸ Create and maintain catalogs

▸ Flag catalogs that are still in draft and not yet assigned to a Transaction PFCG role

▸ Remove CHIPs from homepage or reject changes when in edit mode

Self-Services Catalog

The delivered HR Professional Self-Services catalog contains content available for the ESS, MSS, and HR Professional roles. If your organization requires that the content be separated (i.e., ESS-specific content only on the landing page), then you can create role-specific catalogs and assign that catalog content to the appropriate Transaction PFCG role catalog provider.

For example, if the user accesses ESS and MSS via the SAP Enterprise Portal, he or she would see content either on one landing page (the delivered option) or, if content has been separated into role-specific catalogs, on two tabs containing two distinct landing pages with separate catalog content.

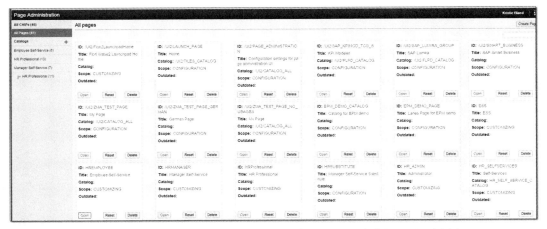

Figure 4.25 Perform Suite Page Builder Page Administration (All Pages Available)

Figure 4.26 Maintain Suite Page Builder Background Image

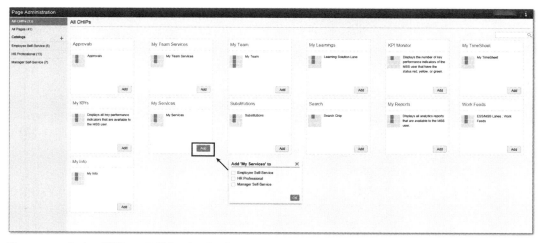

Figure 4.27 Assign CHIPs to Self-Service Catalogs

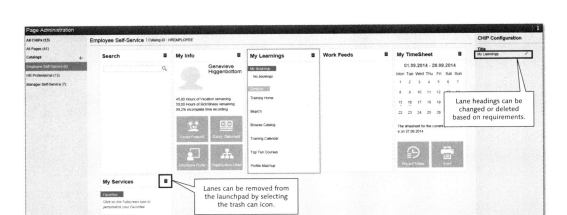

Figure 4.28 Remove CHIP and Change Title

Now that we've looked at the features and functions of both the landing page and Suite Page Builder, exploring how the landing page works and your options for tailoring it to the needs of your user population, we'll take a deeper look at the services delivered for ESS and some basic configuration for those ESS services. As previously mentioned, the focus for this section will be on the SAPUI5 ESS services, but we will also briefly discuss all of the ESS services delivered with the standard ESS role. HR Renewal 2.0 FP 1 is the basis of role functionality for this chapter and, unless otherwise noted, the functionality delivered with ESS on HR Renewal 1.0 FP 4 remains unchanged or further enhanced.

4.4   My Info

We've already mentioned the standard-delivered lanes for ESS, so now we'll take a look at the components that make up each specific ESS lane. We'll start with the

My Info lane, which contains a blend of HR information and a launch area for accessing four predefined services: Employee Profile, Leave Request, Salary Statement, and Organization Chart.

Let's take a more detailed look at the functionality of the services that make up the My Info lane.

4.4.1 Employee Profile

Employee Profile is a new service delivered in HR Renewal 1.0 FP 4; as of HR Renewal 2.0 FP 1, this service has not been changed. It displays a broad snapshot of employee information that covers both personal and organizational data. The information is presented to the user in a multicard view on the overview screen (see Figure 4.29).

Initially, the user would access the Employee Profile by clicking the EMPLOYEE PROFILE button in the My Info lane on the ESS landing page. When you select this option, a separate window is opened, which then shows the expanded Employee Profile. The Talent and Notes/Attachment options are available from this expanded view.

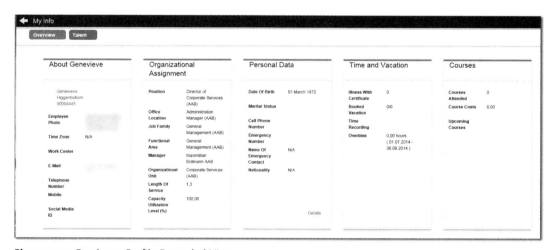

Figure 4.29 Employee Profile Expanded View

From the personal data card, the user can click a hyperlink to launch the Web Dynpro for ABAP version of the Personal Profile in a separate window. If you are an existing user of ESS and you've implemented ESS on EHP 6 and above, then you'll notice that there have been no updates to this service as of the most current release. Any existing configuration and customization will continue to work as they do in your current environment.

The configuration for Employee Profile is located in a shared table that is also used by the MSS and HR Professional roles. Note that we will briefly detail the configuration options for Employee Profile here but will take a longer look at this service in Chapter 6.

To configure data retrieval in Employee Profile, follow the path Transaction SPRO • PERSONNEL MANAGEMENT • EMPLOYEE SELF-SERVICE UI5 • EMPLOYEE PROFILE • CREATE CONFIGURATION WITH FIELD GROUPS in the IMG, as shown in Figure 4.30.

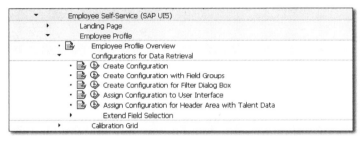

Figure 4.30 Employee Profile Configuration Options

After executing the IMG step, you will be taken to the data retrieval overview configuration table. Highlight the configuration for SAP_ESS_UI5_EMP_OVERVIEW, and then double-click the ADD FIELDS TO A CONFIGURATION folder shown in Figure 4.31.

In the ADD FIELDS TO A CONFIGURATION screen, you will see the corresponding field groups that are displayed on the card view. You can add additional fields to the various groups, remove fields, or reorder the sequence in which the data is presented to the user. See Figure 4.32 for the configuration of field groupings in the Employee Profile.

One of the important things to note is that adding a field group also adds a card on the overview screen, so you have the option of adding additional cards with information that may be more relevant to your organization. If you add a card that was *not* delivered with the standard service, then you'll also need to maintain the BAdI for Card Visibility (see Figure 4.34 later on).

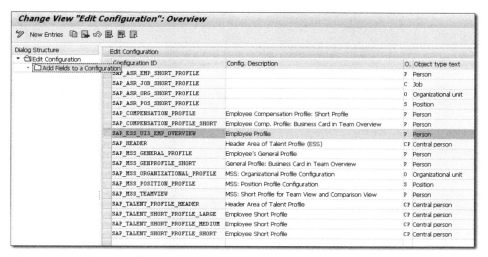

Figure 4.31 Employee Profile Field Group Configuration Overview

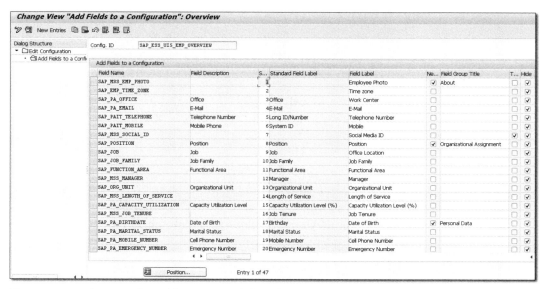

Figure 4.32 Employee Profile Field Group Detailed Configuration

An example of the talent pane within the Employee Profile is seen in Figure 4.33.

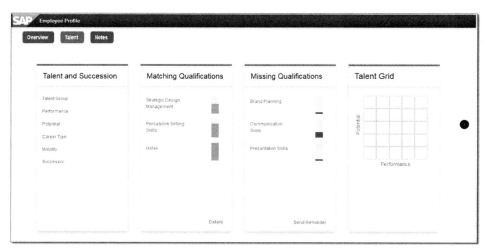

Figure 4.33 Employee Profile—Talent Pane

Talent Profile

The Talent Profile is now part of the Employee Profile service. Along with the refreshed UI, you'll also notice some additional succession planning functionality that had previously only been available to managers and HR personnel.

New to Talent Profile for ESS are the Talent Grid and the Talent and Succession cards. If you have already implemented succession planning, then you will be familiar with the Talent Grid functionality and the information that is displayed in the Talent and Succession cards. There are a few things to be aware of when thinking about this service. In order for information to be displayed in the talent grid, you should have the talent assessment piece configured for MSS. The talent cards for employees are primarily for informational purposes; employees can see how they are rated, but they are not allowed to make changes.

Another item to consider for this service profile are the matching and missing qualifications profile cards. Both cards contain links that assume you have LSO integration turned on and are using it to provide a holistic view from a talent perspective. If you do not have LSO integration active and are not planning to use the succession management component, then you have the option to hide this Talent Profile overview. SAP provides a BAdI that allows you to deactivate the view should this feature not be relevant to your organization (see Figure 4.34).

To configure calibration grid settings in the talent profile, follow the IMG menu path Transaction SPRO • PERSONNEL MANAGEMENT • EMPLOYEE SELF-SERVICE UI5 • EMPLOYEE PROFILE • CALIBRATION GRID (as shown in Figure 4.35).

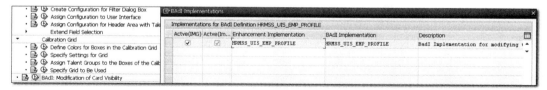

Figure 4.34 BADI: Card Visibility for Removing Talent Profile Overview

Figure 4.35 Calibration Grid Configuration Settings

Tip

The missing qualifications and matching qualifications cards require LSO integration. What if you don't have LSO installed, but you do have your qualifications catalog set up and want to track your employees' qualifications? You can still make use of the previous Talent Profile Web Dynpro for ABAP service that was delivered with EHP 6. You can set up this service to be available to your users via the My Services lane, which we'll discuss in Section 4.5.

4.4.2 Leave Request

The leave request has been a long-standing ESS service; with it, users not only can create leave requests but also can view their leave histories. Beginning in HR Renewal 1.0 FP 4, this service was converted to SAPUI5 and now sports a clean, modern take on the existing leave request. If you're a current ESS user with this functionality enabled, then you should transition into the new service quite easily. Although the interface has been refreshed, the features that were available previously have remained the same. In addition, from a configuration standpoint, if you currently have this service enabled, then your configuration will remain the same as the current Web Dynpro for ABAP service and should require no changes (barring any enhancements or modifications to the ESS service). Let's take a look at some of the features delivered with this service.

Figure 4.36 shows the standard delivered ESS leave request, which includes team calendar and time accounts (quota balances) sections so that the user can determine how much leave is available prior to making the request. In previous releases of ESS, time accounts were a separate ESS service; the SAPUI5 update means that the user is not required to click additional tabs to view this information.

Figure 4.36 Leave Request

Note the LEAVE HISTORY button, which represents a more modern take on the traditional "tab" view. Leave history can be viewed in one of two ways: either via the initial default card view (Figure 4.37) or in a list view (Figure 4.38). Users can toggle between the two views by selecting the CARD VIEW icon in the upper-left corner of the service. As with the previous releases of ESS, users can maintain their leave requests while in the history view by selecting the pencil icon or delete a leave request by selecting the trash can icon.

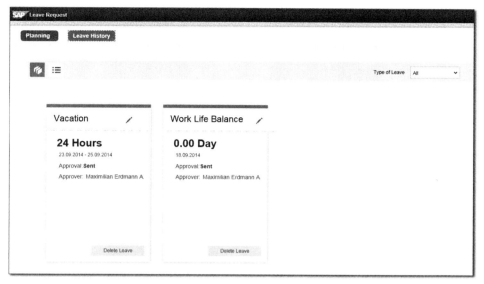

Figure 4.37 Leave History Card View

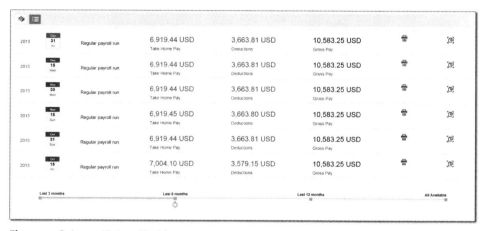

Figure 4.38 Leave History List View

4.4.3 Salary Statement

Another long-standing ESS service that was freshened in HR Renewal is the Pay Statement service, which now has the same clean and modern feel as other SAPUI5 services.

However, this service contains a bit of the old and the new, so it should present little challenge for users to get up to speed on its use. One of the changes with the new update is in the way users will select their pay statements. In previous releases, you could select the number of pay statements available via a dropdown menu, and the available pay statements were displayed in a table format. Now, you can determine which statements to view by using a slider on the overview screen. The default view is presented to users in a card format (Figure 4.39), but users also have the option of viewing the overview in list form (Figure 4.40), as with the leave request.

Figure 4.39 Pay Statement Card View

Figure 4.40 Pay Statement List View

Both views offer two icons—the PRINT icon and the PDF icon—which brings us to the "old" part of what's old and new. The configuration for the pay statement will stay the same as in the previous release if you have ESS implemented with this service enabled. Most organizations have their own take on what their pay statements should look like—a degree of flexibility that's always been available with ESS. If you have a customized form that you're using currently for ESS, then that form will remain the same; the new SAPUI5 service still references the HR Forms Editor (Transaction PE51), so when you click the PDF icon, a separate pop-up screen will open to display your form. The net effect is that users can both print and save their pay statements if they wish.

The print function accessed on the overview screen has seen some enhancements. In the new SAPUI5 version, the PRINT icon directs users to a central batch printer, which typically is useful to payroll personnel but not so much to the individual ESS user. Because some users might assume that clicking the PRINT icon will connect to their default printer and it instead routes to the central batch printer, SAP provides the option to remove the PRINT icon from the overview screen. To access the BAdI shown in Figure 4.41 in order to remove the PRINT icon, follow this IMG path: Transaction SPRO • PERSONNEL MANAGEMENT • EMPLOYEE SELF-SERVICE UI5 • SALARY STATEMENT • FORMS USING HR FORMS EDITOR (PE51) • BADI: DEFINE SETTINGS.

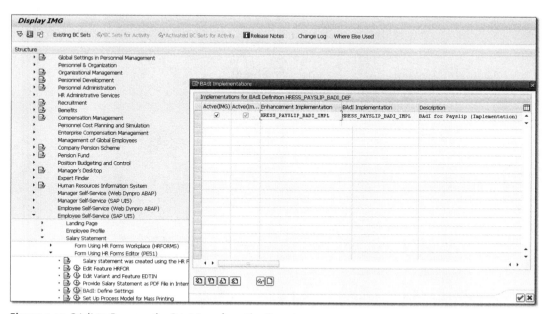

Figure 4.41 BAdI to Remove the Print Icon from the Overview

4.4.4 Organization Chart

As of HR Renewal 1.0 FP 4, ESS users can now view their placement in the organizational chart with the Workforce Viewer. If you're an existing MSS user and your organization implemented either MSS Add-On 1.0 or the initial release of HR Renewal 1.0, then you'll recognize this service as SAP's version of the organizational chart that used embedded Nakisa. This is a shared service with MSS, so we'll spend more time on its configuration in Chapter 5. What's important now is that you can launch it by clicking the My INFO tab in an expanded view.

If the ESS user happens to be a manager, she can also multitask and perform additional functions for her team from the organizational chart. In Figure 4.42, the user and manager Bella Dove can see small business cards within the organizational chart functionality; using these cards, she can access the quick view, which is a shorter version of the Employee Profile, and launch an email from the card view.

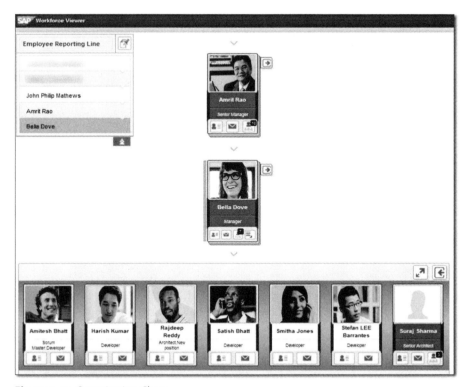

Figure 4.42 Organization Chart

4.4.5 Lane Configuration

The configuration for the services found on the My Info lane is performed in Transaction LPD_CUST (Figure 4.43 and Figure 4.44). If you're an existing ESS customer, you'll no doubt be very familiar with this table and its configuration options. You can access the configuration options for My Info by following the IMG navigation path Transaction SPRO • Personnel Management • Employee Self-Service UI5 • Landing Page • My Information • Configure Launchpad for My Information or using Transaction LPD_CUST.

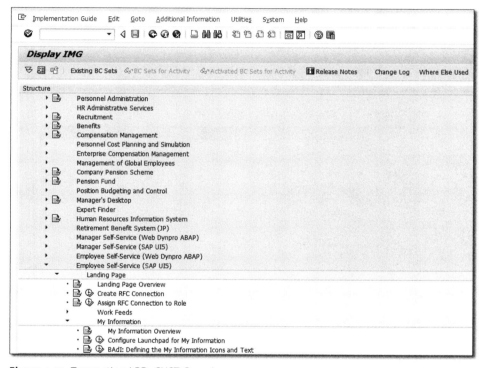

Figure 4.43 Transaction LPD_CUST Overview

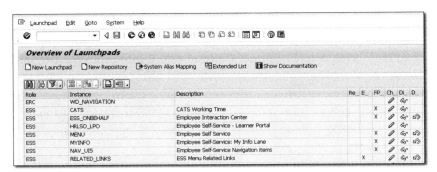

Figure 4.44 Transaction LPD_CUST: ESS Menu Role and Instance Configuration Options

Double-click on the ESS role and MYINFO instance to access the service configuration. Open the MY INFO LANE SERVICES folder, and select the service(s) to be maintained.

The delivered launch page configuration customizes the Employee Profile (Figure 4.45), Leave Request (Figure 4.46), and Salary Statement services (Figure 4.47).

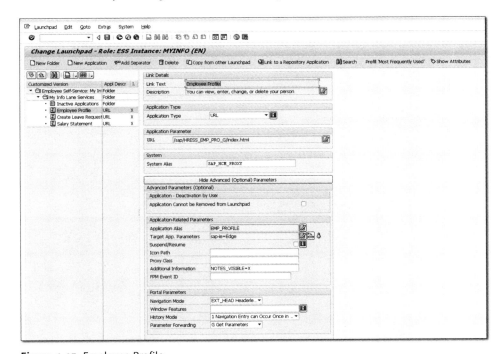

Figure 4.45 Employee Profile

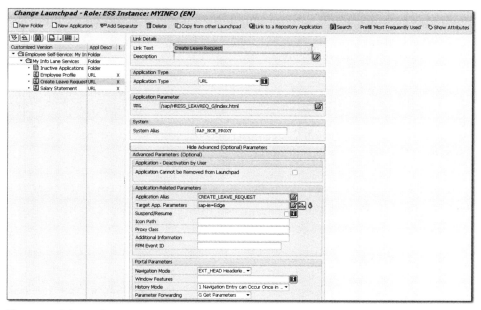

Figure 4.46 Leave Request

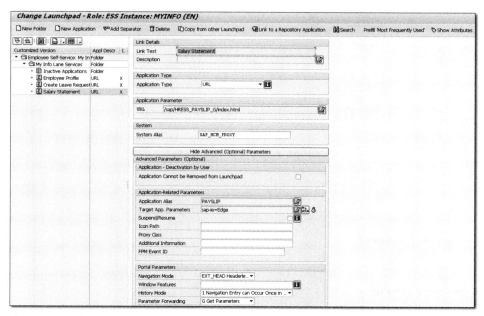

Figure 4.47 Salary Statement

Target Application Parameters

Due to browser-specific changes with Internet Explorer, you will need to maintain the target application parameter for all SAPUI5 services and ESS Web Dynpro for ABAP services with the following entry: `sap-ie=EDGE`.

In HR Renewal 1.0 FP 4, a compatibility error message is displayed that can cause the services to not render or function properly. Maintaining the target application parameter with `sap-ie=EDGE` prevents the compatibility error message from being displayed to the user. With the new SAPUI5 services, users will need to ensure that the "compatibility view" setting is not active.

Now that we've covered the My Info lane, we will move on to the My Services lane and all of its components.

4.5 My Services

My Services is another lane on the central ESS landing page that became available to the user in HR Renewal 1.0 FP 4 (no changes as of HR Renewal 2.0 FP 1). This lane contains a blend of SAPUI5 services and Web Dynpro for ABAP apps that are frequently used by the employee, which can be marked as FAVORITES (Figure 4.48). Some additional functions are available in the expanded view, which displays groupings of services in the same card view available with other converted SAPUI5 services.

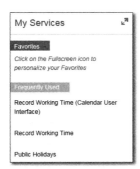

Figure 4.48 My Services Lane

Due to the volume of services available and the global nature of ESS, in the following sections we will take a look at a representative swath of the services that SAP delivers with the My Services lane and what configuration options are available for tailoring the services to your needs. You can view the complete list of services available in Transaction LPD_CUST for the ESS Menu, ESS `LSP_LPO`, and ESS Related Links roles and instances.

The following service area groupings are available in the standard delivery of My Services and are able to be viewed in the expanded lane view shown in Figure 4.49:

▶ Active Applications

▶ My Processes

▶ Related Links

▶ Team

▶ Corporate Information

You can use the ACTIVE APPLICATIONS card on the overview screen for quick links to services that HR would like to make available to employees. The IMG setting to store services in the quick links card is shown in Figure 4.56 in the MY SERVICES configuration section.

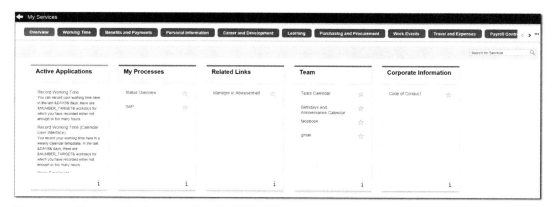

Figure 4.49 Overview Services

4.5.1 Working Time

The Working Time card makes the following time-related service groupings available (see Figure 4.50):

▶ Time Recording

▶ Leave Request & Holidays

- Employment Percentage
- Time Statement
- Clock In/Out Corrections

Figure 4.50 Working Time Services

4.5.2 Benefits and Payment

The Benefits and Payment card displays the following benefits- and pay-related service groupings (see Figure 4.51):

- Benefits Enrollment Overview
- Enroll for Your Benefits
- Submit Claims for Your Benefits
- Payment

Figure 4.51 Benefits and Payment Services

4.5.3 Personal Information

The Personal Information card displays the Personal Information personal info–related service grouping (see Figure 4.52):

- ▶ Employee Profile
- ▶ Personal Profile
- ▶ Personnel File
- ▶ Request Termination
- ▶ Change Permanent Residence
- ▶ Birth of a Child

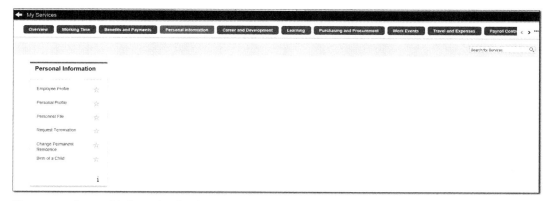

Figure 4.52 Personal Information Services

4.5.4 Career and Development

The Career and Development card displays the following career-related service groupings (see Figure 4.53):

- ▶ Job Opportunities
- ▶ Talent Profile
- ▶ Appraisal Documents

Figure 4.53 Career Services

4.5.5 Learning

The Learning card displays the learning- and training-related service grouping (see Figure 4.54), categorized under Training Home.

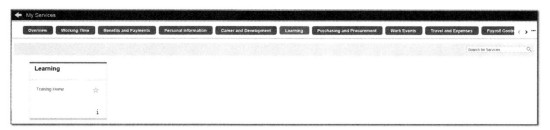

Figure 4.54 Learning Services

4.5.6 Travel and Expenses

The Travel and Expenses card displays the following travel service groupings (see Figure 4.55):

▸ Overview

▸ Create New

▸ General Information

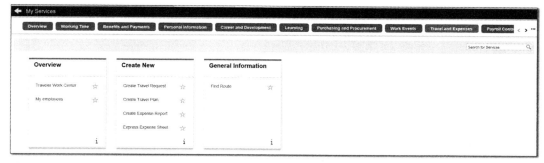

Figure 4.55 Travel and Expenses Services

4.5.7 Lane Configuration

As with the My Info lane, you can configure available services in Transaction LPD_CUST by following the IMG path Transaction SPRO • Personnel Manage-ment • Employee Self-Service UI5 • Landing Page • My Information • Config-ure Launchpad for My Services or using Transaction LPD_CUST (Figure 4.56).

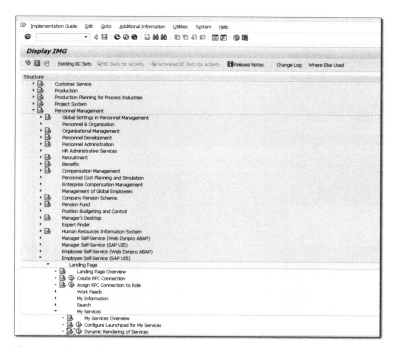

Figure 4.56 Configuring My Services Launchpad Options

The services available in the expanded view are a mixture of SAPUI5, Web Dynpro for ABAP, and external URLs. Transaction LPD_CUST, which is used for both Web Dynpro for ABAP and SAPUI5 services, can be tricky at times; in fact, it doesn't even group all the SAPUI5 services in one specific menu. Figure 4.57 illustrates how the configuration for the SAPUI5 Record Working Time service is delivered. Please note that the application type for all SAPUI5 services will be URL, which can also be used to launch external URLs to access information or even third-party applications. Also, for SAPUI5 services, the application parameter for the URL will reference the relative URL path found in Transaction SICF.

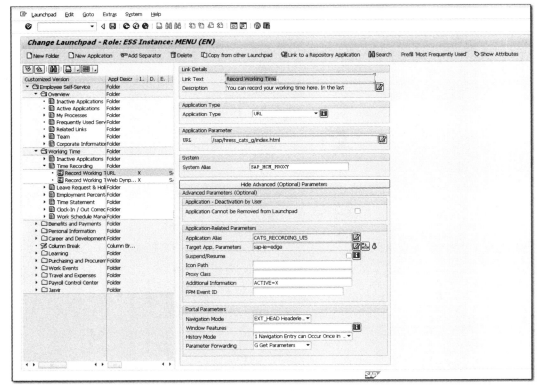

Figure 4.57 ESS Menu in Transaction LPD_CUST

Recall that if you want to flag applications as helpful for employees, you can store them as quick links. In order to display a service in the Active Applications card as a quick link, you must enter an X in the ADDITIONAL INFORMATION field for the service.

SAP delivers a wealth of services out of the box, but you have freedom of choice to use only those services that are relevant to your organization by controlling which cards are displayed and which services are contained within each area grouping card. In the case of the My Services lane, each application grouping card is represented by a folder, and the services are assigned to the folder within Transaction LPD_CUST configuration.

4.6   My Time and the New SAPUI5 Timesheet

HR Renewal 2.0 FP 1 brings a new lane to ESS users for time entry: the My Time lane, shown in Figure 4.58. The lane displays a small calendar view, along with two buttons that launch the users into additional tasks. When a user clicks the RECORD TIMES (clock) button, a separate window showing the full timesheet application opens; when he clicks the PRINT button, the current Web Dynpro for ABAP print functionality launches.

Figure 4.58 My Time Lane

If you're an existing user of ESS and currently using the timesheet service, then you're probably aware of the timesheet's evolution, first through enhancement packs and then the calendar view UI changes in the HR Renewal 1.0 initial shipment release. Now, in HR Renewal 2.0 FP 1, SAP has converted the timesheet into an SAPUI5 service to match all the other SAPUI5 services.

In fact, a lot has changed. One of the updates that SAP had previously made in the Java version of the timesheet removed the ability to display two weeks of time to the user—functionality that had been available in the ITS version. Next, in the Web Dynpro for ABAP update for the timesheet in EHP 6, SAP brought *back* this capability and added the ability to display time vertically or horizontally. In the latest release of the SAPUI5 timesheet (as of HR Renewal 2.0 FP 1), SAP regressed to displaying only one week of the time recording period, forcing manual advance to the next week for a user to enter in his or her time to complete the period if the organization is using biweekly or semimonthly time recording.

Now, let's take a look at the timesheet in its current incarnation. Figure 4.59 displays the new look of the SAPUI5 timesheet. As with the calendar-based Web Dynpro for ABAP timesheet from the HR Renewal 1.0 initial shipment (see Figure 4.60), the revamped SAPUI5 timesheet also presents the user with a calendar view, although it is displayed in weekly increments instead of monthly blocks. Otherwise, the new interface is simpler and makes it easier for a user to quickly view what he or she has entered in previous weeks.

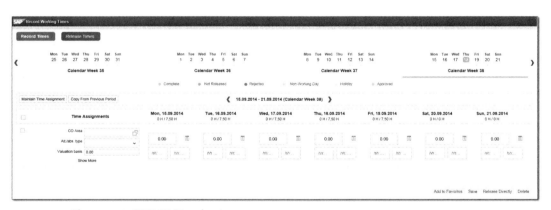

Figure 4.59 SAPUI5 Timesheet

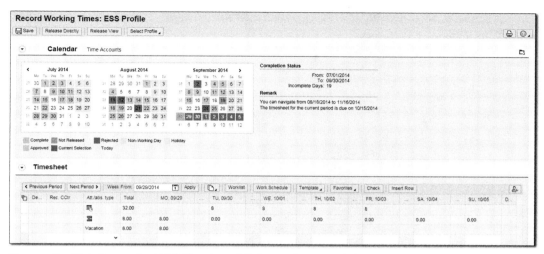

Figure 4.60 Web Dynpro for ABAP Timesheet (HR Renewal 1.0 Initial Shipment)

You can enter time data manually by clicking the MAINTAIN TIME ASSIGNMENT button (see Figure 4.61), or you can click the SUGGESTED tab (see Figure 4.62) and choose from several options.

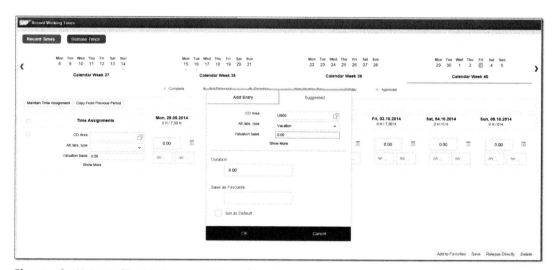

Figure 4.61 Maintain Time Assignments (Manual Entry)

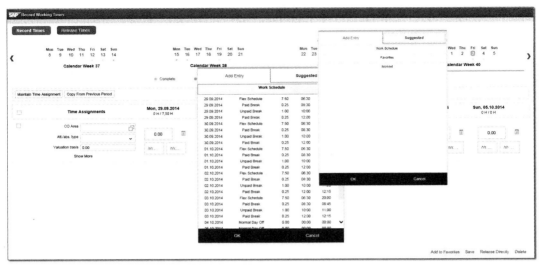

Figure 4.62 Maintain Time Assignments (Suggested)

One piece of timeless functionality is the option to enter weekly time and save it as a favorite, providing a favorite name and selecting either the WITH TIMES or WITHOUT TIMES radio button, as shown in Figure 4.63.

Figure 4.63 Add a Timesheet to Favorites

The SAPUI5 version of the timesheet also gives the employee the option to enter a note about his or her time for the approving manager, as shown in Figure 4.64.

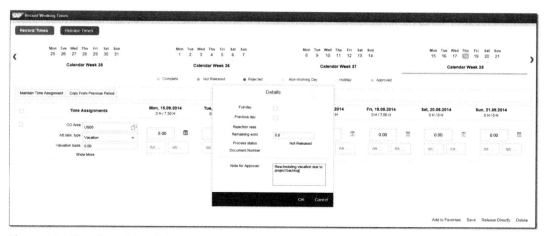

Figure 4.64 Timesheet Notes Feature

Employees can save their timesheets and release their time directly from the Record Times view (see Figure 4.65). As with the previous Web Dynpro for ABAP version, there is also a Release Times view that presents users with all entered time in a tabular format (see Figure 4.66).

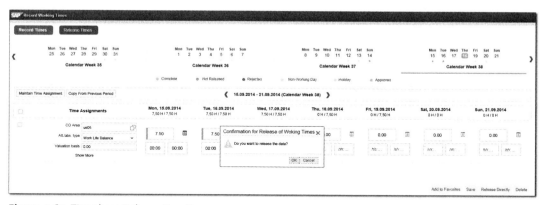

Figure 4.65 Timesheet Release Pop-Up

One additional feature that should be mentioned is the message bar that is displayed on all SAPUI5 services, which can be minimized or expanded by the user. This bar can display a variety of messages, from confirmations to application-specific or Page Builder Suite–related errors. In Figure 4.67, note the YOUR DATA HAS BEEN SAVED message that appears at the bottom of the screen.

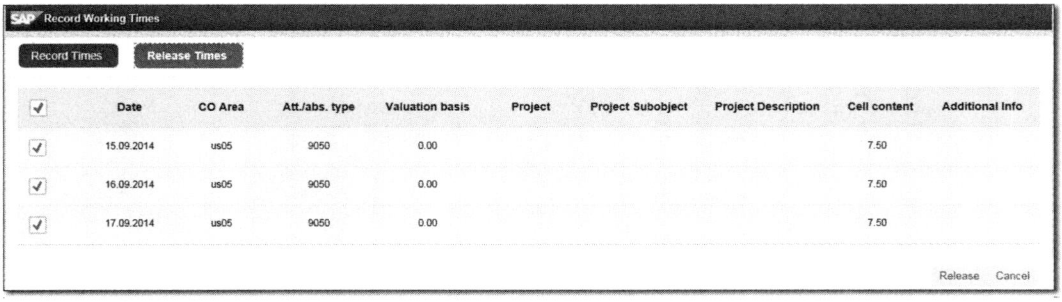

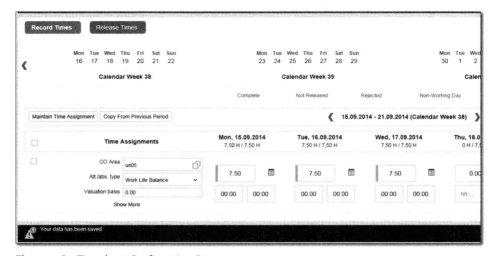

Figure 4.66 Timesheet Release Time View

Figure 4.67 Timesheet Confirmation Bar

If you are currently using the ESS timesheet and, in particular, the Web Dynpro for ABAP Calendar View timesheet delivered with the initial shipment of HR Renewal 1.0, then you only need to update your configuration in one area. If you have your configuration set to display two weeks, simply adjust the profile settings to display only one week. That's it!

You can decide which HR Renewal timesheet (either the older Web Dynpro for ABAP view or the new SAPUI5 conversion) will work best for your organization. If you choose to not use the My Time lane, then you can continue to use your existing timesheet by updating the configuration in Transaction LPD_CUST for My Services.

4.7 My Learnings

HR Renewal 1.0 FP 4 brought the My Learnings lane to the new landing page. This lane shows content that is displayed from an integrated LSO system. As of HR Renewal 2.0 FP 1, on-premise LSO integration is the only option available, and cloud-based SuccessFactors data will not be presented in this view. As with all the lanes on the landing page, the user is presented with additional data or options in the expanded panel. On the lane itself, however, there are two standard category options.

The My Bookings section of the learning lane shows a series of courses, course types, and course dates, as shown in Figure 4.68. The Services portion of the lane delivers additional learning options:

- Training Home
- Search
- Browse Catalog
- Training Calendar
- Top Ten Courses
- Profile Matchup

Figure 4.68 My Learnings Lane

The expanded My Learnings panel displays an overview of an employee's training, along with expiration dates and completion status (see Figure 4.69), in three categories:

- ▸ Classroom

- ▸ E-Learning

- ▸ Curriculum & Course Program

The employee can also launch training from this view; in the case of E-Learning, training is launched in a separate window.

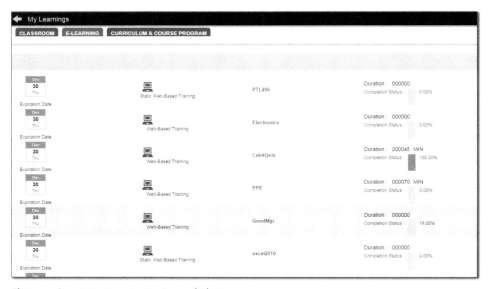

Figure 4.69 My Learning Lane Expanded View

One of the options found in the Services portion of the lane is Training Home, which launches the Web Dynpro for ABAP Training Home service (see Figure 4.70). This application was converted to Web Dynpro for ABAP in the initial shipment of HR Renewal 1.0 and, as of HR Renewal 2.0 FP 1, has not been enhanced.

The configuration options to set which services are presented to the employee in the learning lane are found in Transaction LPD_CUST, using the ESS role and the HRLSO_LPO instance (see Figure 4.71). In the services of the My Learning lane, you can also link to external information (i.e., corporate learning policies, expense reimbursement information, etc.), which can provide additional support to the employee as he or she registers for a course. Additional content links can be set up in Transaction LPD_CUST and assigned to the appropriate role and instance.

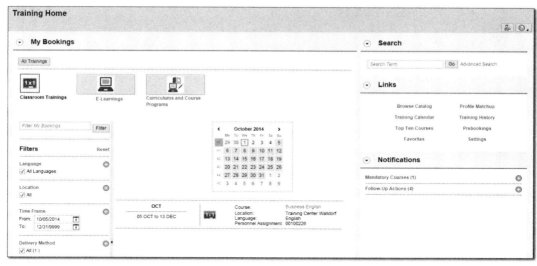

Figure 4.70 Web Dynpro for ABAP My Training Home

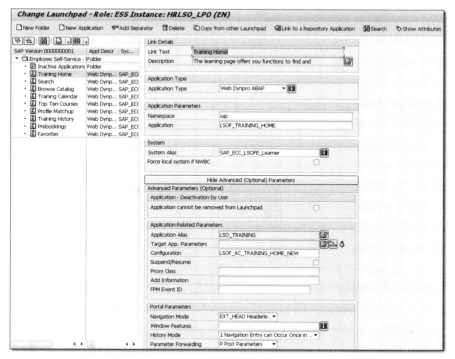

Figure 4.71 Web Dynpro for ABAP Training Home (Transaction LPD_CUST Entry)

4.8   Work Feeds

The Work Feeds lane shown in Figure 4.72 is another shared service lane between ESS, MSS, and HR Professional. The content that is available in the Work Feeds lane can be configured by the administrator, and users can subscribe to or unsubscribe from content updates that are the most or least relevant to them (see Figure 4.73). Typically, for ESS those updates would pertain to the timesheet (timesheet due date), expiring qualifications, salary statements, and so on.

Figure 4.72 Work Feeds Lane

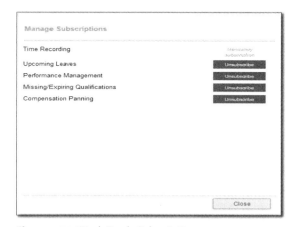

Figure 4.73 Work Feeds Subscriptions

In this chapter, we won't discuss the configuration options for work feeds; instead, we present the configuration information for the necessary configuration settings and the batch program settings for work feeds in Chapter 5.

4.9 Search

Like Work Feeds, the Search lane is another cross-functional service that is shared with ESS, MSS, and HR Professional. This lane became available to ESS users with the delivery of HR Renewal 1.0 FP 4.

The search feature behaves a bit like a Google search, in that it returns any result for any configured "object" (see Figure 4.74). The employee can type in the name of an employee or position that he or she is searching for, and all possible values are returned, with filter options for people, employee, organization unit, and position.

Figure 4.74 Search Lane

When SAP started converting services to Web Dynpro for ABAP, a lot of customers asked what happened to the Who's Who service that allowed employees to search for other employees and view data that was returned based upon query settings for the service. Although SAP thus far has not mentioned plans to update that service, the new search functionality provides a convenient alternative to users because most of the data that had been displayed in Who's Who can be found in the search returns. The employee's position in the organizational structure is available to view by selecting the ORGANIZATIONAL TREE icon in the quick view panel, which launches Workforce Viewer to display the organizational hierarchy and several actionable options.

One important feature of the Search lane is that return value options are also subject to SAP ERP HCM authorizations, so an employee who is not a manager or an HR professional will not have all options available. Figure 4.75 shows an example of how the data that is returned will be presented to the employee.

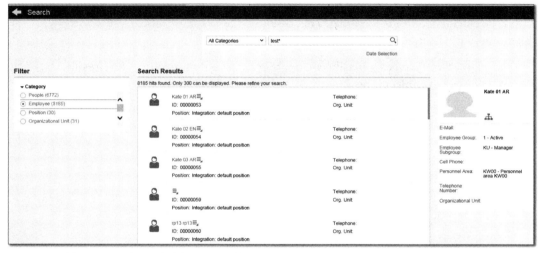

Figure 4.75 Expanded Search Results

SAP has optimized the search functionality for use with embedded search, but you can still use the older, query-based searches if you opt not to use the embedded search model. For additional configuration options for the Search lane, please see Chapter 6.

We've now covered the functionality delivered with the current HR Renewal 2.0 FP 1 and HR Renewal 1.0 FP 4. Now let's discuss the important topic of security authorizations for ESS.

4.10 Managing Security and Authorizations within ESS

The composite role for ESS is SAP_EMPLOYEE_ESS_UI5_1. The ESS composite role contains a set of single Employee Self-Service roles. You should work with your security team to determine which roles are needed for your organization. Table 4.4

lists all of the single roles available in the standard SAP role SAP_EMPLOYEE_ESS_
UI5_1.

Single Role	Description
SAP_EMPLOYEE_ESS_XX_UI5_1	ESS single role containing employee-specific lanes
SAP_EMPLOYEE_OTH_ESS_WDA_1	ESS single role containing non-EA-HR services
SAP_EMPLOYEE_OTH_ESS_WDA_2	Employee role for self-service procurement in SAP ERP
SAP_HR_HAP_PMG_EMPLOYEE_SR	Performance management (generic) single role for employee
SAP_HR_HAP_PMP_EMPLOYEE_SR	Performance management (predefined) single role for employee

Table 4.4 Standard Single Security Roles in the Standard ESS Composite Role SAP_EMPLOYEE_
ESS_UI5_1

The standard Transaction PFCG ESS role can be used by both the SAP Enterprise Portal and SAP NetWeaver Business Client. For uploading instructions of the PFCG role in the portal, please reference SAP Note 1685257 (Upload of SAP Delivered NWBC Roles to the SAP NetWeaver Portal).

We have referred to Transaction LPD_CUST and how to call services with it several times throughout this chapter. There's a link between Transaction LPD_CUST and the user: the personalization option within the role. Personalization is not a new concept to those in security, but for consumers of self-services, it does take on a greater significance.

If you're not a security person, then chances are you haven't really had the opportunity to view the structure of a role. In Section 4.3, we discussed catalogs and their role as a delivery mechanism for content. The tile catalog is assigned to the role menu and is coupled with transaction authorization objects and personalization to provide access to the available roles and instances in Transaction LPD_CUST. This combination is what drives the content that is presented to the end users when they log into ESS.

Figure 4.76 shows the assignment of the HREMPLOYEE catalog to the standard ESS UI5 role. If you created a custom tile catalog in Suite Page Builder, then you would need to replace the HREMPLOYEE catalog with the name of the catalog you created.

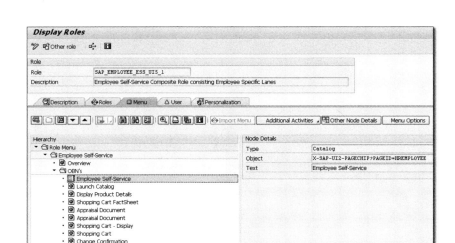

Figure 4.76 Standard Role with Tile Catalog Assignment

As an example, the My Services lane (expanded services) uses the launchpad role and instance name that is derived from the personalization key `HRESS_ACTIONS_LPD` (highlighted in Figure 4.77).

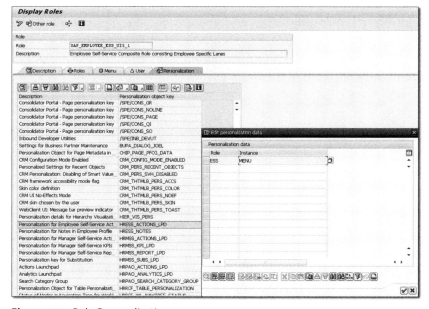

Figure 4.77 Role Personalization

The ESS_MENU role and instance defines the overall layout of the My Services expanded lane and references the launchpad customizing in Transaction LPD_CUST (see Figure 4.78).

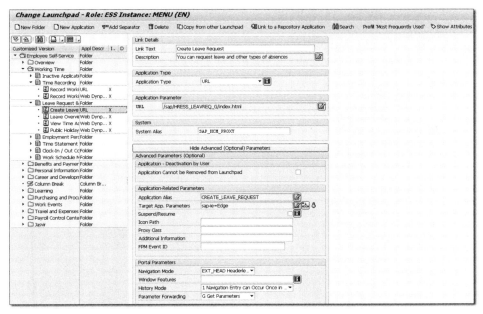

Figure 4.78 ESS LPD_CUST—Create Leave Entry

We've now covered the standard-delivered ESS role and personalization options. Of course, this only covers the basic thoughts behind ESS security, but it provides a good place to start when reviewing how Employee Self-Service will fit into your existing security strategy. If you're a new customer, then you now have a starting place for understanding what authorization is provided out of the box.

4.11 Summary

In this chapter, we reviewed the functionality available in the new Employee Self-Service of HR Renewal. This version of ESS brings a more modern look and feel to the user experience than previous releases of Employee Self-Service. Supported by the concept of lanes, the functionality enables employees to personalize their experiences amidst a new type of web navigation. New services such as Timesheet and Leave Requests have been created in SAPUI5, leveraging the SAP Gateway. Finally, new standard security roles have been provided for customers to model against.

In the next chapter, we will turn our attention from functionality for the employee to functionality for the manager. You will see that there are many similarities between ESS and MSS.

Manager Self-Service provides line management with visibility of their
employees' real-time data and a foundation upon which to deliver key
operational activities, such as workforce planning, performance manage-
ment, and compensation management. This chapter explores the function-
ality available in SAP's latest MSS offering.

5   Manager Self-Service in SAP ERP HCM

Few initiatives within a company offer as many HR transformational opportunities as Manager Self-Service (MSS). MSS functionalities have been around for over
a decade. However, for many organizations MSS is still a challenge to implement
and roll out successfully. Project teams large and small labor around a seemingly
always changing technology stack. Deployment methods also keep changing,
often causing a mix of technology to support. In this chapter, we explore the latest MSS offering based on the SAPUI5 framework as part of HR Renewal.

5.1   MSS Highlights

Before we begin, we want to highlight a few important points about the new
Manager Self-Service functionality part of HR Renewal.

The first highlight you've already encountered in previous chapters, but it bears
reiterating: Navigation for managers can now be completely different from what
you are used to. We will discuss lanes in detail, but the concepts of a lane and
"expanded" lane are new to self-services with SAP.

Another highlight of HR Renewal is the ability to deploy the solution in a variety
of portals. Before self-service was confined to the SAP Enterprise Portal but this
has now changed, and customers have options to deploy these solutions in a variety of ways including using the SAP NetWeaver Business Client, Microsoft Share-
Point, and any other portal that can consume a web service. Also, managers can
access self-services on the go with new mobile capabilities.

A last highlight of MSS is the inclusion of an SAP organization-based structure, called the Workforce Viewer, which has replaced the Nakisa OrgChart. This new organization chart is one of the ways managers can launch forms, profiles, and other functionalities. We'll cover the Workforce Viewer in detail in this chapter.

5.2 Getting Started

Let's begin our discussion of MSS features and functionality with a list of important application areas and deployment options. These will help you navigate the SAP Service Marketplace if you're looking for advanced MSS information. We will also review important SAP Notes, business functions, and the OData services you'll need to activate to get Manager Self-Service functionality out of the box and up and running.

5.2.1 Application Area

Each service within Manager Self-Service is associated with an application area for categorization and support purposes. The application area is used both for searching for SAP Notes and when creating SAP Customer Messages (now referred to as "Incidents") within the SAP Service Marketplace. The application area for the new Manager Self-Service is CA-MSS (Manager Self-Service), which is divided into the following subareas:

- CA-MSS-APL: Manager Self-Service—Application
- CA-MSS-HCM: Manager Self-Service—HR
- CA-MSS-OVR: Manager Self-Service—Workset Work Overview
- CA-MSS-RPT: Manager Self-Service—Reports
- CA-MSS-TEC: Manager Self-Service—Technical
- CA-MSS-TEM: Manager Self-Service—Workset Team

You should also look at the PA-ESS-XX (ESS-Common Parts), PA-AS (HR Processes & Forms), CA-ESS (Employee Self-Service) and CA-TS (Time Sheet) application areas.

Important SAP Notes

We recommend that you reference SAP Note 1965692 (HR Renewal 2.0: Release Information Note), which contains important information about SAP Business Suite release information for HR Renewal, including Manager Self-Service.

If you are interested in SAP's rapid-deployment solution (RDS) for ESS and MSS, refer to SAP Note 2010994. This article includes an attachment titled "Quick Guide to Implementing the SAP Employee and Manager Self-Service Rapid-Deployment Solution." Even if you're not implementing MSS as an RDS, you should take a look at this document.

5.2.2 Deployment Options

Recall from Chapter 2 of this book that deployment options matter. Your company may choose to deploy self-services via the SAP Enterprise Portal, the SAP NetWeaver Business Client, or a third-party portal like Microsoft SharePoint. With each method come pros, cons, and a different approach for deployment. Questions and points to consider when selecting which option is right for you include the following:

▶ The look and feel and the ability to enhance the usability of the portal

▶ Support for mobile devices

▶ The manner in which the standard roles are delivered and maintained

▶ Whether the SAP Gateway should be installed on the same or a different server than SAP ERP

These are just a few of the variables that you will consider when looking at the available deployment options. Of course, sometimes this decision has already been made. Nevertheless, let's quickly review the major areas that need to be activated regardless of deployment.

Business Functions

Business functions are activated typically by an SAP Basis resource using Transaction SFW5 (Switch Framework). It's important that SAP Basis works with a functional resource, because some of these business functions are not reversible (that is, once they are turned on, they cannot be turned off). Business functions have served (and will continue to serve) as the mechanism for delivery of innovation coming from SAP on-premise core. It is common now to switch these business functions on in a sandbox first before switching them on in your development environment, but not all customers have a sandbox in which to "play" in order to test these functions out.

In this chapter, we have assumed that the business functions in Table 5.1 have been switched on as part of an EHP 7 implementation. Please note that there are certain business functions that need to be turned on before others.

Business Function	Name	Business Function Prerequisites
HCM_MSS_WDA_1	HCM, MSS on Web Dynpro for ABAP	None
HCM_MSS_WDA_2	HCM, MSS on Web Dynpro for ABAP 2	HCM_MSS_WDA_1
HCM_MSS_UI5_1	HCM, Manager Self-Service on SAPUI5	HCM_MSS_WDA_2
HCM_MSS_UI5_2	HCM, Manager Self-Service on SAPUI5 2	HCM_ESS_UI5_1 HCM_MSS_UI5_1
HCM_PD_ORGVIS_1	HCM, Workforce Viewer 01	HCM_ESS_UI5_1 HCM_MSS_UI5_1 HCM_PAO_CI_3
HCM_ANALYTICS_3	HCM, Analytics for Manager	FND_ANALYTICS_TOOLS
HCM_MSS_OADP_1	HCM, Manager Self-Service Performance Optimization with OADP	HCM_MSS_WDA_2
HCM_PD_UI_1	HCM, PD UI Visualization 01 Technical	None
HCM_PD_UI_2	HCM, PD UI Visualization 01 Technical	HCM_PD_UI_1

Table 5.1 Business Functions Relevant for Manager Self-Service

In addition to business functions, several MSS services will need to be activated as well. We will discuss those now.

Business Functions and Applications

Please reference Appendix A for a thorough list of key business functions and applications for ESS, MSS, and the HR Professional role.

Activation of Services

Before you can use any of the new self-service functionality, you need to activate the services on SAP Gateway. Regardless of whether your SAP Gateway is on the same instance or not, the activation steps are the same.

In the IMG, go to the activity under SAP NetWeaver • Gateway • OData Channel • Administration • General Settings • Activate and Maintain Services or use Transaction /IWFND/MAINT_SERVICE (see Figure 5.1). The following OData services need to be activated for Manager Self-Services:

▸ HROVIS_ORGCHART_SERVICE

▸ HRESS_EMP_WORK_FEEDS_SERVICE

▸ HROVIS_ORGCHART_SERVICE

▸ HRXSS_PERNR_MEMID_SERVICE

▸ HRXSS_PERS_KEY

▸ HRMSS_OTHER_APPROVALS_SERVICE

▸ HRMSS_LEAVE_APPROVAL_SERVICE

▸ HRESS_TEAM_CALENDAR_SERVICE

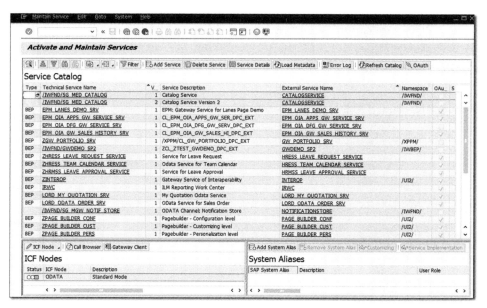

Figure 5.1 Transaction /IWFND/MAINT_SERVICE for Maintaining and Activating OData Services

- HRESS_EMP_PROFILE_SERVICE

- HRMSS_EMPLOYEE_NOTES_SERVICE

- PAO_SEARCH_SERVICE

- PAO_ACTIONMENU

- HRGEN_QUICK_VIEW_SERVICE

- /IWPGW/TASKPROCESSING

- /IWFND/NOTIFICATIONSTORE

- /UI2/LAUNCHPAD

- /UI2/QUICKVIEW

- HROVIS_ORGCHART_SERVICE

- HRGEN_QUICK_VIEW_SERVICE

Again, you will need to work with your SAP Basis or developer resource for this activation, because the SAP Gateway system may or may not be coupled with your SAP ERP system. We do not discuss the advantages or disadvantages of a coupled versus decoupled SAP Gateway system in this book.

From a technical perspective, there is a business server page (BSP) that encapsulates the call to the OData service (or services). Figure 5.2 shows the HRMSS_MY_TEAM_G BSP application, which is making a call to the /sap/opu/OData/sap/HROVIS_ORGCHART_SERVICE/ OData service. When you activate the service via the OData transaction listed previously, the corresponding BSP service will be activated automatically in Transaction SICF.

Other MSS-related BSPs that are activated include the following:

- HRMSS_MY_TEAM_G

- HRMSS_TASKS_G

- HRESS_WRKFEED_G

- HRMSS_TEAMSRV_G

- HRMSS_TEAMCDR_G

- HRMSS_LR_APPR_G

- HRESS_EMP_PRO_G

- HRMSS_MGRANA_G

- HRMSS_LPD_C

- HRMSSATTACH

- HRMSS_SUBS_G

- HRMSS_CATSAPR_G

- HRORGVIS_CHART

- HRGEN_QUICKVIEW

- HRPAO_SEARCH_C

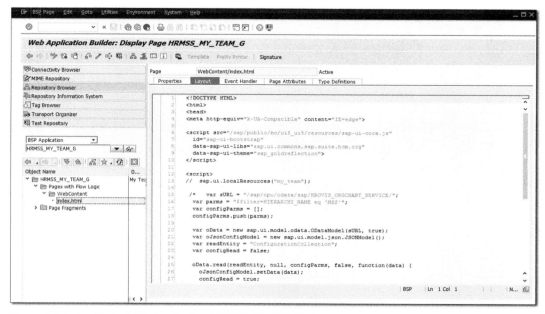

Figure 5.2 index.html of BSP Application HRMSS_MY_TEAM_G

Additional References

To learn more about OData services, including the use of the SAP Gateway and SAPUI5, refer to two available SAP PRESS books:

- *OData and SAP NetWeaver Gateway* by Carsten Bönnen, Volker Drees, André Fischer, Ludwig Heinz, and Karsten Strothmann (2014)
- *Getting Started with SAPUI5* by Miroslav Antolovic (2014)

These are technical guides that can help a development resource get up to speed on the newer technologies that support ESS and MSS within HR Renewal.

Now that we have covered the major items needing activation, let's discuss the MSS landing page, which is the starting point for the new Manager Self-Service functionality.

5.3   MSS Landing Page

In contrast with self-service functionality in the past, which was based on portal tabs, the navigation within the new SAPUI5-based home page is different. The new landing page is lane based, which some users think has a more modern look and feel. (Other users are confused by this layout and prefer the original tabular home page approach.) As with Employee Self-Service, the Suite Page Builder framework provides a foundation for the new lane navigation, look and feel, and overall user experience for Manager Self-Service.

> **New Framework**
>
> If you are familiar with the Homepage framework or portal content navigation delivered via business packages, then note that SAP no longer delivers self-service in this manner. It's important to understand how the new framework is delivered, including the launchpad customizing (Transaction LPD_CUST), security roles, and personalization keys. These are all discussed later in this chapter.

Though they were covered in Chapter 4, let's briefly review the lanes and extended lane concept next, because it is a foundation concept within the new self-service delivery framework, including MSS.

A lane in self-service is simply a widget with information. The lane has a title and the ability to expand to an "expanded lane" in the upper-right corner of the lane. All lanes are scrollable (if the information spills past the border of the lane). Many lanes have FAVORITES and RECENTLY USED sections, which help managers access commonly used applications more quickly.

In the standard delivery of MSS, the manager role has the following lanes available (see Figure 5.3):

▶ My Team

▶ My Reports

▶ Approvals and Substitution

- My Team Services
- My KPIs
- Search (also available for ESS)
- KPI Monitor
- Work Feeds

Figure 5.3 Landing Page Example for Manager Self-Service

It is up to your organization to determine which of these lanes to make available to managers. Depending on your implementation scope, you may not deploy all of these lanes. In fact, in most cases, you will not go live with of all the MSS lanes, because doing so would mean including a lot of functionality in one go.

The expanded lanes contain a deeper dive of information of the lane that was launched. For example, the My Team lane contains a stacked set of employee photos. The user can get access to the Employee Profile (when the user clicks on the photo) from the lane itself.

When the lane is expanded, however, it launches the Workforce Viewer, from which many Manager Self-Service transactions can be initiated. The expanded lane is an "overlay," meaning that it does not display in a new browser window but rather takes over the screen "on top of" all lanes, while the manager does the work in that lane. Once in the expanded lane, the user can click on the back arrow to return to the landing page, with all of the lanes again available.

Let's now discuss each lane available within Manager Self-Service.

5.4 My Team

The My Team lane provides a manager with a view of his or her direct reports. Each employee card within the lane contains photos of the employee (assuming you have stored these photos in SAP). The standard SAP ArchiveLink storage area is where these pictures are sourced from. If the employee photo is not in SAP, then a generic silhouette will appear instead, as shown in Figure 5.4.

> **Tip**
>
> For more information on using employee photos in SAP, reference the "How to Upload Employee Photo in SAP HCM" wiki post on the SAP Community Network at *http://wiki.scn.sap.com*. This will help you begin to use SAP ArchiveLink for photo storage. Make sure you work with your SAP Basis team on this, because it does involve database sizing.

The My Team application is an SAPUI5 application with the technical name `HRMSS_MY_TEAM_G`. It calls OData services `HROVIS_ORGCHART_SERVICE` and `HRXSS_PERNR_MEMID_SERVICE`.

Figure 5.4 My Team Lane

Within the My Team lane, clicking on an employee photo brings you to the Employee Profile (see Figure 5.5).

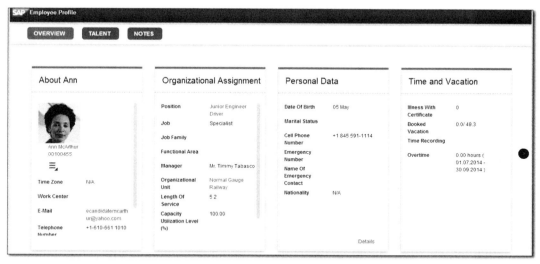

Figure 5.5 Employee Profile—Accessed from the My Team Lane of MSS

5.4.1 Employee Profile

The Employee Profile is covered in detail in Chapter 4. The important thing here is that employees have access to the same Employee Profile application. However, you can implement logic so that the manager can see additional cards and/or information that won't be available for the employee. We will review where and how to do this near the end of the chapter.

The Employee Profile is an SAPUI5 application with technical name `HRESS_EMP_PRO_G`. It calls OData services `/UI2/LAUNCHPAD`, `HRESS_EMP_PROFILE_SERVICE`, and `HRMSS_EMPLOYEE_NOTES_SERVICE`.

New to this release of Manager Self-Service is the ability for managers to create notes from within the tool (see Figure 5.6). These notes are stored in table `HRMSS_D_NOTES`. Attachments within these notes, if used, are stored within the SAP ArchiveLink. The notes features call the `HRMSS_EMPLOYEE_NOTES_SERVICE` OData service.

Figure 5.6 Manager Notes for an Employee

5.4.2 Employee Profile Action Menu

The Employee Profile has an action menu, which allows a manager to perform many self-service actions, including those actions that can be performed "on behalf of" the employee, as shown in Figure 5.7. We will discuss each of these services later in this chapter.

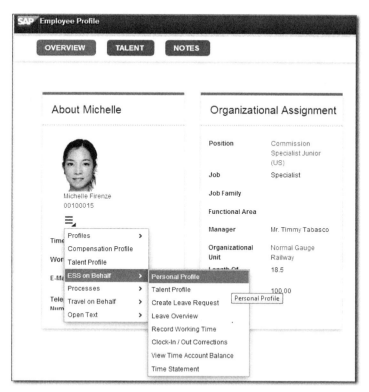

Figure 5.7 Action Menu of the Manager's View of the Employee Profile

5.4.3 People View

The expanded lane within the My Team view launches SAP's Workforce Viewer. This is what we'll call SAP's own manager launchpad, and it's new with the SAPUI5 delivery. The business function HCM_PD_ORGVIS_1 (HCM, Workforce Viewer 01) needs to be activated in Transaction SICF before this Workforce Viewer is available.

The Workforce Viewer is a significant application within Manager Self-Service because it is one of the mechanisms for launching many different services. Alternatively (or additionally), you can launch services via the My Team Services lane, which we will discuss later in the chapter. The default view (shown in Figure 5.8) is the People view, but you can also toggle to the Organization view via the ORGANIZATION button.

The Workforce Viewer is an SAPUI5 application with the technical application name HCM_PD_ORGVIS_1. It calls OData services /UI2/LAUNCHPAD, /UI2/QUICKVIEW, HROVIS_ORGCHART_SERVICE, HRGEN_QUICK_VIEW_SERVICE, and PAO_ACTIONMENU.

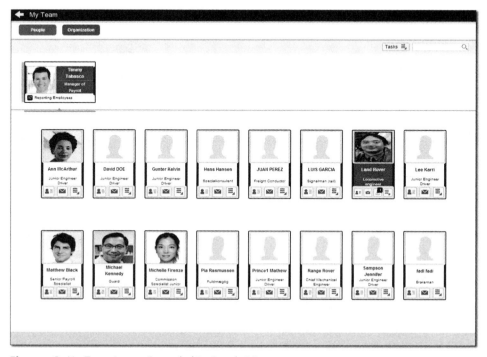

Figure 5.8 My Team Lane—Expanded to People View

Quick View

The quick view option from the Employee Profile (Figure 5.9) allows the manager to see a short profile of an employee within his or her span of control. The information that is shown on the quick view card is configurable in the IMG. The standard configuration ID SAP_PA_SHORT_PROFILE (Employee Quickview) is used and can be copied and enhanced. To configure, follow this IMG path: PERSONNEL MANAGEMENT • MANAGER SELF-SERVICE (SAPUI5) • EMPLOYEE PROFILE • CONFIGURATIONS FOR DATA RETRIEVAL • CREATE CONFIGURATION.

This quick view calls OData service HRGEN_QUICK_VIEW_SERVICE.

Figure 5.9 Quick View from the Expanded My Team Lane

Email

The EMAIL icon will appear for all employees who have valid employee addresses in the system. Clicking on this link will launch the user's default local email program, such as Microsoft Outlook or Lotus Notes.

Action Menu

The action menu (see Figure 5.10) within the Workforce Viewer is the launching point for accessing many applications for the selected employee. Clicking on the right-hand icon below the employee's photo will launch the following out-of-the-box menu options: PROFILES, ESS ON BEHALF, PROCESSES, TRAVEL ON BEHALF, and OPEN TEXT.

The action menu calls OData service PAO_ACTIONMENU. You can view profiles (Talent Profile, Compensation Profile, or Employee Profile; see next subsection) and perform actions on multiple employees. You can configure the standard actions in the launchpad (Transaction LPD_CUST), using the MSS launchpad role and the instances EMPLOYEE_MENU, POSITION_MENU, and ORGANIZATION_MENU.

Figure 5.10 Action Menu within the My Team Expanded Lane

Profiles

From the PROFILES menu option, the manager can open any of the following employee profiles:

- Employee Profile (launches the standard Web Dynpro Application HRMSS_EMP_OVER_PROFILE)

- Compensation Profile (launches the standard Web Dynpro Application HCM_ECM_PROFILE)

- Talent Profile (launches the standard Web Dynpro Application HRTMC_LONG_PROFILE_MSS_NEW)

These profiles were all available in prior releases of MSS but are now consolidated into one place within the Workforce Viewer. Enhancements to any of these profiles can be achieved through the normal ABAP enhancement framework. These profile views are frequently enhanced to exclude certain sections and/or tabs that will not be used by the customer.

ESS on Behalf

The ESS ON BEHALF menu option enables the manager to update the employee's own services on their behalf. This may or may not be an option for your organization, depending on your policies and business requirements.

The services listed in Table 5.2 are available as part of the standard delivery.

Service	Technical Name
Personal Profile	HRESS_A_PERSINFO
Talent Profile	HRTMC_LONG_PROFILE_MSS_NEW
Leave Request	HRESS_A_PTARQ_LEAVREQ_APPL
Leave Overview	HRESS_A_PTARQ_LEAVREQ_APPL
Record Working Times	HRESS_A_CATS_1
Clock-In/Out Corrections	HRESS_A_CORRECTIONS
Time Account Balances	HRESS_A_PTARQ_TIMEACC
View Time Statement	HRESS_A_TIME_DATESEL
Total Compensation Statement	HRESS_A_TCS

Table 5.2 Employee Services Available from the ESS on Behalf Menu

Processes

The manager can launch a form from the PROCESSES link of the employee card within the Workforce Viewer of the My Team expanded lane. A sample list of forms is provided in Table 5.3.

Service	Technical Name
Search Employee Processes	ASR_PROCESSES_DISPLAY
Start Employee Processes—Adobe	ASR_PROCESS_EXECUTE_FPM
Start Transfer	ASR_PROCESS_EXECUTE_OVP
Create Special Payment	ASR_PROCESS_EXECUTE_OVP

Table 5.3 Process Links Available from the Processes Menu

The START TRANSFER and CREATE SPECIAL PAYMENT links launch some example forms that are part of the Floorplan Manager (Web Dynpro for ABAP-based) framework. These forms can be extended as necessary since they are part of the HCM Processes and Forms framework.

More Information

HCM Process and Forms is covered extensively in the SAP PRESS book *SAP ERP HCM Processes and Forms* by Brandon Toombs and Justin Morgalis (2013).

The START EMPLOYEE PROCESSES—ADOBE option is available for customers who want to use the Adobe-based forms. That said, the Adobe Interactive Forms are no longer the technology choice of many organizations for a variety of reasons, but that shouldn't necessarily stop you from using them if your organization believes that doing so is the best option available. SAP will continue to support the Adobe-based forms.

Travel on Behalf

SAP Travel and Expense is not covered in this book, because it is typically handled within the Finance module. However, within the TRAVEL ON BEHALF menu option the manager has the following menu options for initiating travel-related services on behalf of the employee: TRAVEL PROFILE, CREATE EXPENSE REPORT, CREATE EXPRESS EXPENSE SHEET, CREATE TRAVEL PLAN, and CREATE TRAVEL REQUEST.

> **More Information**
>
> For more information on SAP Travel Management, refer to the SAP PRESS book *Configuring Financial Accounting in SAP* by Narayanan Veeriah (2nd edition, 2015).

OpenText

OpenText is a vendor that provides solutions for enterprise information management. The OPENTEXT menu provides the following options for the manager: DIGITAL PERSONNEL FILE, UPLOAD OPENTEXT DOCUMENT, and DISPLAY OPENTEXT PERSONNEL FILE. Through these links, the manager can display filed documents stored within the OpenText solution. Your company needs to have a licensing agreement with OpenText and the associated software installed for these links in order to leverage OpenText options.

Mass Processing from Workforce Viewer

Managers can also start certain forms (such as the special payment form) with multiple employees at the same time. The mass processing feature within the Workforce Viewer is only available for employees (and not for organizational objects). In Figure 5.11, an example is shown in which the manager has added several employees to start a special payment (e.g., a spot bonus). To initiate this transaction, the manager selects the TASKS dropdown list on the top right of the screen. The subsequent screens are the standard HCM Processes and Forms mass processing.

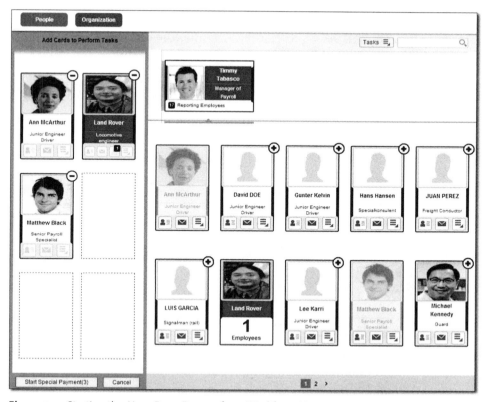

Figure 5.11 Starting the Mass Form Process from Workforce Viewer

Standard SAP delivery offers three applications: Compare Profiles, Start Special Payment, and Start Address Change. You can configure the standard actions in the launchpad (Transaction LPD_CUST) by using the MSS launchpad role and the NAV_UI5 instance.

Mass Processing

If you are using the mass processing functionality, reference SAP Note 2004572 (Launching a Mass Process for Multiple Employees in the "My Team" Lane Results in a Dump), which contains useful information.

Now that we have covered the People view of the Workforce Viewer, let's address the Organization view, which includes transactions and information on both organizational units and positions.

5.4.4 Organization View

From the Organization view, you can choose either the manager's organizational unit hierarchy or the positions view.

Each box in the Organizational Units view (Figure 5.12) represents an organizational unit and shows the following information:

▸ Organizational unit text

▸ Organization unit ID

▸ Manager of the organizational unit

▸ Number of subordinate organizational units

▸ Number of positions within the organization unit

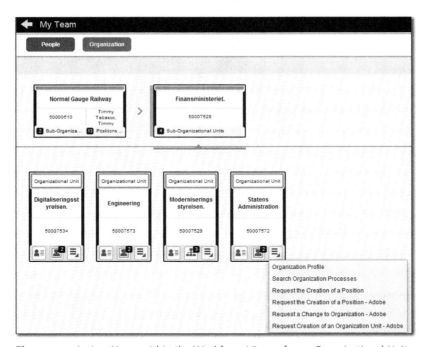

Figure 5.12 Action Menu within the Workforce Viewer for an Organizational Unit

The organizational view (for readers familiar with evaluation paths, this is the O-O structure) provides the ability for the manager to display additional information on his or her organizational unit(s) and performing actions. For example, the manager can view detailed information on the organizational unit (such as enterprise structure, description, qualifications, and cost distribution), request the creation of a position in an organizational unit, or request the creation of an additional organizational unit. These requests are integrated with the HCM Processes & Forms functionality (both Adobe and Web Dynpro for ABAP-based form integration is supported).

Within the Positions view of the Workforce Viewer (see Figure 5.13), the manager's position hierarchy is displayed. (For readers familiar with evaluation paths, this is the O-S-P structure.)

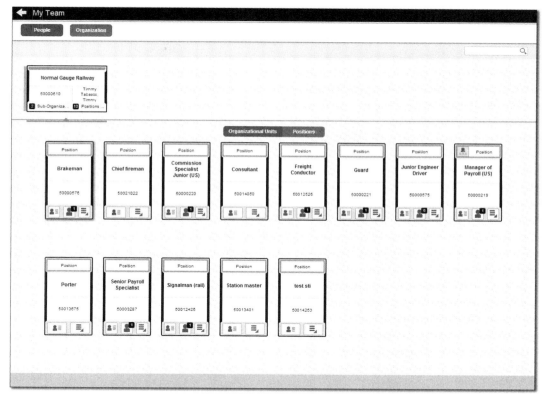

Figure 5.13 Positions View of the Workforce Viewer

As with the Organizational view, the Positions view also gives the manager the ability to perform certain organizational management actions, such as viewing the position profile and requesting a change (or move) to a position within the organizational structure (see Figure 5.14).

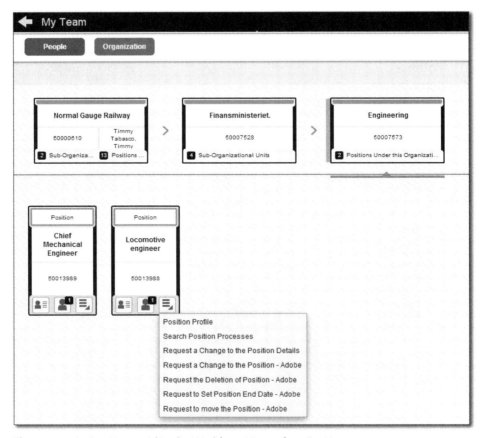

Figure 5.14 Action Menu within the Workforce Viewer for a Position

Next, we will discuss the Workforce Viewer configuration.

5.4.5 Configuration of the Workforce Viewer

Workforce Viewer configuration is new in the SAPUI5 delivery but leverages the familiar Object and Data Provider (OADP). The configuration is split into three visualization IDs that correspond to the three views accessible from within the application (see Figure 5.15). Visualization configuration of the Workforce Viewer is performed in the IMG, via the following path: PERSONNEL MANAGEMENT •

MANAGER SELF-SERVICE (SAPUI5) • LANDING PAGE • MY TEAM • CONFIGURE SETTINGS FOR WORKFORCE VIEWER.

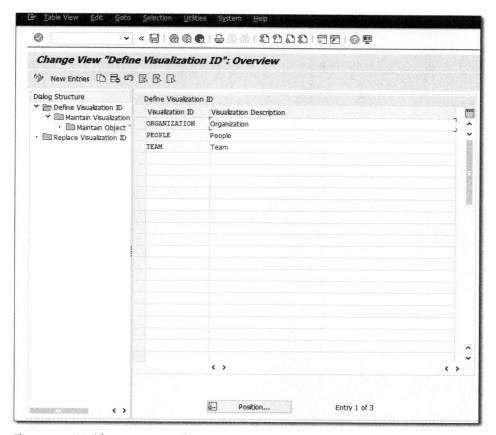

Figure 5.15 Workforce Viewer Configuration within the IMG

Now that you have an overview of the My Team lane within the new HR Renewal functionality, let's jump to the My Team Services lane and the functionality it offers.

5.5   My Team Services

The My Team Services lane provides the manager with options to view information and initiate actions on his or her direct and indirect reports. It offers a way to access applications for employees without using the Workforce Viewer. You will need to determine which services you will want to access here, which services you will access from the Workforce Viewer, and which services you will want available in both areas.

The lane itself (see Figure 5.16) contains a FAVORITES and FREQUENTLY USED section. Once a link is selected, a new browser window is displayed for the application, regardless of whether you are calling a Web Dynpro for ABAP or an SAPUI5 application.

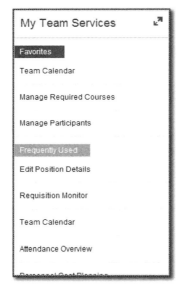

Figure 5.16 My Team Services Lane

The launchpad role and instance name are picked up from the personalization key HRMSS_ACTIONS_LPD on the SAP role (in Transaction PFCG). In the standard shipment, the MSS role and TEAM_MENU instance is assigned, and OTYPE is empty. The personalization key is assigned to the SAP_MANAGER_MSS_CR_UI5_1 MSS composite role. You can update your customized role and instance by replacing the MSS role and TEAM_MENU instance in the HRMSS_ACTIONS_LPD personalization key. See Section 5.10 for more information about how personalization keys are managed within security roles.

My Team Services is an SAPUI5 application with the technical application name HRMSS_TEAMSRV_G. It calls the /UI2/LAUNCHPAD and HRXSS_PERS_KEY OData services.

Once expanded, the My Team Services lane contains the following applications in the standard delivery:

- ▶ Team
- ▶ Recruiting
- ▶ Talent Management
- ▶ Planning
- ▶ Projects
- ▶ Budget
- ▶ Organization

We will review each section of the My Team Services expanded lane now.

Non-HR Services

The Planning, Projects, and Budget lanes can be categorized as non-HR services, so although they provide managers with additional self-service functionality, we won't cover them here.

5.5.1 Team

By default, the TEAM section of the My Team Services expanded lane offers the services shown in Figure 5.17, but we want to highlight a few in the following list:

- ▶ **Attendance Overview**
  The Attendance Overview service (Figure 5.18) offers the manager a summary of the absence and attendance status of their direct and indirect reports. There is an option to display a pie chart with this information as well. Attendance Overview is a Web Dynpro for ABAP application, HRMSS_ATTENDANCE_OVERVIEW.

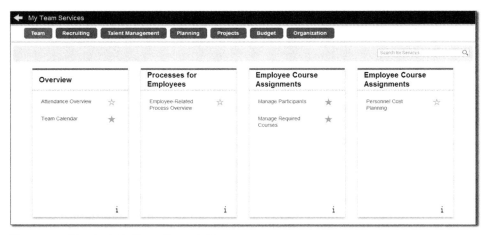

Figure 5.17 Standard My Team Expanded Lane

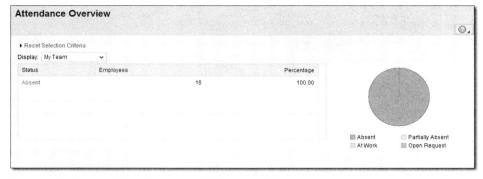

Figure 5.18 Standard Web Dynpro for ABAP Service Attendance Overview

► **Team Calendar**

This Team Calendar service in Figure 5.19 allows the manager to view the absence and attendance data for his or her direct reports at a glance in a calendar format. The manager can filter specific types of absences and direct reports using the filter feature.

The team calendar is an SAPUI5 application available for managers (as of business function HCM_MSS_UI5_1). The technical name of the SAPUI5 application is HRESS_TEAMCDR_G and it calls the HRESS_TEAM_CALENDAR_SERVICE OData service.

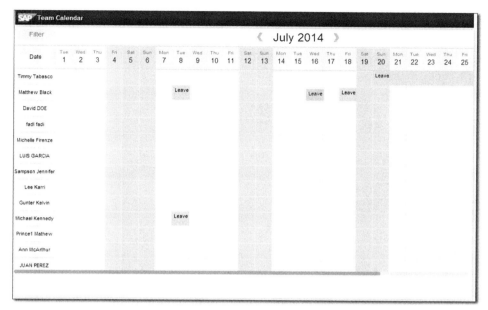

Figure 5.19 Team Calendar Application via Business Function HCM_MSS_UI5_1

▶ **Employee-Related Process Overview**

The Employee-Related Process Overview in Figure 5.20 is the standard Web Dynpro for ABAP service ASR_PROCESSES_DISPLAY from the HCM Processes and Forms framework. Here again we recommend the SAP PRESS book *SAP ERP HCM Processes and Forms* for more detailed information on this and other HCM Processes and Form functionalities.

Figure 5.20 Process Overview for the Manager (HCM Process and Forms)

▶ **Other Services**

Other standard delivered services for the manager in the My Team expanded lane include the Manage Participants (LSO_MANAGE_PARTICIPANTS) and Managed

Required Courses (`LSO_MANAGE_MANDATORY_ASSIGN`) Learning Solution services and the `WDA_HCP_DET_PLAN` Personnel Cost Planning (PCP) service.

The PCP service is pictured in Figure 5.21 and is only available for those customers who have implemented that module.

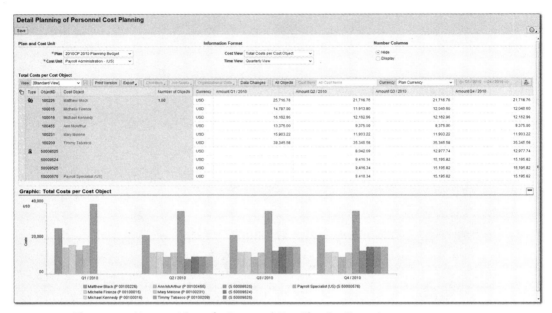

Figure 5.21 Manager View of a Personnel Cost Planning Scenario

5.5.2 Recruiting

The recruiting section in Figure 5.22 contains the following three standard services:

- **Requisition Monitor**
  Web Dynpro for ABAP service `HRRCF_A_REQUI_MONITOR`

- **Requisition Requests Overview**
  Web Dynpro for ABAP service `HRRCF_C_REQUEST_BROWSER`

- **Create Requisition Request**
  Web Dynpro for ABAP service `ASR_PROCESS_EXECUTE_FPM`

All three of these services are related to the applicant tracking and administration available within the on-premise SAP ERP HCM E-Recruiting module.

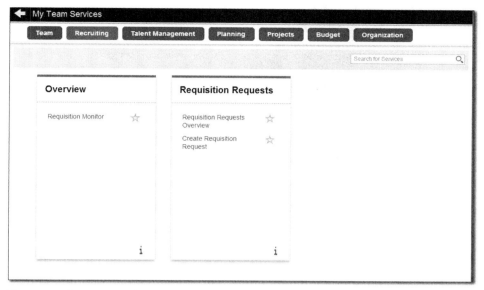

Figure 5.22 Recruiting under My Team Services

5.5.3 Talent Management

The following services are available in the TALENT MANAGEMENT areas within My Team Services. This section (see Figure 5.23) contains links to the on-premise SAP ERP HCM Talent Management functionality.

- ► **Talent Management Page**
  Web Dynpro for ABAP service `HRMSS_TALENT_HOME_PAGE`; includes details on performance management and competency matchups

- ► **Talent Assessment**
  Web Dynpro for ABAP service `HRTMC_TA_DASHBOARD`; includes Assessment, Development Plan, and the Calibration Grid

- ► **Performance Management**
  Web Dynpro for ABAP service `HAP_A_PMP_OVERVIEW`; predefined performance management process

- ► **Compensation Planning**
  Web Dynpro for ABAP service `HCM_ECM_PLANNING_UI_GAF`

- ► **Compensation Planning Overview**
  Web Dynpro for ABAP service `HCM_ECM_PLANNING_OVERVIEW_OIF`

> ► **Compensation Information**
> Web Dynpro for ABAP service `HCM_ECM_TEAMVIEWER_OIF`

Figure 5.23 Talent Management under My Team Services

5.5.4 Organization

The Organization area shown in Figure 5.24 contains some important organizational-related services for Manager Self-Service:

► **Organization Information**

Within the Organization Information service (Figure 5.25), the manager is presented with a list of organizations within his or her span of control. For each organization, information on the organizational unit, including the company code, personnel area, personnel subareas, and cost center, is displayed. In addition, the main screen provides information on summary information for the organizational unit, including positions, working time, and qualification data.

The Web Dynpro for ABAP application name for this service is `HRMSS_ORGPRO-FILE_TEAMVIEWER`.

Figure 5.24 Organization under My Team Services

Figure 5.25 Manager's View of Organizational Information

▶ **Organization-Related Processes**
Like the Employee-Related Process Overview service, the Organization-Related Processes service (see Figure 5.26) also contains information from

HCM Processes and Forms, but only for the organizational management objects (organization, position, job, etc.).

The Web Dynpro for ABAP application name for this service is ASR_PA_PD_ PROCESSES_DISPLAY.

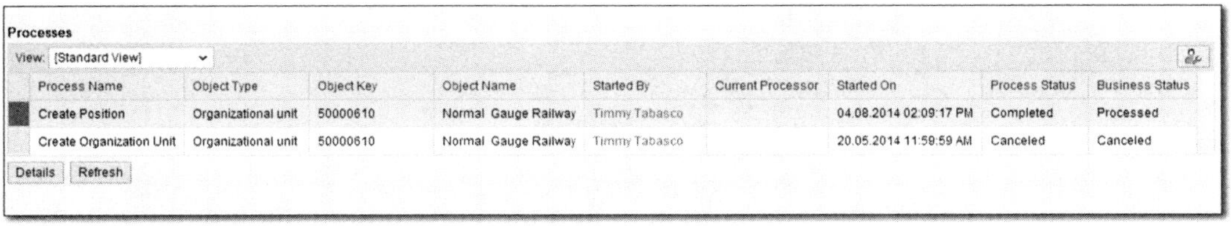

Figure 5.26 Organizational-Related Processes Started by the Manager

▸ **Position Information**

Like the Organizational Information service, the Position Information service in Figure 5.27 contains indicative position information, including company code, personnel area, personnel subarea, employee group, employee subgroup, vacancy information, working time, compensation, qualifications, and others.

The Web Dynpro for ABAP application name for this service is HRMSS_POSPRO- FILE_TEAMVIEWER.

Figure 5.27 Position Profile of One of Manager's Reports

- ▶ **Search Organizational Processes**

  Using the Search Organizational Processes service (Figure 5.28), you can conduct a deep search for any object type in organizational management. You can then start a form, using the HCM Processes and Forms framework.

  The Web Dynpro for ABAP application name for this service is ASR_SRCH_PD_PROCESS.

- ▶ **Edit Position Details**

  The Edit Position Details service is an example form for editing the position information for a position within the manager's own span of control. The Web Dynpro service technical name for the Edit Position Details service is MAINTAIN_POSITION_REQ.

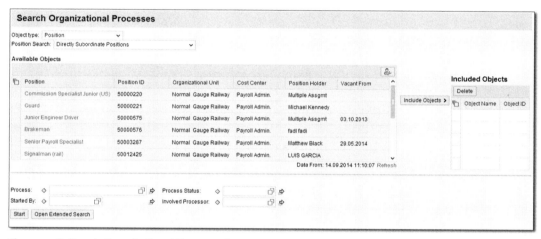

Figure 5.28 Search Organizational Processes Service

5.5.5 Search for Services

One feature within the My Team Services expanded lane is the ability to perform a deep search on any service you have the authorization to initiate.

In Figure 5.29, you can see that the user has begun to search for *position*. A type-ahead feature has already come back with five different available services with the partial word "pos". This is one of the most appreciated features within the tool, because we are all accustomed to similar search functionality on websites and in many web browsers.

Figure 5.29 Search for Services within the My Team Services Area

5.5.6 Lane Configuration

The configuration of the My Team Services lane of MSS is performed in the IMG under the following path: Personnel Management • Manager Self-Service (SAPUI5) • Landing Page • My Team • Configure Launchpad for My Team Services. It uses the standard launchpad framework (Transaction LPD_CUST). The standard role MSS is used with instance TEAM_MENU as a default; this role should be copied into your own customer namespace and enhanced.

Figure 5.30 shows an example of the SAPUI5 service Team Calendar (with associated attributes). Note that the folder structure within LPD_CUST mimics the navigation within the self-service application.

This concludes our discussion of the My Team Services lane of Manager Self-Service. Next, we discuss the analytics capability available within Manager Self-Service, including KPIs and reporting. With advanced reporting capabilities, managers have more information at their fingertips, which allows them to make more informed decisions. SAP has long struggled with providing robust MSS reporting. Now, let's discuss whether SAP has finally met customers' reporting needs challenges.

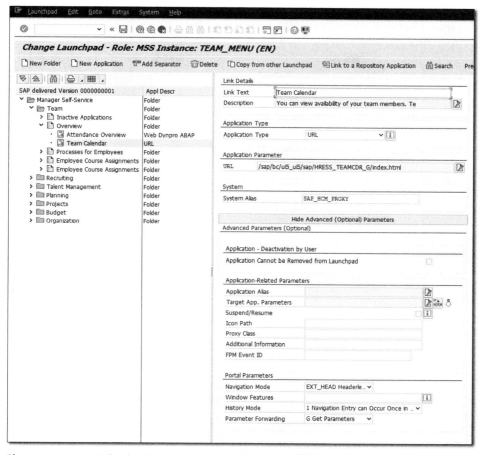

Figure 5.30 Team Calendar (Launchpad Role MSS, Instance TEAM_MENU)

5.6   Analytics Lanes

The analytics functionality included within the new Manager Self-Service is available from the following lanes:

- My Reports
- My KPIs
- KPI Monitor

Each of these lanes offers different value for the manager. The My Reports lane is the launching pad for a variety of reporting sources (query, SAP BusinessObjects BI, SAP HANA, etc.), whereas the My KPIs and KPI Monitor lanes provide key statistics on important HR metrics, such as headcount, turnover, and illness rate.

We will discuss each of these lanes in the following sections.

5.6.1   My Reports

The reports lane, called My Reports, contains report favorites that can be launched directly from the lane (see Figure 5.31). Clicking on any report in the lane will automatically launch that report in a new browser window.

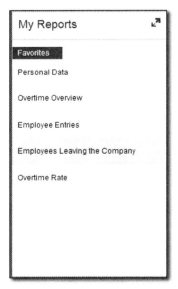

Figure 5.31 My Reports Lane

Expanding the My Reports lane provides the manager with access to the Reporting Launchpad. This service displays all of the reports that have been customized in the launchpad configuration (Transaction LPD_CUST). Figure 5.32 shows a partial list of reports that are available out of the box.

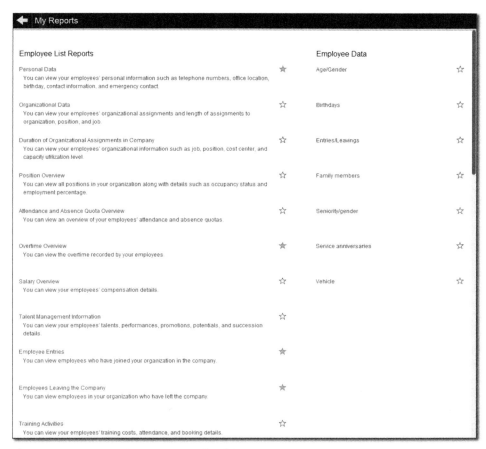

Figure 5.32 Manager's Reporting Launchpad Reports

The following three kinds of reports are available within the Reporting Launch-pad:

▶ **Employee List Reports**
The Employee List is based on the Operational Reports Provisioning concept, which is relatively new. Employee List reports use Web Dynpro service HRMSS_ ANLY_LIST_REPORTING.

Table 5.4 lists the reports that are available in the Employee List Reports.

Report Name	Target Application Parameters
Personal Data	BSA_QUERY=0HCM_PA_T01_Q0008
Organizational Data	BSA_QUERY=0HCM_PA_T01_Q0006
Duration of Organizational Assignments in Company	BSA_QUERY=0HCM_PA_T01_Q0007
Position Overview	BSA_QUERY=0HCM_OS_T01_Q0001
Attendance and Absence Quota Overview	BSA_QUERY=0HCM_PT_T01_Q0001&BSA_ROLE=MSS&BSA_INSTANCE=TIME_NAV
Overtime Overview	BSA_QUERY=0HCM_MP02_Q0001
Salary Overview	BSA_QUERY=0HCM_PA_T05_Q0001&BSA_ROLE=MSS&BSA_INSTANCE=COMP_NAV
Talent Management Information	BSA_QUERY=0HCM_PA_T01_Q0009&BSA_ROLE=MSS&BSA_INSTANCE=TALENT_NAV
Employee Entries	BSA_QUERY=0HCM_PA_T02_Q0003
Employees Leaving the Company	BSA_QUERY=0HCM_PA_T02_Q0004
Training Activities	BSA_QUERY=0LSO_MP04_Q0002
Expiring Qualifications	BSA_QUERY=0HCM_LSO_T01_Q0003

Table 5.4 Standard Employee List Reports

These queries are included in the MSS role and new instance REP2 within the launchpad customizing (Transaction LPD_CUST).

▶ **Employee Data Reports**
Employee Data Reports are based on the Manager's Desktop framework and leverage the SAP query tool for data extraction. Table 5.5 contains the reports that are available in the Employee Data Reports.

Report Name	Target Application Parameters
Age/Gender	FCODE=* HIS REZZ/S 18&FTYPE=FUNC&SCENARIO=RPT0
Birthdays	FCODE=* HIS REZZ/S 10&FTYPE=FUNC&SCENARIO=RPT0
Entries/Leavings	FCODE=* HIS REZZ/S 9&FTYPE=FUNC&SCENARIO=RPT0
Family Members	FCODE=* HIS REZZ/S 17&FTYPE=FUNC&SCENARIO=RPT0
Maternity	FCODE=* HIS RELMUT 13&FTYPE=FUNC&SCENARIO=RPT0

Table 5.5 Standard Employee Data Reports

Report Name	Target Application Parameters
Nationality (Q)	FCODE=* HIS REZZ/S 20&FTYPE=FUNC&SCENARIO=RPT0
Powers of Attorney	FCODE=* HIS REZZ/S 15&FTYPE=FUNC&SCENARIO=RPT0
Seniority/Gender	FCODE=* HIS REZZ/S 19&FTYPE=FUNC&SCENARIO=RPT0
Service Anniversaries	FCODE=* HIS REZZ/S 11&FTYPE=FUNC&SCENARIO=RPT0
Vehicle	FCODE=* HIS REZZ/S 12&FTYPE=FUNC&SCENARIO=RPT0

Table 5.5 Standard Employee Data Reports (Cont.)

The Employee Data Reports service uses the Web Dynpro service HRMSS_OADP_ REPORTING. You can see the configuration parameters needed for a typical employee data report in Figure 5.33.

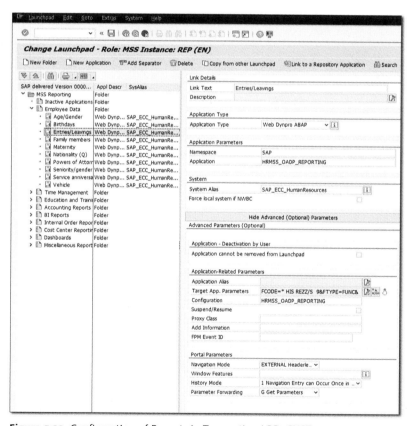

Figure 5.33 Configuration of Reports in Transaction LPD_CUST

These queries are included in the MSS role and instance REP within the launch-pad customizing (Transaction LPD_CUST).

▸ **BW Reports**
The reports listed in Table 5.6 are available as SAP Business Warehouse (BW) Reports. These queries are included in the MSS role and instance REP within the launchpad customizing (Transaction LPD_CUST).

Report Name	SAP BW Web Template
Headcount	0TPLS_0PA_C01_Q0110_V02_C
Headcount FTE	0TPLS_0PA_C01_Q0110_V07_C
Entries	0TPLS_0PA_C01_Q0103_V02_C
Leavers	0TPLS_0PA_C01_Q0104_V02_C
Illness Rate	0TPLS_0PT_C01_Q0101_V02_C
Illness Costs	0TPLS_0PY_MC02_Q0101_V02_C
Overtime Rate	0TPLS_0PT_C01_Q0102_V02_C
Overtime Costs	0TPLS_0PY_MC02_Q0102_V02_C
Number of Qualifications	0TPLS_PAPD_C01_Q0101_V0101_C
Average Proficiency of Quals	0TPLS_PAPD_C01_Q0101_V0201_C
Course Participations and Costs	0TPLS_PE_C01_Q0101_V0101_C
Course Cancellations and Costs	0TPLS_PE_C01_Q0101_V0201_C

Table 5.6 Standard SAP BW Reports

5.6.2 My KPIs

New to HR Renewal is the My KPIs lane. The KPIs can be configured to pull in information from either an SAP BW or an SAP HANA system. The following two important SAP Notes should be referenced for more information; they contain detailed information and "how-to" documents for creating the actual KPI metrics:

▸ **SAP Note 1852087**
Data from SAP HANA views for KPIs on the KPI lane in MSS. There are detailed configuration steps specified in the document "How to Use Data from HANA for MSS KPIs" for SAP HANA–specific queries.

▶ **SAP Note 1852088**

Data from easy queries for KPIs from the KPI lane in MSS. There are detailed configuration steps specified in the document "How to Use Data from Easy Queries for MSS KPIs" for BI-specific queries.

You can find both documents on the SAP Service Marketplace. Go to *http://service.sap.com/erp-hcm* and navigate to CORE HR & PAYROLL • MANAGER SELF-SERVICE (MSS) • RESOURCES • OTHER INFORMATION.

Figure 5.34 contains an example of the My KPIs lane, which contains certain predefined metrics that you have the ability to change through configuration.

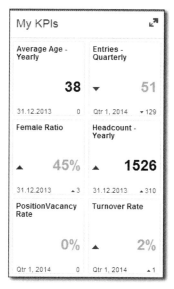

Figure 5.34 My KPIs Lane

Once expanded, the My KPIs lane widens into a screen that show more detailed information for each of the KPIs in the lane (Figure 5.35). You can hover your mouse to get more information as well. For example, for the HEADCOUNT— YEARLY KPI in the top left, hovering over each of the plots will show you the headcount for that particular year. In this way, you can see the actual numbers that are used to calculate the statistic.

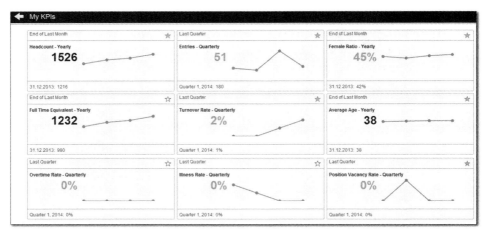

Figure 5.35 Expanded Lane for My KPIs

5.6.3 KPI Monitor

The KPI Monitor lane (Figure 5.36) shows managers their KPIs per specific status (red, yellow, or green). Managers can then easily determine whether they need to drill down into one or more of their KPIs more closely without having to open the expanded KPI lane first. The system calculates the status of a KPI based on the threshold values stored in the IMG.

Figure 5.36 KPI Monitor

5.6.4 Lane Configuration

The configuration of the My Reports lane of MSS is performed in the IMG, under the following path: PERSONNEL MANAGEMENT • MANAGER SELF-SERVICE (SAPUI5) • LANDING PAGE • ANALYTICS.

As with the other areas of self-service, the reporting and KPIs use the standard launchpad framework (Transaction LPD_CUST). The personalization of the role should be copied into your own customer namespace and enhanced with the HRMSS role and `KPI` instance for the KPI lane, and the HRMSS role and `REPORTING` instance for the reports lane.

SAP delivers two feeder classes (Figure 5.37) that are important within the analytics lanes. A *feeder class* allows filtering or modifying of the launchpad content at runtime, which can prove useful if you need to perform data manipulation. These feeder classes are `CL_MSS_ANALYTICS_LPD_FEEDER` for the standard KPI launchpad (HRMSS role, `KPI` instance) and `CL_HRPAO_ACTIONS_LPD_FEEDER` for the standard report launch pad (HRMSS role, `REPORTING` instance).

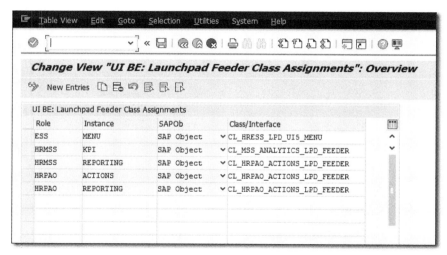

Figure 5.37 Feeder Classes, Including for the KPI and REPORTING Instances

5.7 Approvals and Substitution

No MSS implementation would be complete without approvals and substitution functionality. Allowing the manager to select a delegate for their work item approval has long been functionality required for MSS, and substitution, too, has been available within MSS for many years. We will now talk about another aspect of delegation called *transactional delegation*, which allows managers to initiate transactions on their behalf.

The Approvals and Substitution lane is an SAPUI5 application with the technical application name HRMSS_TASKS_G. It calls OData services /UI2/LAUNCHPAD, HRMSS_ OTHER_APPROVALS_SERVICE, /IWPGW/TASKPROCESSING, and HRMSS_CATS_APPROVAL_ SERVICE.

Approvals Functionality

Please note that in order to use the approvals functionality you must have installed the component IW_PGW 100 SP 3 in SAP Gateway system and the component IW_BEP 200 SP 6 in the backend SAP ERP system.

The Approvals and Substitution lane (see Figure 5.38) provides the manager with a quick view of favorite and recently used applications.

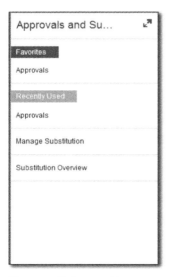

Figure 5.38 Approval Lane

Expanding the lane (Figure 5.39) brings you to the following three services that support the approvals and substitution functionality within the system:

▸ **Approvals**
Approvals (or the approval inbox) is seen in Figure 5.40. It is a Web Dynpro for ABAP service based on the POWL concept. This inbox has several queries above it that allow the manager to quickly filter out certain tasks (e.g., only show Leave Approval requests).

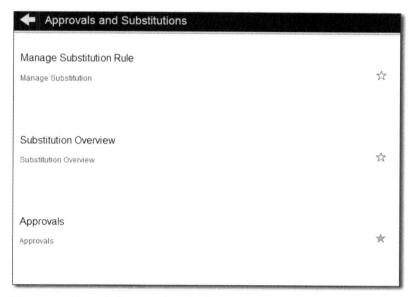

Figure 5.39 Expanded Approvals and Substitutions Lane

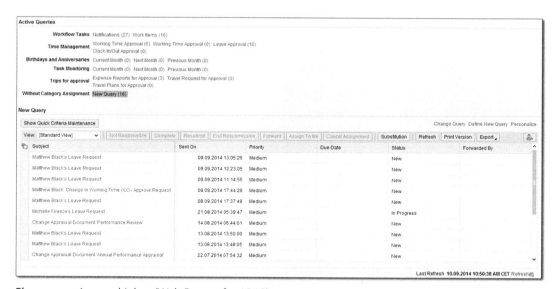

Figure 5.40 Approval Inbox (Web Dynpro for ABAP)

▶ **Manage Substitution Rules**

The manager can manage the substitution of approvals for chosen delegates via the Manager Substitution Rules service (see Figure 5.41). When selecting the substitute, the manager can select which types of approval tasks the substitute should have access to.

▸ **Substitution Overview**
The Substitution Overview service, shown in Figure 5.42, contains the names of the people to whom you have assigned substitutions and the names of those who have assigned substitutions to you, including substitutions that you are ready to initiate.

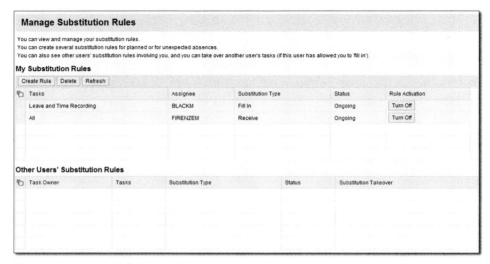

Figure 5.41 Manage Substitution Rules

Figure 5.42 Substitution Overview

As of business function HCM_MSS_UI5_2 (HCM, Manager Self-Service on SAPUI5 2), a new lane is available for managers that enables full substitution for both approvals and workflow. The ability for managers to now initiate services on behalf of other managers is a significant step forward for SAP's Manager Self-Service solution set; previously, only approval delegation was offered.

The SAP standard role `SAP_MANAGER_MSS_SUBST_SR_NWBC` contains the Substitution Overview and Work Overview applications and the authorizations needed for the substitute to perform his or her work on behalf of the manager.

The Approvals lane is an SAPUI5 application with the technical application name `HRMSS_SUBS_G`. It calls OData services `HRMSS_SUBS_ACTION_MENU` and `HRMSS_SUBSTITUTION_SERVICE`.

In the Approvals expanded lane, you must make the necessary settings in Transaction SWFVISU to enable the work item to be visible. Maintain the visualization parameter `APP_PATH` and the visualization parameter value `/sap/bc/ui5_ui5/sap/HRMSS_LR_APPR_G/index.html` in this transaction. For the decision options maintained for each task, you must implement the Workflow BAdI Used before Update (`/IWWRK/BADI_WF_BEFORE_UPD_IB`).

5.8   Search

The Search lane allows managers to search for any configured "object," including employees, positions, jobs, and organizational units. As seen in Figure 5.43, the user can type in a word and click the magnifying glass (search) icon to immediately perform a search for the entered keyword.

Figure 5.43 Search Lane from the MSS Landing Page

Let's look at an example. In Figure 5.44, a search for "ann" returns all employees, positions, and organizational units that contain the phrase "ann". Therefore, employees, positions, or org units that have "ann" in their names, position titles, or organizational unit texts will show up in the result set. This includes the employees with names such as Annette Sturm, Anne Albert, and so on.

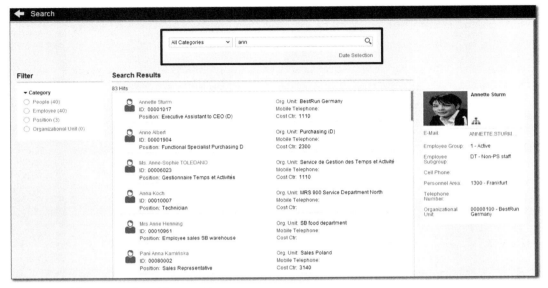

Figure 5.44 Searching as a Manager

Within the expanded Search lane, the manager also has the option of filtering the search by certain configured "search categories" (e.g., Employee, Position, and Organizational Unit). These are configured in the IMG, under the path Personnel Management • Employee Self-Service (SAPUI5) • Search • Define Search Categories and path Personnel Management • Employee Self-Service (SAPUI5) • Search • Group Search Categories.

By using filters, the manager could weed out all *employees* that contain "ann" and only see the *positions* that contain "ann." We can tell from the left side of the search results that there are three of these positions.

5.9 Work Feeds

The Work Feeds lane (Figure 5.45) displays notifications that the manager can act on (such as missing time entries, missing qualifications, and/or performance appraisal updates), which are pushed from the system (via configuration that you set up). Recall from Chapter 4 that this lane is available in the ESS role, but additional content can be pushed to managers for alerts and information about employees within their span of control.

Figure 5.45 Work Feeds Lane

The Work Feeds application is an SAPUI5 application with the technical name HRESS_WRKFEED_G. It calls OData services HRESS_EMP_WORK_FEEDS_SERVICE, HRESS_WRK_FEED_SUB_OVERVIEW_SERVICE, and /IWFND/NOTIFICATIONSTORE.

Work Feeds Functionality

Please note that in order to use the work feeds functionality you must have installed the IW_FND 250 SP 6 and GW_CORE 200 SP 6 components in the SAP Gateway system and the IW_BEP 200 SP 6 component in the backend SAP ERP system.

The expanded Work Feeds lane displays all configured work feeds to the manager. The work feeds in Table 5.7 are available to the manager as part of the standard delivery. Each work feed is listed with its message (stored in the system as an OTR text) and with the BAdI implementation that generates the logic for the feed. Developers should also reference the HRESS_B_WORK_FEED enhancement spot in Transaction SE18 for additional details about these BAdI implementations.

Work Feed	Message Text	BAdI Implementation
HRMSS_CATS	Time Sheet not filled out for the period &START_DATE&-&END_DATE&: &NUM_EMP& employees	HRESS_WORK_FEED_EMP_CATS
HRMSS_COMPENSATION	You must complete compensation planning by &END_DATE&	HRMSS_WORK_FEED_COMPENSATION
HRMSS_EXPIRNG_QUALIF	&EMP_NAME& has qualifications expiring in the next &NUM_DAYS& days	HRMSS_WORK_FEED_QUALIFICATIONS
HRMSS_LEAVE	&NUM_EMP& employees are on leave during &START_DATE&-&END_DATE&	HRESS_WORK_FEED_LEAVE
HRMSS_MISSNG_QUALIF	&EMP_NAME& has missing qualifications	HRMSS_WORK_FEED_QUALIFICATIONS
HRMSS_PRM	Appraisal documents of &NUM_EMP& employees are open and pending closure	HRMSS_WORK_FEED_PERFORMANCE

Table 5.7 Standard MSS Work Feeds and BAdI Implementations

However, you're not bound by these standard-issue work feeds; you may create new feeds based on your specific requirements. To do so, you must define your own work feeds, under the configuration in the IMG, reached via the following path: Personnel Management • Manager Self-Service (SAPUI5) • Work Feeds • Define Work Feeds.

You also need to define the attributes of the work feed, including the notification text, the priority (low or high), and whether the user can unsubscribe to the feed.

Then, schedule program RPC_ESS_WORK_FEED_GENERATOR as a batch job, which performs the generation of the work feeds for a particular subscription key (specified in the program's variant). The report reads all subscribed users and then generates feeds for these users. The BAdI Defining the Text for Work Feeds (HRESS_B_WORK_FEED) is used during the generation of work feeds.

You can use Transaction HR_FEED_SUBSCRIPTION (program RPU_WORK_FEED_SUBS_ONBEHALF), as shown in Figure 5.46, to perform a mass subscribe or unsubscribe to one or more of the standard or customized work feeds.

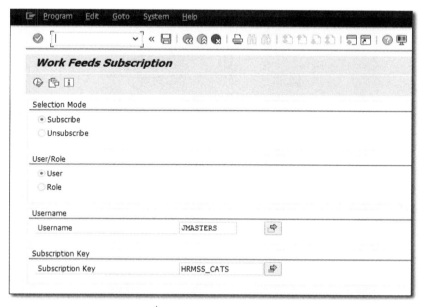

Figure 5.46 Work Feeds Subscription Program

Important SAP Note

Reference SAP Note 2032336; the Birthday and Anniversary work feed can't be generated unless the background job is executed by the subscribed user.

The expanded Work Feeds lane is shown in Figure 5.47.

Managers can also subscribe to and unsubscribe from all the of work feeds available in the system (see Figure 5.48) by clicking on the gear icon on the top right of the expanded Work Feed lane.

Figure 5.47 Expanded Work Feeds Lane

Figure 5.48 Subscription/Unsubscription

Lane Configuration

The configuration of the Work Feeds lane of MSS is performed in the IMG, under the following path: PERSONNEL MANAGEMENT • MANAGER SELF-SERVICE (SAPUI5) • LANDING PAGE • WORK FEEDS (Figure 5.49). It uses the standard launchpad framework (Transaction LPD_CUST). In order to get set up the subscription to work feeds, you must add the work feed subscription key to personalization key HR_ WORK_FEEDS. Only then will the user be able to subscribe or unsubscribe to a work feed.

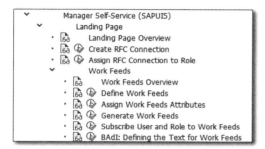

Figure 5.49 Work Feeds Configuration

Now that we have reviewed everything available within MSS in detail, let's discuss the important topic of security and authorization management.

5.10   Managing Security and Authorizations

Security is hugely important to the success of any SAP project, and self-service is no different. Authorization management within a self-service context involves expert knowledge in both SAP ERP HCM and structural authorizations. It is important that you work alongside your security experts at your company, because there are many changes to the roles in ESS, MSS, and HR Professional Self-Services. These changes will be required in order for a smooth transition for go-live.

In the following sections, we'll cover the single and composite roles available in the standard system.

5.10.1 Security Authorizations

The composite role for Manager Self-Service is `SAP_MANAGER_MSS_CR_UI5_1`. You should copy this role into your customer namespace for security.

Standard Roles

As with other composites, the MSS composite role contains a set of single Manager Self-Service roles. It is likely that you will not need copies of all of these single roles for your own implementation. For example, if you are not using SAP Learning Solution (LSO), then you can exclude the `SAP_HR_LSO_HR-MANAGER` and `SAP_HR_LSO_MANAGER` single roles from your customer composite.

Table 5.8 lists all of the single roles available in the standard SAP role `SAP_MANAGER_MSS_CR_UI5_1`.

Single Role	Description
SAP_ASR_MANAGER	HR Administrative Services: Manager
SAP_FI_TV_WEB_APPROVER_2	Approving Manager
SAP_HR_CPS_DET_PLAN_L_SR_NWBC	Personnel Cost Planning: Detail Planning of Personnel Costs by Line Managers
SAP_HR_LSO_HR-MANAGER	SAP Learning Solution: HR Manager Training
SAP_HR_LSO_MANAGER	SAP Learning Solution: Manager
SAP_MANAGER_MSS_OTH_NWBC	Manager Single Role for the Applications from Remote systems
SAP_MANAGER_MSS_SR_ANA_1	MSS Analytics Lane
SAP_MANAGER_MSS_SR_NWBC_3	Single Role for the Manager Containing Menu Structure for SAP NetWeaver Business Client
SAP_MANAGER_MSS_SR_UI5_1	Manager Self-Service Single Role Containing Manager specific lanes
SAP_RCF_MANAGER	Manager
SAP_SR_TMC_MANAGER_6	Manager in Talent Management
SAP_TIME_MGR_XX_ESS_WDA_1	Time Approval Role for ESS

Table 5.8 Standard Singles Security Roles in SAP_MANAGER_MSS_CR_UI5_1

Please note that the delivery strategy of SAP role content is now via a single delivery channel, the PFCG role. The roles, menu structure, and so on defined in

Transaction PFCG are consumed by both the SAP Enterprise Portal and the SAP NetWeaver Business Client. This means that no additional portal roles need to be created and assigned, and the Transaction PFCG roles need to be uploaded to the SAP Enterprise Portal.

> **Additional Information**
>
> For more on this, reference SAP Note 1685257 (Upload of SAP Delivered NWBC Roles to SAP NetWeaver Portal). Detailed steps for how to upload an SAP NetWeaver Business Client role to the SAP Enterprise Portal can be found on the SAP Community Network at *https://scn.sap.com/docs/DOC-31973*.

Personalized Roles

With the new self-services functionality, more logic has been embedded within Transaction PFCG and associated framework to drive functionality based on the configuration in the personalization of the role. Personalization at the role level may be a new concept to you, but it's important to know how it determines the functionality available for ESS, MSS, and HR Professional self-service, especially with respect to navigation and taxonomy.

For My Team Service, for example, the launchpad role and instance name are picked up from the personalization key HRMSS_ACTIONS_LPD (see Figure 5.50).

Within the My Team Services Organizational Viewer functionality, the POSITION_MENU instance under the MSS role provides the menu options for the position; the ORGANIZATION_MENU instance under the MSS role provides the menu options for the organizational view; and the EMPLOYEE_MENU instance under the MSS role provides the menu options for the employee dropdown list.

The TEAM_MENU instance under the MSS role with no object defined defines the overall layout of the My Team Services expanded lane (see Figure 5.51). You'll probably need to copy the MSS role and/or instance into your customer namespace and alter the contents, navigation, and parameters. If you do, make sure that you update the personalization key at the role level again. The TEAM_MENU instance referenced in the personalization key drives the navigation and attributes of the service.

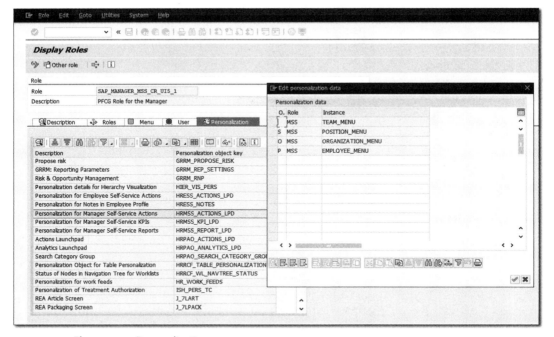

Figure 5.50 Personalization

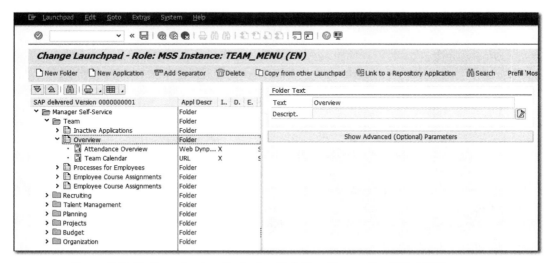

Figure 5.51 My Team Services Navigation Definition (Transaction LPD_CUST)

We have covered the standard roles and role personalization, both of which are important for Manager Self-Service. Let's now discuss structural authorizations within Manager Self-Service—a common area of confusion for many folks.

5.10.2 Structural Authorizations

Some SAP customers (and consultants!) are under the mistaken belief that structural authorization is a prerequisite for deploying Manager Self-Service. Although structural authorizations offer benefits that standard authorization alone does not, you should only consider structural authorizations when there is a strong business reason to do so.

When is that? Structural authorization allows you to restrict authorizations based on underlying structures (for example, organizational structures, business event hierarchies, and qualification catalogs, to name a few). Structural authorization access in the form of authorization profiles is granted at the position or user level. In turn, access to organizational objects (organizational units, positions, jobs, and so on from SAP ERP HCM Organizational Management) are granted based on this access. A root object (e.g., an organizational unit) is sometimes explicitly specified along with an evaluation path (e.g., SBESX, Staffing Assignments along Organizational Structure) to return all objects in a given time period (all, today, current month, current year, past, and future). At other times, objects can be determined dynamically based on a function module set in the authorization profile.

SAP delivers two standard function modules for this purpose: RH_GET_MANAGER_ASSIGNMENT determines all organizational units for which the user is the chief manager, and RH_GET_ORG_ASSIGNMENT determines which organizational unit the user is assigned to. From any root node that is returned from these functions, you can use an evaluation path (such as SBESX) to retrieve all objects (organizational units, positions, and employees) underneath that user's span of control. These returned objects are used *in conjunction with* the user's standard authorizations to present a complete authorization check from both the standard authorization side (authorization objects P_ORGIN, PLOG, P_PERNR, etc.) and from the structural authorization side (the structures hierarchy). The intersection of these authorization checks provides SAP customers with added security.

In the next subsections, let's discuss function module RH_GET_MANAGER_ASSIGNMENT in greater detail and learn how it can be used within a Manager Self-Service context. We can get a better idea of how and why this authorization can be used.

RH_GET_MANAGER_ASSIGNMENT

As part of the manager's structural authorization profile, the standard function module RH_GET_MANAGER_ASSIGNMENT (or a customized version of it) is typically granted. As previously mentioned, this function retrieves all organizational units for which the user is the chief manager. If the manager is a chief of multiple organizational units, then all organizational units will be returned as root nodes. The manager can sit anywhere in the organizational structure; the 012 Manages relationship on his or her position in an organizational unit drives the identification of managed organizational units. Within this function module, the standard evaluation path MANASS is used to retrieve the organizational units.

Once the root node (or nodes) are retrieved, an evaluation path is used to identify all underlying objects that should be available for the user's authorization. Figure 5.52 shows an example authorization profile, Z_MANAGER, with evaluation path SBESX. The following parameters are used to fully define the authorization profile:

▶ Authorization Profile: Z_MANAGER
▶ No.: (sequence number of your choice)
▶ Plan Version: 01
▶ Object Type: O
▶ Object ID: (leave blank)
▶ Maintenance Flag: (unchecked)
▶ Evaluation Path: SBESX
▶ Status Vector: 12 (where 1 is active and 2 is planned)
▶ Depth: blank (meaning there is no restriction in depth)
▶ Sign: blank (meaning objects are processed top down, not bottom up)
▶ Period: blank (meaning there is no time period restriction)
▶ Function Module: RH_GET_MANAGER_ASSIGNMENT

You can build additional authorization profiles and assign them to users in a similar fashion.

According to the Z_MANAGER authorization profile, a manager can view his or her entire organizational structure scope (i.e., full span of control, including organizational units, positions, and employees). Together with the authorizations from his or her standard authorization, this profile would form the total picture of back-end security for the user.

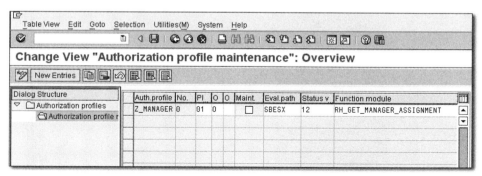

Figure 5.52 Authorization Profile Z_MANAGER within Table T77PR Containing Function Module RH_GET_MANAGER_ASSIGNMENT

In some cases, a combination of standard and structural authorizations is not enough; in such cases, context-sensitive authorizations come into play.

Context-Sensitive Authorizations

A context-sensitive solution is required when you need to associate individual standard and structural authorization profiles together within the same context.

A classic example is that of a payroll manager. The payroll manager has certain responsibilities for the organization in his or her role as a manager of corporate payroll and different responsibilities for his or her direct and indirect reports in his or her role as a people manager (i.e., a chief). This segregation of duties is typically within the HR function. In order to handle this issue, you can either issue two separate user IDs for this employee or implement context-sensitive authorizations.

In Figure 5.53, authorization P_ORGINCON contains read and search access to Infotypes 0000, 0001, and 0002, but only for the objects (that is, employees) available within structural authorization profile Z_MANAGER. Another P_ORGINCON authorization could give this user access to update Infotype 0002 for a different contextual scenario.

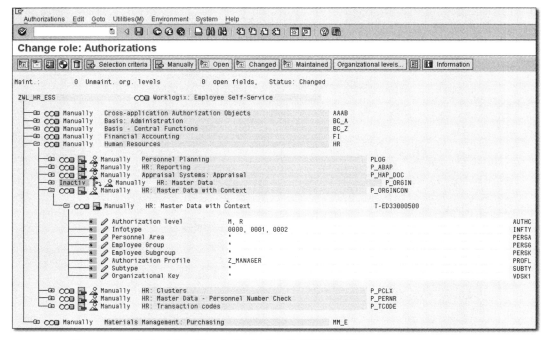

Figure 5.53 Context-Sensitive Authorization P_ORGINCON

We have seen how context-sensitive authorizations can provide a segregation of duties without the need to create duplicate user IDs. By maintaining context-sensitive authorizations, you can more tightly integrate standard and structural authorizations together. This might be pertinent to your Manager Self-Service implementation if the same manager (for example, the payroll manager we mentioned) who uses MSS functionality will also be using backend HR transactions.

Performance Management

If you are implementing on-premise SAP ERP HCM Performance Management, then you can only activate structural authorizations within this module. In other words, structural restrictions can be made to access appraisals only, but in the SAP ERP HCM Personnel Administration module no checks are performed. To turn on for performance management only, you must activate the HAP00/AUTHO switch in table T77S0 by placing an X as the value (see Figure 5.54). In addition, because no structural authorizations checks need to be performed in Personnel

Administration, you use authorization object P_ORGIN for your infotype checks (and not P_ORGINCON, which includes an authorization profile).

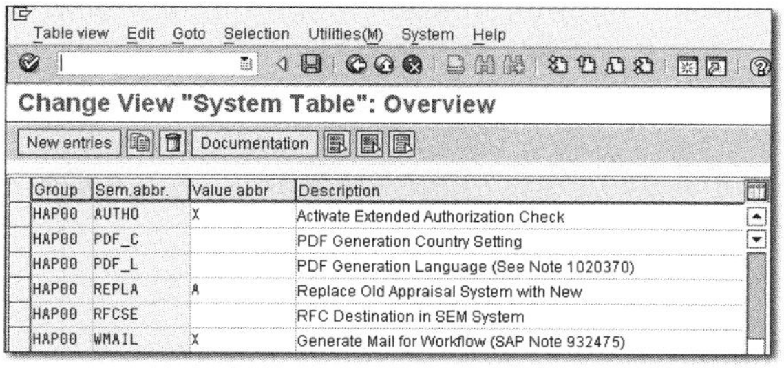

Group	Sem.abbr.	Value abbr	Description
HAP00	AUTHO	X	Activate Extended Authorization Check
HAP00	PDF_C		PDF Generation Country Setting
HAP00	PDF_L		PDF Generation Language (See Note 1020370)
HAP00	REPLA	A	Replace Old Appraisal System with New
HAP00	RFCSE		RFC Destination in SEM System
HAP00	WMAIL	X	Generate Mail for Workflow (SAP Note 932475)

Figure 5.54 Determining Structural Profile Use

When the HAP00/AUTHO switch is turned on, a structural profile must be entered in the PROFL authorization field for authorization object P_HAP_DOC. In addition, the user must have an entry in table T77UA. Also, be sure that the correct authorization profile is defined in P_HAP_DOC itself. If the HAP00/AUTHO switch is turned on and no authorization profile (or a wrong authorization profile) is defined in P_HAP_DOC, then users with the identified authorization profile will be unable to access appraisals.

It's clear that structural authorizations provide a more robust way to handle complex, context-sensitive security requirements. However, if you're going to use structural authorizations for your implementation, then give yourself additional testing time for unexpected challenges to surface. Remember that you should be careful to only implement structural authorizations if there is a clear business need to do so. Implementing structural authorizations is a major shift in the backend security approach. There is also additional maintenance involved in supporting a security design with structural authorizations.

Let's turn our attention now to some of the more important areas within MSS that can be enhanced. These are called enhancement spots, and they are a part of the overall enhancement framework provided standard by SAP.

5.11 Enhancement Spots

Enhancement spots (and their respective BAdIs) provide you with a way to introduce customer-specific logic into standard processing rules without the need for modifications to the system. During system upgrade time, this ensures that your customer-specific code is not affected when SAP code gets patched.

There are several enhancement spots available within Manager Self-Service. Speak with your developer about the list provided in Table 5.9 to determine if any of these could be of use to you for your own implementation.

Enhancement Spot Name	Description
HRMSS_CALENDER_APPOINTMENT	Enhancement Spot for Deadline Monitor and Reminder of D
HRMSS_CALENDER_ENTRY	Enhancement Spot for Birthday and Work Anniversaries
HRMSS_CATS_APPR_EMAIL_ENH	Enhancement Spot for Approval Dashboard Email
HRMSS_DEADLINE_MONITOR_MGR	BAdI Definitions Used in MSS Deadline Monitor
HRMSS_MODIF_BUSINESS_PARAMS	To Modify Business/Application Parameters while Calling
HRMSS_MODIFY_EMAIL_CONTENT	Enhancement Spot for Changing the Email Content
HRMSS_SUBSTITUTION	BAdI: Determine Substitution Rules and Application for User
HRMSS_UI5_EMP_PROFILE	BAdI: Modification of Card Visibility

Table 5.9 Enhancement Spots for Manager Self-Service

To view the technical details about these enhancement spots, go to Transaction SE18. You will need to work with a developer for enhancing an enhancement spot. An *enhancement spot* is a part of the enhancement framework that allows you to place your customer-specific logic within standard SAP. These are enhancements, *not* modifications to the SAP system.

One of the most important BAdIs within the MSS, HRMSS_UI5_EMP_PROFILE, influences what is displayed on the employees' cards in the Employee Profile and who can see the data. The enhancement has two methods: MODIFY_CARD_PARAMETERS (modify cards assignment) and SET_NOTES_VISIBILITY (control the visibility of the NOTES tab in the Employee Profile). Within the MODIFY_CARD_PARAMETERS method (see Figure 5.55), each card ID (specified by the LS_CARDS_UI_ID parameter) is set to be either displayed or not for each user type (employee, manager, or other). Within the SET_NOTES_ VISIBILITY method, you control whether or not the employee and/or manager have access to view and maintain the notes functionality in the Employee Profile.

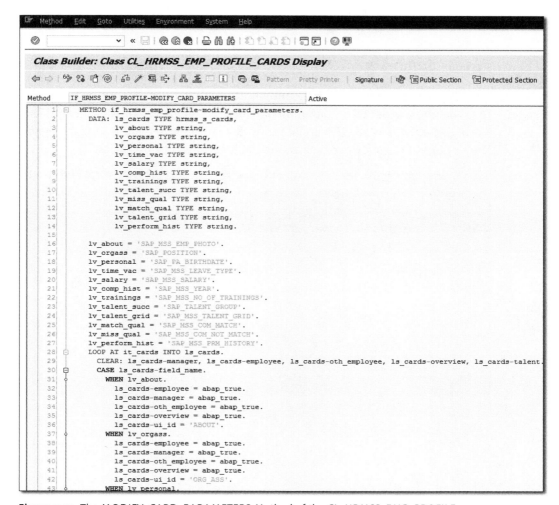

Figure 5.55 The MODIFY_CARD_PARAMETERS Method of the CL_HRMSS_EMP_PROFILE_
CARDS Class within the HRMSS_UI5_EMP_PROFILE BAdI

You will need to work with your development team in order to influence the information displayed on and the user access to the employee cards on the Employee Profile page.

We have covered a lot of the technical areas within Manager Self-Service, but in many cases it's not the technology that will determine success; instead, it's organizational readiness.

5.12 Summary

In this chapter, we explained the functionality available in Manager Self-Service. SAP offers new out-of-the-box functionality in its delivery of Manager Self-Service, including new SAPUI5 applications, the lane concept, and a heavier reliance on PFCG and roles for personalization and navigation.

The next chapter provides an in-depth look at the HR Professional role within HR Renewal. Before HR Renewal, there was no dedicated web-based role for an HR business partner and/or administrator. This makes the HR Professional functionality an important leap forward in core SAP ERP HCM.

HR administrators typically interact with SAP ERP HCM more than anyone else. In this chapter, we talk about how SAP has rebuilt the user interface for that interaction.

6   HR Professional Self-Service in SAP ERP HCM

HR Professional self-service is the area that has undergone the greatest level of development in recent years by SAP. In fact, the HR Renewal initiative was centrally intended as a refreshing of the UI for users who work with SAP ERP HCM the most: those who work in HR.

In this chapter dedicated to explaining HR Professional self-service, we will start by explaining the case for transitioning your organization to the new HR Professional role and away from Transactions PA30 and PA40, because describing the new functionality becomes irrelevant without making this case. Once we have you on board, we will describe the new functionality and available adjustment options.

6.1   The Case for Change

Before we walk through all of the new ways that HR can interact using the new user interface (UI), we need to address an obvious question that many readers will have. Many SAP ERP HCM installations are now 10 years old or older—and aging still. This means that many HR professionals have become quite conversant in SAP's current methods for getting around; most organizations have made peace with the transaction code method of navigating and the classical way—that is, the SAP Windows GUI method—of getting things done.

In response to this intransience, SAP has largely left the HR administrator UI unchanged for the better part of two decades. (Consider that Employee Self-

Service is currently on its fourth generation, yet in most organizations HR administrator functions remain unchanged.) An HR Administrator role that had some functionality was added to the SAP Enterprise Portal several years ago, but it simply was not comprehensive enough to credibly serve as a replacement for the classical way of getting around. In fact, if you were trained in SAP in 1998 and then decided to take a 15-year nap, you would have no trouble picking up right where you left off in working with SAP HR data when you woke up.

However, in the marketplace at large the march of technology has continued unabated. Users' expectations of the ways that they interact with their applications has evolved. We are accustomed to browser-based solutions with intuitive, user-friendly designs. When contrasted with those solutions, classical SAP ERP HCM Personnel Administration now looks as dated as a house with gold appliances and shag carpeting.

As you know, SAP recognized this trend and decided to invest heavily in a rewrite of the core HR applications, calling this initiative HR Renewal. For HR Professional self-services, the changes are significant and wide-ranging. We will go through all of these changes in greater detail later in the chapter, but we want to hit the highlights here first. Then, we'll talk about the business benefits that can accrue for organizations that adopt the new frontend.

6.1.1 HR Professional Highlights

The HR Professional role is the combination of an entirely new set of applications centered on how users in real-world situations work with HCM data. It bears little resemblance to the old way of doing things and centers on two features:

- **Unified search**
  Unified search is a time-saver. By typing in a search term, the user can reach almost any HR object in the system, and, unlike search tools in SAP ERP HCM, you can search for and retrieve results from either Personnel Administration or Organizational Management, as shown in Figure 6.1.

- **Summarized employee profiles**
  One of the longstanding complaints about Transaction PA30 is that it presents little information on existing employees. In Figure 6.2, showing "old-school" HCM, you only see via checkmarks that data exists on for the infotype, not what the data is. In contrast, with HR Renewal (see Figure 6.3), you are provided with summary information on key infotypes. This can answer many

questions without requiring the user to click through to the individual infotype and can allow the user to readily take action when it's necessary to do so.

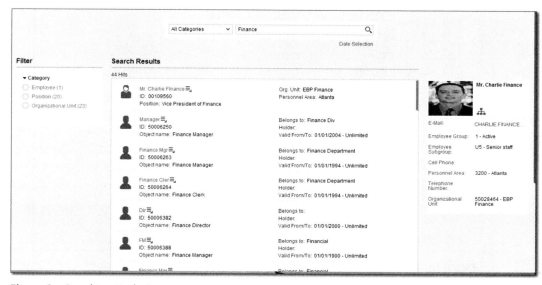

Figure 6.1 Searching Made Easy

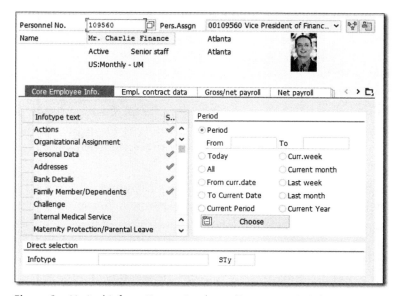

Figure 6.2 Limited Information on Employee (Transaction PA30)

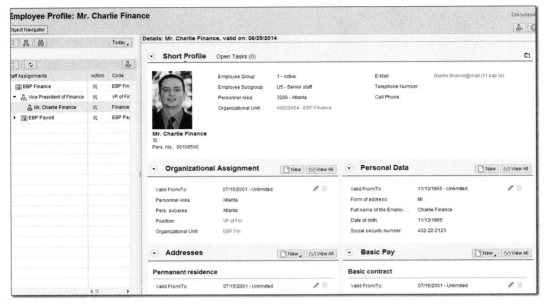

Figure 6.3 Summary Information at Your Fingertips (HR Renewal)

HR Renewal has some great functionality for capturing data from the HR professional. The following list presents some highlights; we'll delve much deeper later:

▶ **Roadmap forms**

As any administrator will tell you, sometimes you must do more than survey the data or make a small change to an infotype. Sometimes you will need to update several related pieces of information together.

For example, for a promotion you may need to update the position (Infotype 1), the work schedule (Infotype 7), and the pay (Infotype 8). In the classical model, you'd do this via Transaction PA40, which strings together the necessary screens to accomplish the task at hand.

In contrast, the process has been refreshed with some key improvements in HR Renewal. The new multiscreen forms are known as roadmap forms and will be discussed in more detail in Section 6.13. For starters, the actions are launched off of the employee profile screen shown in Figure 6.3. Where you once had to launch an action from a separate screen (Transaction PA40), now you can launch a form that has the infotypes listed down the left side and the current infotype being processed on the right (see Figure 6.4).

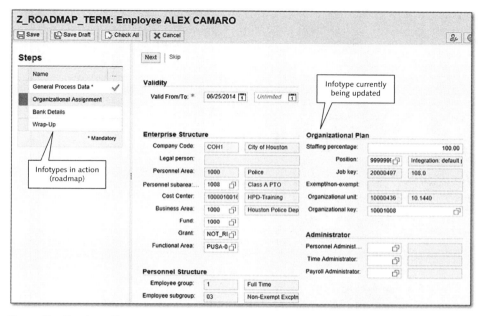

Figure 6.4 Roadmap Forms

You can configure roadmap forms so that any or all of the infotypes in the roadmap must be completed before the transaction is committed to the system. In Transaction PA40, users can get halfway through the action, discover that they are missing key information, and exit the transaction—resulting in in half-finished transactions in the system.

Another key improvement from Transaction PA40 for roadmap forms is the ability to save a draft. When you save the roadmap form as a draft, all of your values are retained. The draft form is stored in your Workflow Inbox, to be completed when you are ready to do so.

▶ **Floorplan Manager forms**
  With Floorplan Manager (FPM) forms, your organization has abundant flexibility to tailor forms with the precise fields you require. You can build out forms that can be started by managers, employees, or HR administrators. The forms are dynamic and intuitive and can readily bring HR business processes online.

▶ **Digital personnel files**
  As we move from a paper-based world to an electronic one, we need a way to store and access scanned documents and the personnel request forms related to

the employee. In the classical model, you must access digital documents through a separate transaction. With the new HR administration, the digital file can be accessed from the same place in which you access the key employee information (see Figure 6.5 for an example).

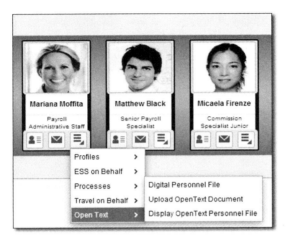

Figure 6.5 Digital Personnel Files

That completes our quick summary of some of the key new functions that we will cover in depth later in the chapter. However, HR IT managers who want to make such a significant change as refreshing how core HR works need better talking points than "the screens are much prettier" when proposing a project. How does the new functionality translate into business benefits?

6.1.2 Business Benefits from the New HR Professional Role

There are two major business impacts from moving from the old Windows-based processes to the new HR Professional frontend:

▶ **HR Renewal makes HR users more productive.**
Numerous improvements will make the HR administrator more productive. The application was built to allow the user to handle numerous types of requests within a few clicks. For the first time, Organizational Management data and Personnel Administration data can both be maintained from one main screen. The new integrated search pulls back both position and personnel results. The net effect is a faster, more efficient HR administrator.

▶ **HR Renewal reduces the learning curve.**
Classical SAP ERP HCM takes some getting used to. When do you use /o or /n?
What does the yellow up arrow mean versus the green side arrow? What's the
infotype number for the work schedule? The new UI is designed to eliminate
points of confusion such as these and offers intuitive menus in place of transaction codes and infotype numbers, as shown in Figure 6.6.

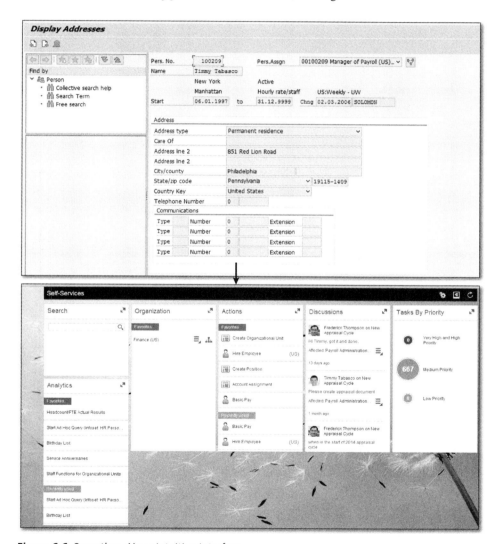

Figure 6.6 Smoother, More Intuitive Interface

Because users no longer need to learn obscure numbering or transactions, the distance between the user and the completed task becomes shorter. The organizational impact of this is twofold:

▸ **New users can become productive in a shorter period of time.**
Every organization has a story of the sudden loss of a key resource who was responsible for a portion of key HR processes. With HR Renewal, you can reduce the time required to bring a new user up to speed and can focus more on training on your company's business process and less on how the screens work.

▸ **Responsibility for rollout to more casual users can enable organizational realignment.**
A more intuitive interface can change the equation for who is a potential HR administrator. If creating a new position can be handled in just a few clicks in most cases, then a part-time field administrator who receives infrequent change requirements should be capable of handling most requests without assistance. Rather than develop experts whose only job is to comprehend and interact with SAP ERP HCM, companies can realign their HR organizations closer to the field so that they can assist with more strategic operational initiatives.

Now that we've presented this high-level summary of the business benefits, we'll look at the steps involved in getting started. Then, we transition into the "meat" of the chapter, looking in depth into each area of functionality.

6.2 Getting Started

As with the chapters on ESS and MSS, it's important to know where to begin. We'll take a quick look at the application area and deployment possibilities for HR Professional.

6.2.1 Application Area

Each service within the HR Professional role is associated with an application area for categorization and support purposes. The application area is used both for searching for SAP Notes and when creating SAP Customer Incidents. The application area for the new HR Professional is PA-PAO (HR Renewal—Personnel & Organization).

SAP Business Suite and HR Renewal

We recommend that you reference SAP Note 1965692 (HR Renewal 2.0: Release Information Note), which contains important information about SAP Business Suite release information for HR Renewal.

6.2.2 Deployment Options

For HR Professional, you'll want to do some soul searching on the same dilemmas covered in the MSS deployment, related to the UI and usability of the portal, support for mobile devices, the way roles are delivered and maintained, and the site of SAP Gateway.

Let's turn our attention to the business functions that need to be activated for HR Professional.

Business Functions and Applications

Please reference Appendix A for a thorough list of key business functions and applications for ESS, MSS, and the HR Professional role.

Business Functions

Again, as with ESS, you'll want to have your SAP Basis resource activate a few business functions using Transaction SFW5.

In this chapter, we have assumed that the business functions in Table 6.1 have been switched on, as part of an EHP 7 implementation. Please note that there are certain business functions that need to be turned on before others.

Business Function	Name	Business Function Prerequisites
HCM_PAO_CI_1	HCM, Personnel & Organization (Reversible)	HCM, Administrative Services 04 (HCM_ASR_CI_4)
HCM_PAO_CI_2	HCM, Personnel & Organization 02 (Reversible)	HCM_PAO_CI_1
HCM_PAO_CI_3	HCM, Personnel & Organization 03 (Reversible)	HCM_PAO_CI_2

Table 6.1 Business Functions Relevant for HR Professional Self-Service

Business Function	Name	Business Function Prerequisites
HCM_PAO_CI_4	HCM, Personnel & Organization 04 (Reversible)	HCM_PAO_CI_3
HCM_PAO_CI_5	CM, Personnel & Organization 05 (Reversible)	HCM_PAO_CI_4
HCM_PAO_CI_6	CM, Personnel & Organization 06 (Reversible)	HCM_PAO_CI_5
HCM_PD_ORGVIS_1	HCM, Workforce Viewer 01	HCM_ESS_UI5_1 HCM_MSS_UI5_1 HCM_PAO_CI_3
HCM_ANALYTICS_3	HCM, Analytics for Manager	FND_ANALYTICS_TOOLS
HCM_PD_UI_1	HCM, PD UI Visualization 01 Technical	None
HCM_PD_UI_2	HCM, PD UI Visualization 01 Technical	HCM_PD_UI_1

Table 6.1 Business Functions Relevant for HR Professional Self-Service (Cont.)

In addition to business functions, several services need to be activated as well. We will discuss those services next.

Activation of Services

Before you can use any of the new self-service functionality, you need to activate the services on SAP Gateway. Regardless of whether your SAP Gateway is on the same instance or not, the activation steps are the same.

In the IMG, go to the activity under SAP NETWEAVER • GATEWAY • ODATA CHANNEL • ADMINISTRATION • GENERAL SETTINGS • ACTIVATE AND MAINTAIN SERVICES or use Transaction /IWFND/MAINT_SERVICE (see Figure 6.7). The following OData services need to be activated for the HR Professional:

▶ HRPAO_COMMON_JS

▶ HRPAO_DISC_C

▶ HRPAO_LPB_JS

▶ HRPAO_LPB_C

▶ HRPAO_LPB_G

- HRPAO_ORGFAVS_G

- HRPAO_ORGFAVS_G HRMSS_TASKS_G

- HRPAO_ORGFAV_C

- HRPAO_PROCESS_G

- HRPAO_PROC_C

- HRPAO_SEARCH_C

- HRPAO_SEARCH_G

- HRPAO_SWFDUPD_G

- HRPAO_TASKSWD_G

- HRPAO_TASKS_C

- HRPAO_TASKS_G

- HRPAO_TDFT_C

- HRORGVIS_CHART

- HRGEN_QUICKVIEW

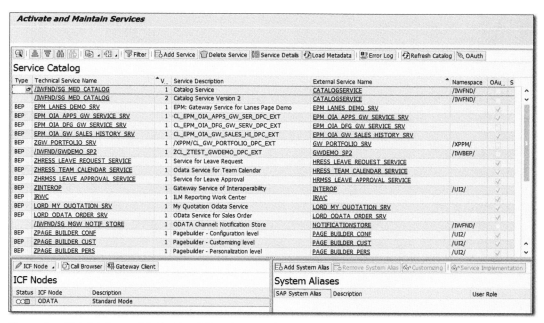

Figure 6.7 Maintaining and Activating OData Services (Transaction /IWFND/MAINT_SERVICE)

From a technical perspective, there is a business server page (BSP) that encapsulates the call to the OData service (or services). BSPs that are activated within the HR Professional role include the following:

- HRPAO_OS
- HRPAO_COMMON_JS
- HRPAO_DISC_C
- HRPAO_LPB_JS
- HRPAO_LPD_C
- HRPAO_LPD_G
- HRPAO_ORGFAVS_G
- HRPAO_ORGFAV_C
- HRPAO_PROCESS_G
- HRPAO_PROC_C
- HRPAO_SEARCH_C
- HRPAO_SEARCH_G
- HRPAO_SWFDUPD_G
- HRPAO_TASKSWD_G
- HRPAO_TASKS_C
- HRPAO_TASKS_G
- HRPAO_TDFT_C
- HRPAO_PAOM_MASTERDATA
- HRPAO_99RU_STANDARD_TEXTS
- HRSSC_A_PAOM_MENU
- PAOC_TRV_SRV
- PAO_ACTIONMENU
- PAO_ORGANIZATION_FAVORITES
- PAO_PROCESSES
- PAO_SEARCH_SERVICE
- PAO_USERCONTEXT
- HRPAO_SEARCH_C

▶ HRORGVIS_CHART

▶ HRGEN_QUICKVIEW

▶ HRPAO_SEARCH_C

▶ HRPAO_TASKS_G

▶ HRPAO_TDFT_C

Now the guided tour begins. For each area of the HR Professional role, we will introduce the functionality and features. We then will explain what configuration options exist.

We are going to cover the new lanes first. As we have discussed in earlier chapters, the lanes are independent applications that coexist side by side. Taken together, the lanes provide powerful capabilities to the user.

6.3   Search

We begin the tour with one of the best features of the new HR Professional role: the Search lane, shown in Figure 6.8. Recall from Chapter 4 and Chapter 5 that within this lane, the user can search across both organizational and personnel information simultaneously.

Figure 6.8 Very Simple Search Screen

SAP clearly intends this lane to be a simple way for you navigate to the person or organizational object that you need to view or maintain. The idea here is that administrators know the name of what they're looking for most of the time and want quick access to it via a complete name, a partial name, or an ID.

Once you have entered your search term, you are taken to the results screen, which has a simple, logical structure. You can filter the results based on what type of object you're looking for (person, organizational unit, or position) by using the radio button shown on the left in Figure 6.9.

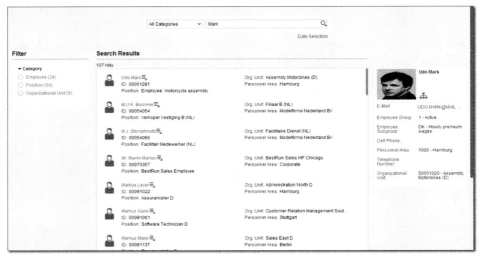

Figure 6.9 Search Results Screen

In the middle section, you'll see the results from your search on the lane. Clicking on the name of the object will launch the detailed screen, from which you can review the employee, position, or organization profile, depending on the item you've selected. However, as you can see in Figure 6.10, if you only need to take action on the object, then you can do so without drilling into the detail.

Figure 6.10 Navigate to Actions Directly from Search Results

In addition, on the right side of the results screen you can see a quick summary of key details for whatever object is currently highlighted in the results section, using something that SAP refers to as a *Bizcard*. Figure 6.11 shows all of the Bizcard types (an employee, position, and organizational unit) presented in the search results.

Figure 6.11 Bizcard Examples

> **Job Maintenance**
>
> You'll notice when you use the search that the job objects are not presented as a category of search results. In most organizations, jobs are centrally maintained by a small group of experts (often the compensation team) and not by the HR administrators who make up the target audience of this portal role.

6.3.1 Lane Configuration

You can access the configuration for this section in the IMG via Transaction SPRO • PERSONNEL MANAGEMENT • EMPLOYEE SELF-SERVICE (SAPUI5) • SEARCH.

Figure 6.12 illustrates the relationships among the search configuration elements. An overall *category group* bundles into SAP_STANDARD for SAP Query, and SAP_STANDARD_ES is for Embedded Search (to be defined shortly). *Search context* associates the categories with specific applications. For example, Full Search is for the Search lane. The *search category* is the specific unit of search. It is at this level that we define what type of object we will be searching for in the category.

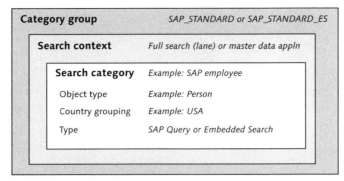

Figure 6.12 Search Configuration

The good news is that if you are using the search function that is delivered you don't need to do any configuration. This gives us time to decide *which* search type you'll want to use: SAP Query or Embedded Search.

If you have been working with Personnel Administration, you are probably no stranger to SAP Query. It is the key ad hoc reporting tool for most organizations. SAP Query has one key downside, though: its performance can degrade if you have a large group of employees.

In contrast, Embedded Search is a high-speed search tool based on SAP's TREX search engine. It indexes the information in your system so that when it is queried the results are near instantaneous. The downside is that TREX requires a separate server to be created and maintained. However, if you are only using TREX for HR search, then the server requirements will be relatively small.

Which search type should you use? There are a couple of key considerations. If you have a large organization, then you will likely want to go the TREX route, whereas smaller companies can probably get by with SAP Query. Our recommendation is to enable HR Renewal in a sandbox that contains the full employee population in your organization, use SAP Query search, and evaluate the performance. If it is not acceptable, then you will want to set up a TREX server.

To designate whether you want to use the SAP Query search or the Embedded Search, you need update the personalization for HRPAO_SEARCH_CATEGORY_GROUP on the SAP role in which the lanes are assigned to HR administrators, as shown in Figure 6.13.

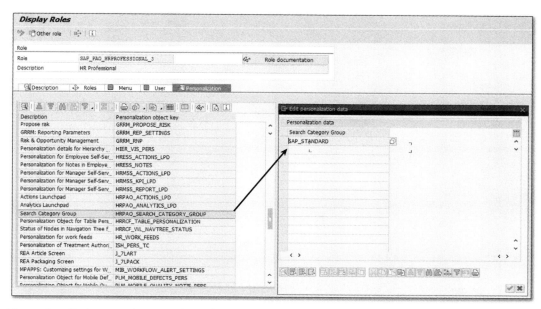

Figure 6.13 Designating the Type of Search

To assign the lane to users, assign the SAP_PAO_SR_HRLANE_SEARCH role or a copied version with equivalent menus, personalization, and authorization objects to the users.

6.4 Organization

If search is the most common way for people to access information, then viewing based on the organizational structure would be a close second.

The organizational structure shows both people and the ways that they are organized (that is, as organizational units). In the classical frontend, you have to go to a separate transaction (Transaction PPOSE) to get to organization information, but with the new interface the Organization lane can exist right beside employee information. The Organization lane is a summary of the organizational units that you access the most. For example, if you're an HR administrator responsible for Maintenance, Customer Service, and Finance, then your Organization lane might look like the one shown in Figure 6.14.

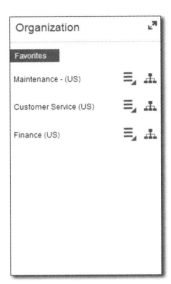

Figure 6.14 Organization Lane

You can take four possible actions from within the Organization lane:

► Clicking on the EXPAND icon (two arrows) in the upper-right corner takes you to an expanded view of your favorites; an example is shown in Figure 6.15. This expanded view includes information about who is managing the organization, the cost center assignment, and which organizational units are reporting to this one.

► Access the profile for the organizational unit (the Employee Profile application) by clicking on the name of the organizational unit. Designate the organizational unit on the profile screen by clicking on the star next to the organizational unit name. We will discuss the Organizational Unit Profile in more detail later in the chapter.

► The ACTION icon (three horizontal lines) includes a menu from which you can launch an action directly, such as launching a form to create a new position directly from the lane.

► Clicking on the ORGANIZATIONAL STRUCTURE icon takes you to the Workforce Viewer that we discussed in Chapter 4.

Figure 6.15 Expanded Organization Lane

6.4.1 Lane Configuration

There's only one configuration option we need to cover for the Organization lane. To assign the lane to users, assign the SAP_PAO_SR_HRLANE_SEARCH role or a copied version with equivalent menus, personalization, and authorization objects to the users.

6.5 Actions

The Actions lane gives you access to any applications available to the user. The lane contains FAVORITES and RECENTLY USED sections. Clicking on the EXPAND icon (two arrows, shown in Figure 6.16) in the upper-right corner takes you to the expanded view of applications.

By expanding the Actions lane, the user can designate which applications should be in his or her favorites by clicking the star beside the service. The delivered list of transactions from SAP contains most if not all of the applications delivered from HR Renewal, so the expanded Actions lane in Figure 6.17 serves as a good starting point for reviewing the applications and deciding which ones are required at your organization.

You can adjust the menu by adding or removing actions. It is important to note that any web-based transactions can be added to this Actions menu, not only those from HR Renewal.

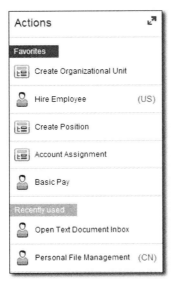

Figure 6.16 Actions Lane

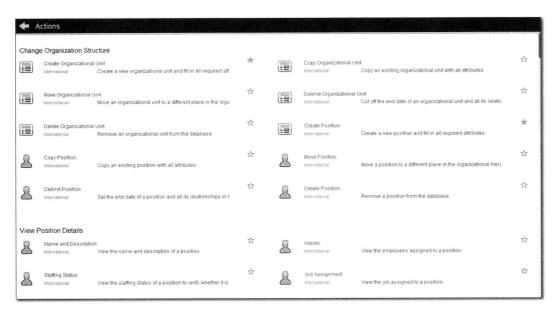

Figure 6.17 Expanded Actions Lane

6.5.1 Lane Configuration

There are several configuration options for the Actions lane.

To assign the lane to users, assign the SAP_PAO_SR_HRLANE_PROCESSES role or a copied version with equivalent menus, personalization, and authorization objects to the users.

The list of available applications is stored in the launchpad configuration in SAP (Transaction LPD_CUST). You need to designate the role and instance. As shown in Figure 6.18, the delivered example from SAP is the HRPAO role and the ACTIONS instance; we recommend using this example as a starting point and copying it to your own versions. Once you have set up your role/instance, you need to supply this information to the personalization for the HRPAO_ACTIONS_LPD role parameter.

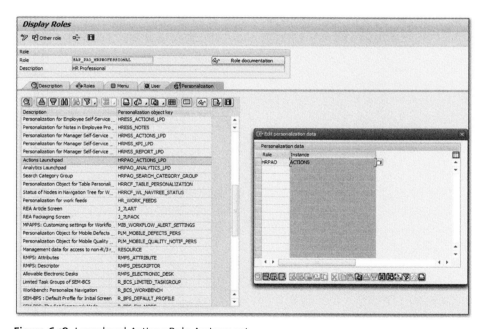

Figure 6.18 Launchpad Actions Role Assignment

In the context of the Actions lane, the list of available applications is static, meaning that whatever is in the role/instance will be presented to the user. In certain cases, you may want to make the application assignments more dynamic—for example, if only a company division needs to have visibility to and maintenance of a certain infotype. For instances such as this, you can replace the delivered feeder class from SAP (CL_HRPAO_ACTIONS_LPD_FEEDER) with your own implementation by going to IMG • Personnel Management • Personnel & Organization • Role • Assign Feeder Class to Launchpad.

6.6   Analytics

The Analytics lane is the portal to reporting for HR administrators. Some prebuilt reports are available, and companies can add in their own reports as well. Similar to the Actions lane, the Analytics lane also contains Favorites and Recently used sections, as shown in Figure 6.19.

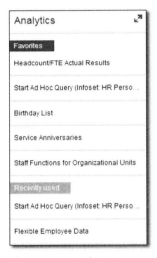

Figure 6.19 Analytics Lane

The expanded view of the lane displays the full inventory of available reports. Although organizations are free to create whatever type of reports they choose to provide to users, there are two primary types of reports delivered by SAP: classical reports and ODP reports.

6.6.1   Classical SAP Reports

Several HR reports have been available from SAP for a number of years and have been made available to users in the Analytics lane, including the following:

- SAP Query-based reports, such as Service Anniversaries (JUBILEE_LIST)
- Traditional reports, such as Flexible Employee Data (RPLICO10)
- Ad Hoc Query reports

Table 6.2 lists an example of each of the classical SAP reports with a short description.

Report	Description
Date Monitoring (DATE_MONITOR)	Lists all upcoming dates from Infotype 19 (Monitoring of Dates)
Infoset Query	Query tool based on SAP Query (Figure 6.20)
Flexible Employee Data (RPLICO10)	Long-term key report with variable selection and output possibilities

Table 6.2 Classicial SAP Reports

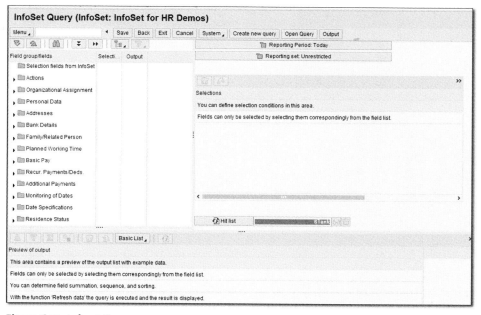

Figure 6.20 Infoset Query

Remember that the classical reports were originally designed for the classical model. Years back, SAP created the Internet Transaction Server (ITS) in order to render classical transactions over the web. ITS works well and is certainly road tested by now, but as we saw in early chapters of this book, its interface is dated. Using these classical reports prolongs the use of the ITS, which some organizations want to sunset.

6.6.2 Operational Data Reporting

The Operational Data Provisioning (ODP) reports were first made available in EHP 6, but they are not widely known. These reports provide SAP BW–like functionality for HR reporting without the need for a separate, dedicated SAP BW system.

Describing the process for implementing ODP reports is beyond the scope of this book, but we can summarize it: in addition to activating the HCM_ANALYTICS_2 switch in Transaction SFW5, you must also install a BI add-in (SAP NetWeaver 7.0 BI Content Add-On 6, as of the writing of this book). SAP also recommends that you use TREX to index your data in order to speed up the results.

6.6.3 Lane Configuration

There are several configuration options for the Actions lane.

To assign the lane to users, assign the SAP_PAO_SR_HRLANE_PROCESSES role or a copied version with equivalent menus, personalization, and authorization objects to the users.

The list of available applications is stored in the launchpad configuration in SAP (Transaction LPD_CUST). You need to designate the role and instance. The delivered example from SAP is the HRPAO role and REPORTS instance; we recommend using this as a starting point and copying it to your own versions. Once you have set up your role/instance, you need to supply this information to the personalization for the HRPAO_REPORTS_LPD role parameter.

In the context of the Actions lane, the list of available applications is static, meaning that whatever is in the role/instance will be presented to the user. In some cases, you may want to make the application assignments more dynamic—for example, if only a company division needs to have visibility to and maintenance of a certain infotype. For instances such as this, you can replace the delivered feeder class from SAP (CL_HRPAO_ACTIONS_LPD_FEEDER) with your own implementation. The SAP-delivered implementation tailors the reports based on a country

that has been passed in as a parameter. You will do this in the IMG step under
Personnel Management • Personnel & Organization • Role • Assign Feeder
Class To Launchpad.

6.7 Discussions

The Discussions lane shows the most recent conversations related to HR objects
over SAP's collaboration tool, SAP Jam, in which the user is involved. You'll first
have to set up SAP Jam, which is outside of the scope of this book, but once SAP
Jam is set up, discussions are an easy way to keep track of the back and forth
among participants in HR processes. However, the discussions are started from
the master data application. The lane and the expanded view of discussions are
essentially the same, but the expanded view (see Figure 6.21) shows more details.

Figure 6.21 Expanded Discussions Lane

6.7.1 Lane Configuration

There's only one configuration option we need to cover for the Discussions lane. To assign the lane to users, assign the SAP_PAO_SR_HRLANE_SWFD role or a copied version with equivalent menus, personalization, and authorization objects to the users.

6.8 Tasks

The Tasks lanes are a streamlined version of the workflow inbox. They provide a quick, graphical overview of the work items assigned to the user.

As Figure 6.22 shows, there are three separate Tasks lanes: tasks summarized by the priority of the task (Tasks by Priority), tasks summarized in relation to their due date (Tasks by Time), and draft-only tasks (Tasks by Drafts).

Figure 6.22 Task Lanes

Clicking on one of the circles takes you to an expanded, filtered view of the user's workflow inbox, as seen in Figure 6.23. The expanded tasks view is similar to the universal worklist (UWL) in the SAP Enterprise Portal, with which many of the readers of this book are no doubt familiar. At the top left are various options available to filter the view, such as OVERDUE TASKS and OPEN TASKS. To access a work item, click on the description of the work item. You can also reserve or unreserve the work item by highlighting it and clicking either CLAIM or RELEASE.

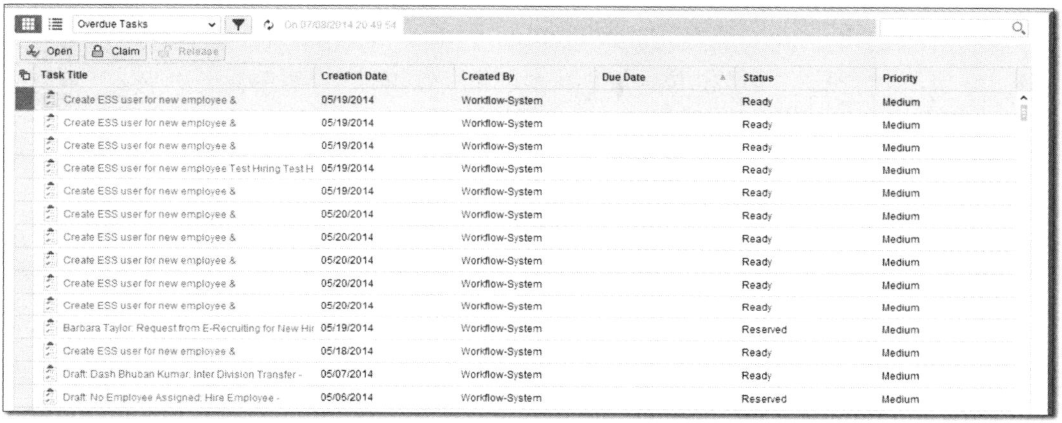
Overdue Tasks
Open
Claim
Release
Task Title
Creation Date
Created By
Due Date
Status
Priority
Create ESS user for new employee & 05/19/2014 Workflow-System Ready Medium
Create ESS user for new employee & 05/19/2014 Workflow-System Ready Medium
Create ESS user for new employee & 05/19/2014 Workflow-System Ready Medium
Create ESS user for new employee Test Hiring Test H 05/19/2014 Workflow-System Ready Medium
Create ESS user for new employee & 05/19/2014 Workflow-System Ready Medium
Create ESS user for new employee & 05/20/2014 Workflow-System Ready Medium
Create ESS user for new employee & 05/20/2014 Workflow-System Ready Medium
Create ESS user for new employee & 05/20/2014 Workflow-System Ready Medium
Create ESS user for new employee & 05/20/2014 Workflow-System Ready Medium
Create ESS user for new employee & 05/20/2014 Workflow-System Ready Medium
Barbara Taylor: Request from E-Recruiting for New Hir 05/19/2014 Workflow-System Reserved Medium
Create ESS user for new employee & 05/18/2014 Workflow-System Ready Medium
Draft: Dash Bhuban Kumar: Inter Division Transfer - 05/07/2014 Workflow-System Ready Medium
Draft: No Employee Assigned: Hire Employee - 05/06/2014 Workflow-System Reserved Medium

Figure 6.23 Expanded Tasks View

The Tasks by Drafts lane is a specialized view that shows draft work items. A draft work item gets created whenever an HR form is started and is saved via the SAVE AS DRAFT option before it is submitted. Clicking on the hyperlink for the item launches the work item itself, allowing the user to complete the task. The Tasks by Priority lane groups assigned work items based on the priority of the work items. The Tasks by Time lane groups assigned work items based on the due dates of the work items.

The Tasks lanes are an attractive and compelling addition to the HR administrator role, because they effectively simplify the functions that HR administrators will value in the tasks view. However, compared to the UWL they are not without their limitations. For example, there is no way to manage substitutions from this frontend, as you can in the UWL. You will need to log in to the SAP GUI to do this. Also, there is no section at the bottom in which a detailed explanation of the work item can be seen, such as you see in the UWL.

6.8.1 Lane Configuration

By default, all of the items assigned to the user are visible in the tasks views. If you decide that some work items should not appear, employ a filter to limit the workflow inbox to only certain work item types by following this IMG path: SAP NETWEAVER • GATEWAY SERVICE ENABLEMENT • CONTENT • MAINTAIN TASK NAMES AND DECISION OPTIONS.

In addition, there are a couple of minor configuration settings in the IMG under PERSONNEL & ORGANIZATION • LANDING PAGE • TASK LANES • DEFINE GROUPING OF TASK PRIORITIES. Within this step, you determine how to sort the tasks and what the composition will be for the status groupings.

To assign the lane to users, assign the SAP_PAO_SR_HRLANE_TASKS role or a copied version with equivalent menus, personalization, and authorization objects to the users.

6.9   Processes

The Processes lane shows all of a given user's ongoing and completed processes. The narrow view displays the items that are effective today through the next seven days, although you can change the number of days via a parameter. Figure 6.24 shows the narrow Process lane view.

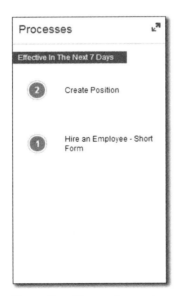

Figure 6.24 Narrow Process Lane

The expanded view of the Process lane is where the real value lies. This view shows a larger number of fields, and if you click on the FILTER icon in the upper-left corner of the screen you are taken to a filtered view, in which you have the flexibility to search based on processor, status, date, or the affected ID (position, organization, or employee).

6.9.1 Lane Configuration

You can adjust the number of days into the future that the narrow lane will show results by going to the IMG node PERSONNEL & ORGANIZATION • LANDING PAGE • PROCESS LANE.

To assign the lane to users, assign the SAP_PAO_SR_HRLANE_PROCESSES role or a copied version with equivalent menus, personalization, and authorization objects to the users.

We have successfully driven through all of the lanes, so we can exit the vehicle with a good sense of the information at the HR administrator's fingertips. Let's move on to Personnel and Organization Master Data Application and the new services we can access from there.

6.10 Master Data with POMDA

After 20 years and countless transactions, it's time to meet the new core master data maintenance screen, the Personnel and Organization Master Data Application. For our purposes, we'll shorten this to POMDA, even though the abbreviation makes the application sound somewhat like a new music group.

The redesign was based on direct feedback from HR administrators about what information would be most helpful and what functions need to be accessed most often. Notice in Figure 6.25 that the Employee Profile in ESS is a rethinking of the employee view.

Since we've been using Transactions PA20 and PA30 for the past 20 years, there's a possibility that the POMDA screen needs to last us a couple decades, so we should explore a little, beginning with the overall structure of the screen. We'll discuss how to influence POMDA's functionality shortly.

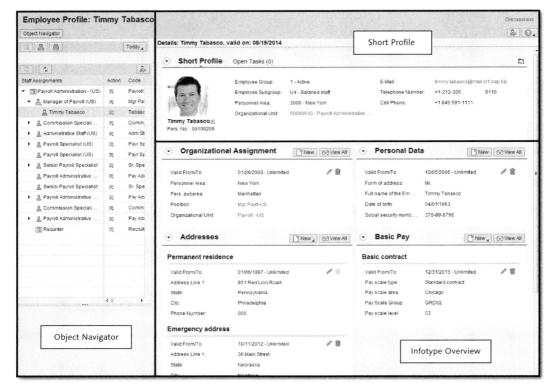

Figure 6.25 POMDA Employee Profile

Let's discuss each of the areas:

- **Object Navigator**

  The Object Navigator serves a similar purpose to the left-hand navigation in PA30, with a key difference: this view can launch detailed views of positions, organizational units, or employees interchangeably.

  There are three types of views for the object navigator:

  - The tree view is the default view. It is the traditional hierarchical view, with the organizational unit at the top and the positions below the position occupants in increasingly subordinate status. If you are launching the Employee Profile from the Employee Search lane, then the Object Navigator automatically defaults to this view, showing the employee in the context of his or her organizational unit.

▶ The hierarchy view is the Adobe Flash Island view, also known as the Nakisa view. We will therefore not cover the functionality or configuration options related to the Nakisa view, because those will soon be obsolete. The organizational structure view is on its way out. At the time of writing of this book (fall 2014), SAP is in the process of rewriting the organizational structure view to use the new Team Viewer we covered in Chapter 4.

▶ The last option for navigation is the unified search, which uses the same logic that we discussed in Section 6.3. Regardless of which option is chosen from the Object Navigator, the user can pull up the full profile by clicking the name of the object from the Object Navigator.

▶ **Short Profile/Open Tasks**
The top-right section of POMDA is a composite view that consists of two elements that you can toggle between using either the transparent tabs or the folder icon at the top of the screen. SHORT PROFILE presents key details on the object in a single view. OPEN TASKS shows any open workflow items that pertain to the selected object.

▶ **Infotype Overview**
INFOTYPE OVERVIEW contains Bizcard views for the key infotypes of the object in question. The business card displays a few key details for the infotype. Each infotype view also provides options for displaying, editing, deleting, and creating, depending on the nature of the infotype. Because the Infotype Overview features very similar to the Employee Profile features in ESS, please see Chapter 4 for further elaboration on the editing and maintenance capabilities. Table 6.3 provides a summary of the infotypes that are delivered for maintenance by object type.

Because we're talking about infotype maintenance, it's important to note that the Actions menus that we referenced earlier in the chapter are available in POMDA as well. The Actions menus appear in the Object Navigator results and in the Short Profile; they can be used to provide access to infotypes that need to be maintained less frequently. In the next section, we will discuss how to configure both the Actions menu and the Employee Profile.

Employee	Position	Organizational Unit
▶ Org. Assignment	▶ Name and Description	▶ Name and Description
▶ Personal Data	▶ Master Cost Center	▶ Master Cost Center
▶ Address	▶ Job	▶ Department/Staff
▶ Basic Pay	▶ Account Assignment Holder	▶ Account Assignment
▶ Bank Details	▶ Staffing Status	▶ Work Schedule
	▶ Employee Group/Subgroup	
	▶ Staff	
	▶ Planned Compensation	
	▶ Managed Org. Units	
	▶ Work Schedule	

Table 6.3 Infotypes Maintainable by Object Type

Now that we have described POMDA's functionality, let's shift our focus to customizing it to fit your organization's requirements. We will first tackle the three meatiest topics for configuration: Short Profile alterations, Bizcard edits, and Object Navigator configuration.

6.10.1 Short Profile Configuration

As we will see in this section, the "short" in Short Profile refers to the amount of data typically included in the form—not the configuration options that get it there. Unfortunately, this is one area in which the path forward is not readily deduced from the SAP documentation, so we'll walk through it here.

The Short Profile was built using the Floorplan Manager (FPM), which is in turn a part of the Web Dynpro framework. You can adjust Web Dynpro screens using component configurations and application configurations. If you need to review basic Web Dynpro configuration, we recommend doing so, because we'll move right to the basic linkages that take a field from SAP and present it on the screen. To make the process as clear as possible, we will start at the overall Web Dynpro application and end up at the field, employing a specific example. For the Employee Profile, we will trace the mobile phone field from the application all the way through the configuration in the following steps:

1. First, call the Web Dynpro application HRPAO_PAOM_MASTERDATA, which references application configuration HRPAO_PAOM_MASTERDATA.

Transaction SE80

The upcoming application and component configurations can be located in Transaction SE80 • Web Dynpro • FPM_OVP_COMPONENT.

2. Application configuration HRPAO_PAOM_MASTERDATA then calls component configuration HRPAO_PAOM_MASTERDATA. This component configuration is the overall design for all of POMDA. It is broken into multiple smaller components, which are called *user interface building blocks* (UIBBs).

As you can see in Figure 6.26, the Short Profile can be found in UIBB HRPAO_PAOM_TABBED_SHORTPRF. To navigate from the application configuration to the component configuration (or between component configurations), use the hyperlinks within Transaction SE80.

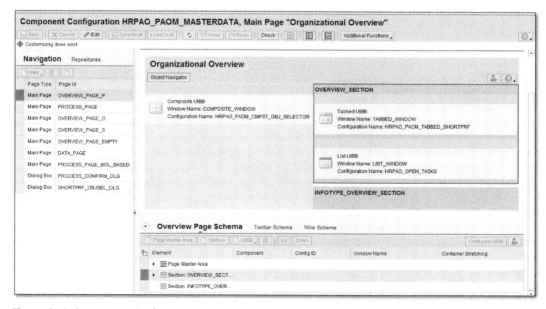

Figure 6.26 Component Configuration

> **Making Overall Profile Changes**
>
> Because POMDA is based on component configuration, there are virtually no limits to the adjustments that could be made to it, if the configurator or developer has the requisite knowledge. For example, you could develop a new UIBB with special graphics or so on, but general Web Dynpro developments such as this are outside of the scope this book.

3. UIBB `HRPAO_PAOM_TABBED_SHORTPRF` is a tabbed UIBB, which means that another UIBB can be embedded within it. That embedded UIBB, `HRPAO_PAOM_MASTERDATA`, is called and in turn references application configuration `HRPAO_PAOM_MASTERDATA` (see Figure 6.27).

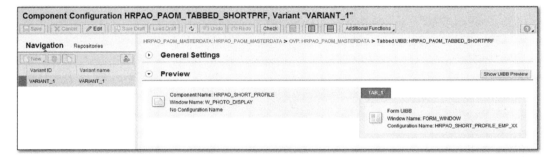

Figure 6.27 Tabbed Short Profile Component Configuration

4. We have finally arrived at the key point for configuration of the Short Profile — at least on the Web Dynpro side. For employees, the standard-delivered profile is `HRPAO_SHORT_PROFILE_EMP_XX`. This component configuration is an FPM UIBB, which means that it is designed to allow users to design the form. As seen in Figure 6.28, the fields for the UIBB are available in a left-side panel named Repositories. In the Preview section, the user can drag and drop the fields and design the form. In the Attributes section at the bottom of the screen, you can see specifics about any highlighted field. In our case, we have highlighted the Cell Phone field, which has an ID of SAP_PAIT_MOBILE.

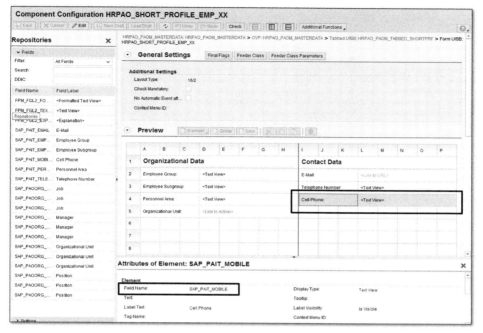

Figure 6.28 Short Profile FPM Configuration

5. Now that we can see the list of fields, it's time to see how the fields get there. Readers familiar with FPM forms know that the fields are obtained through a specialized ABAP class called a feeder class. The feeder class is responsible for obtaining the catalog of fields when you're designing the form and retrieving the data for the fields when the form is being run. The feeder class can be determined by clicking on the FEEDER CLASS PARAMETERS button in Form Designer (at the top of Figure 6.28). In our example, the feeder class is CL_HRPAO_GUIBB_SHORTPRF_FORM and the parameters are a PERSON object type of and an SAP_PA_SHORT_PROFILE configuration ID (see Figure 6.29).

Without going into a deep dive of the code in the class itself, the short of it is that SAP looks into a table in the IMG and finds the fields that are associated with this object type and configuration ID. This is the link between the FPM form and the IMG configuration.

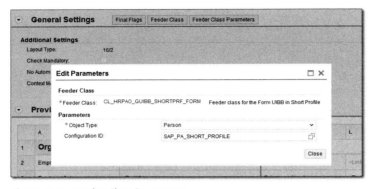

Figure 6.29 Feeder Class Parameters

6. Exiting Transaction SE80, we arrive at more comfortable surroundings, the IMG. In our example, the feeder class is looking for an entry for the PERSON object type and with the SAP_PA_SHORT_PROFILE configuration ID, which can be found at IMG step PERSONNEL MANAGEMENT • PERSONNEL & ORGANIZATION • MASTER DATA APPLICATION • OBJECT PROFILE PAGE • SHORT PROFILE • CREATE CONFIGURATIONS FOR DATA RETRIEVAL. Highlight this row, and select ADD FIELDS TO A CONFIGURATION from the left-side navigation in the same view to see all of the fields assigned to the configuration. Our example field, SAP_PAIT_MOBILE, is one of the fields listed.

7. For every field that needs to be retrieved for the FPM form, SAP first figures out what category it belongs to, which gives an indication of which class gets called to do the actual lookup. The field's category gets defined in PERSONNEL MANAGEMENT • PERSONNEL & ORGANIZATION • MASTER DATA APPLICATION • OBJECT PROFILE PAGE • SHORT PROFILE • EXTENDED FIELD SELECTION • ADD FIELDS TO FIELD SELECTION CATALOG.

As you can see in Figure 6.30, the SAP_PAITF_MOBILE field is assigned to the SAP_PAITF category and the SAP_MOBILE BAdI field.

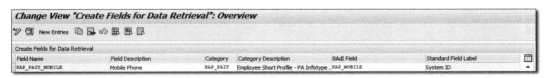

Figure 6.30 Field Assignment to Category/BADI Field

8. Once the field is assigned to a category and a BAdI field, the next step is to define the BAdI in which the actual processing will take place. The BAdI is assigned in the IMG (under Personnel Management • Personnel & Organization • Master Data Application • Object Profile Page • Short Profile • Extended Field Selection • BAdI: Evaluate Fields For Data Retrieval).

Launching the IMG shows you numerous BAdI implementations, so which one is doing the work for your particular field? You have to drill into the individual BAdI and find the one assigned to do the work for the field category. In our case, the SAP_PAIT field category is being processed by the HRPAO_DR_FIELDS_PA_INFTY_DATA enhancement implementation, as Figure 6.31 shows.

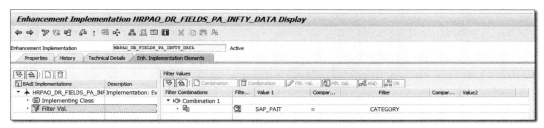

Figure 6.31 BAdI Assignment to Category

9. Because the processing for the BAdI is ABAP based, the possibilities are (almost) limitless for how field values can be derived. The downside to this is that you need to have a programmer write code whenever you need a new field. What happens in cases in which you only need to pull a simple infotype value?

This is actually the case in our example, in which we only want the Mobile Phone field from Infotype 105 Subtype 0010. SAP has provided a special processing class for these cases. This processing class calls the IMG step Personnel Management • Personnel & Organization • Master Data Application • Object Profile Page • Short Profile • Extended Field Selection • Maintain Infotype Fields For Employee Short Profile. If you only need to add in a basic field, you can simply add a field to this IMG step and then add the field to the field selection catalog for the SAP_PAIT category, and the field will be available to your FPM form.

6.10.2 Bizcard Configuration

Bizcards fill in the detail in the bottom right of the profile, as seen in Figure 6.32.

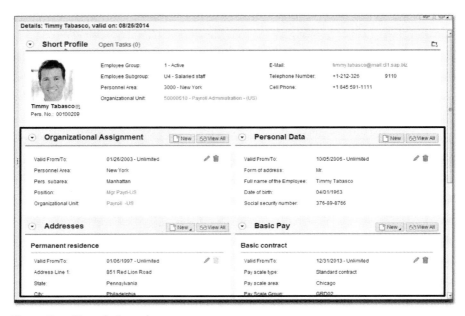

Figure 6.32 Bizcards Example

Some organizations elect to adjust which infotypes should appear in the profile based on the object type. Fortunately, SAP provides an easy way to do this via configuration by providing an override table. As with other override tables, SAP divides the process into two steps:

1. Review what SAP has delivered. This information can be found at PERSONNEL MANAGEMENT • PERSONNEL & ORGANIZATION • MASTER DATA APPLICATION • BIZ CARDS • SAP: BIZ CARDS FOR OBJECT PROFILE PAGES. Any required changes would be made by updating the customer override table, which is the next step in the same IMG node: CUSTOMER: SPECIFY BIZ CARDS FOR OBJECT PROFILE PAGES. To make adjustments, replace all of the entries for the given infotype version, which almost always will correspond to the Molga (country) version. As an example, let's say that we want to replace bank details (Infotype 9) on the US Employee Profile with date specifications (Infotype 41). Identify the entries for the US in the SAP table, as shown in Figure 6.33.

2. Create entries in the override table identical to the ones delivered by SAP, but override the sequence 5 value to be Infotype 41 rather than Infotype 9, as shown in Figure 6.34.

Change View "SAP Configurations for Object Profile Pages": Overview

New Entries

SAP Configurations for Object Profile Pages

Obj.Type	IT Version	Variable Key	Seq	Ord	Configuration ID	Variable Key
P	10		1	1	IT0001	
P	10		2	2	IT0002	
P	10		3	3	IT0006	
P	10		4	4	IT0008	
P	10		5	5	IT0009	

Figure 6.33 SAP-Delivered Bizcard Values for US Employee Profile

Change View "Customer Configurations for Object Profile Pages": Overvi

New Entries

Customer Configurations for Object Profile Pages

Obj.Type	IT Version	Variable Key	S...	O..	Configuration ID
P	10		1	1	IT0001
P	10		2	2	IT0002
P	10		4	4	IT0008
P	10		5	5	IT0041

Figure 6.34 Customer Override for Employee Profile Business Card Display

This explains how to change which Bizcards appear, but what if we want to change the fields that appear in the Bizcard? We'll cover this functionality as part of our infotype UI discussion in Section 6.12.

6.10.3 Object Navigator Configuration

The Object Navigator configuration can be found at PERSONNEL MANAGEMENT • PERSONNEL & ORGANIZATION • ORGANIZATIONAL CHART/TREE. To adjust the display of the tree, you will first review the delivered values in the CHECK STANDARD CONFIGURATION FOR ORGANIZATIONAL TREE step. The hierarchy name for the master data application is `PAO_ORG_TREE`. Then, overwrite the values in the CONFIGURE ORGANIZATIONAL TREE IMG step. Although you won't have to adjust this view in most circumstances, you might need to if you have custom relationships that need to be included in the hierarchy.

The configuration of the search portion of the Object Navigator is handled through IMG node Personnel Management • Personnel & Organization • Search. The categories we're using are the same ones we discussed earlier in the chapter, which can be found in the Group Search Categories IMG step. The difference here is that we will be concerned with the Master Data Application search context. Within this search context, we see SAP_EMPLOYEE, SAP_ORGANIZATION, and SAP_POSITION search categories. These categories are the same ones used in the search application we reviewed in the Search lane (see Section 6.3). Adding new search categories is beyond the scope of this book.

6.11   Actions Menu

To recycle an overused metaphor, explaining the HR Professional role is like peeling an onion. Until now, we have peeled away the layers of the lanes and the POMDA. Now, we want to discuss the Actions menu, which we introduced in a couple of contexts previously in this chapter. Following the design principle of giving users multiple avenues to access the most common functions, SAP has embedded the Actions menu in at least five different places, as Figure 6.35 illustrates.

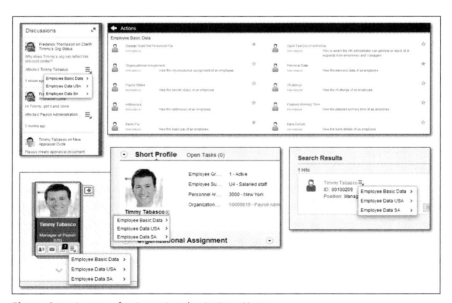

Figure 6.35 Avenues for Accessing the Actions Menu

As we learned earlier in Section 6.5, the Actions menu is assigned to a role. If no menu is assigned, then the standard menu is used instead (the HRPAO role and Actions menu). You maintain the role and menu in Transaction LPD_CUST, which you'll remember from Chapter 4 and Chapter 5.

Because the menu simply launches other applications, the possibilities for the Actions menu are endless, but there are a few common elements that often get added to the Actions menu in the HR Professional role:

- Direct infotype maintenance (Section 6.12)
- Forms: FPM, Adobe, and roadmap (Section 6.13)
- Personnel files (Section 6.14)

We will cover each of these in depth in the sections that follow, but for now let's review the role structure in Transaction LPD_CUST.

If you compare Figure 6.36 to the menu for a user in Figure 6.35, you'll notice that the menus that users see for the given employee are much smaller. This is because the menu items are automatically filtered based on parameters assigned to the individual services inside the respective folders. The service must be for both the right object type (O, S, or P) and for the country grouping for the employee or object in question. You can see where these parameters are located in Figure 6.37.

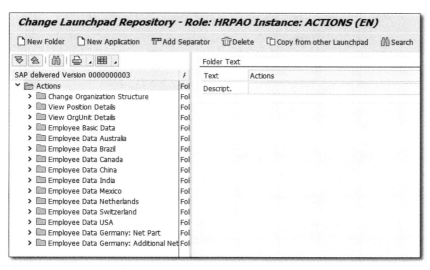

Figure 6.36 HRPAO Role in Transaction LPD_CUST

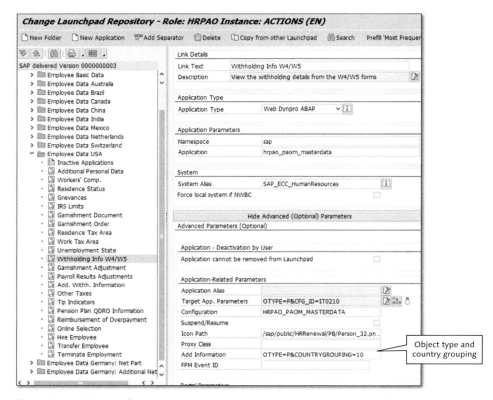

Figure 6.37 HRPAO Role in Transaction LPD_CUST (Application Detail Example)

The OTYPE parameter denotes the object type, whereas the COUNTRYGROUPING parameter denotes the location in which the service is relevant. If either of these parameters is omitted, then the service is globally available for that context. For example, if the COUNTRYGROUPING parameter is omitted, then the service is available for all countries. The individual folders themselves only appear in the employee or object's context menu if they contain a service that is relevant to that context. The most effective way to build out your own application entries is to copy the existing values provided by SAP. You do this by right-clicking the LPD_CUST entry and choosing COPY.

As we mentioned earlier, the LPD_CUST entries can contain a variety of functionality. Now, it's time to delve into this smorgasbord. First up is direct infotype maintenance.

6.12   Direct Infotype Maintenance

Earlier in this chapter, we discussed editing key infotypes from the Employee Profile; now we will spend more time talking about the infotype edit functions. The ability to directly edit infotypes is crucial for companies that want to move from the classical model to the HR Professional role, so SAP has invested in the time and effort to build out infotype maintenance screens for a number of infotypes across a number of countries. As of the time of writing (fall 2014), over 150 infotypes have been converted to Web Dynpro across 33 countries, and additional countries and infotypes are being added every quarter.

The maintenance of infotypes is designed to be straightforward. To describe the functionality and illustrate how the maintenance works, we'll walk through the Address infotype shown in Figure 6.38.

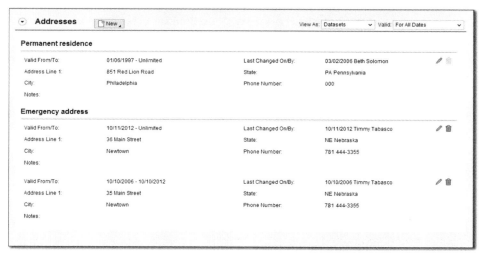

Figure 6.38 Address Overview Screen

Note the NEW button in the top-left corner next to the infotype name. This button will be driven by the infotype in question, including whether it has subtypes and what the time constraints are for the infotype and/or subtypes.

The VIEW AS field appears further to the right and has two options. The datasets view shown in Figure 6.38 uses the Bizcard display for the infotype. The table view shows a table at the top of the screen with all of the valid records. Users can highlight the record at the top, and the detail screen for the record appears on the bottom half of the screen.

On the far right, the VALID field allows users to designate what records they want to see. Table 6.4 describes the options available in the drop-down and the logic behind them.

Date Option	What It Does
For all Dates	Shows all records: past, current, and future
As of Today	Lists any records that are valid as of today's date plus any future entries
In the Past	Lists any records that are no longer active

Table 6.4 Valid Field Options

The detail screens are "web" versions of the familiar classical screens, with one noticeable change: the notes functionality is much more prominent than in PA30. The NOTES section appears at the bottom of the detail screen, as you can see in Figure 6.39. In Transaction PA30, you can only create new notes via a menu path (TOOLS • OPTIONS).

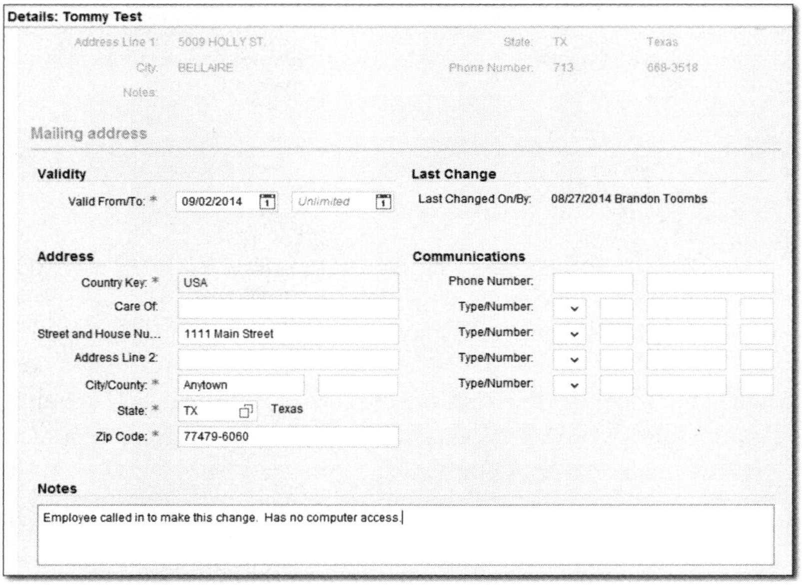

Figure 6.39 Address Infotype Detail Screen

In most material respects, the infotype maintenance behaves similarly to infotype maintenance in PA30, but there are a few key differences. For example, the web-based infotype maintenance screens do not have COPY and DELIMIT buttons. Because new users often find these buttons confusing, however, many view their removal as a positive development.

There are several layers of configuration that go into infotype maintenance. We will start with a discussion of the screen control configuration, and we will then review the configuration step in which the component configurations get tied in to POMDA.

6.12.1 Screen Control Configuration

One of the complaints about other areas of web-enabled screens, such as ESS and MSS, was about the inability to influence the field properties through configuration rather than having to update the application directly through development.

There's a fix! SAP has addressed this in the infotype maintenance screens, delivering screen control configuration that serves a purpose similar to what the screen control table T588M does for the classical model. The configuration can be found at PERSONNEL MANAGEMENT • PERSONNEL & ORGANIZATION • INFOTYPES • INFOTYPES FOR EMPLOYEES • INFOTYPES IN THE DECOUPLED INFOTYPE FRAMEWORK. As in other areas of configuration, you'll first reference the SAP values and then enter your values in an override table.

The SAP values can be found in SAP: FIELD PROPERTIES, with the overrides occurring in the next step, under CUSTOMER: DEFINE FIELD PROPERTIES. Copy all of the fields from the SAP table for the infotype, country version, or subtype you want to adjust, and then paste the copied fields into the customer override. Check the column that pertains to the field property that you require for the field. As of the time of writing, the column names in table T588MFPROPC are displaying in German, but because the column names will likely eventually be translated to their English equivalents, we will present them based on their order rather than their label:

▶ The first column (MUSSEINGABE) marks the field as required.

▶ The second column (AUSGABE) makes the field read-only.

▶ The third column (UNBENUTZT) hides the field.

If you want a field to be visible, editable, and not required, leave all of the columns blank. Figure 6.40 is an example of a customer entry for a US address, with the telephone number marked as required. Note that if you omit a field from your table the value from SAP table will govern the display. Our recommendation is to include all fields for any country versions or infotypes that you are going to override to make it easier to reference later.

HR: Field Properties						
Version	S...	Struktur	Field Name	Musseingabe	Ausgabe	unbenutzt
10		P0006	ANSSA	☑	☐	☐
10		P0006	BUSRT	☐	☐	☑
10		P0006	COM01	☐	☐	☐
10		P0006	COM02	☐	☐	☐
10		P0006	COM03	☐	☐	☐
10		P0006	COM04	☐	☐	☐
10		P0006	ENTKM	☐	☐	☑
10		P0006	LAND1	☐	☐	☐
10		P0006	NUM01	☐	☐	☐
10		P0006	NUM02	☐	☐	☐
10		P0006	NUM03	☐	☐	☐
10		P0006	NUM04	☐	☐	☐
10		P0006	ORT01	☐	☐	☐
10		P0006	PSTLZ	☑	☐	☐
10		P0006	STATE	☑	☐	☐
10		P0006	STRAS	☑	☐	☐
10		P0006	WKWNG	☐	☐	☑
10		P0006	TELNR	☑	☐	☐
				☐	☐	☐
				☐	☐	☐

Figure 6.40 Screen Control for Address

Screen Control

For readers who have been using Transaction PA30, this process probably looks similar to table T588M, in which we maintain field visibility for PA30. It's important to note that the new process does not replace the screen control process for PA30.

This screen control provides a simple way to make basic changes to how the infotypes function, which in most cases should be sufficient to allow organizations to tailor infotypes to meet their needs. However, what happens when you need more in-depth changes? You'll need to update the infotype UI configurations.

6.12.2 Infotype UI Configuration Table

Infotype UI configurations can best be described as the nerve center for the Web Dynpro infotype UI. This is where all of the Web Dynpro definitions are stored, along with information on the business logic. Infotype UI configurations can be located at PERSONNEL MANAGEMENT • PERSONNEL & ORGANIZATION • INFOTYPES • INFOTYPE UI CONFIGURATION FOR MASTER DATA APPLICATION.

As with the screen control, the IMG has two steps: one to view the standard configuration and one for customer overrides. Both of the tables contain the fields listed in Table 6.5. Because the table handles a lot of tasks, Figure 6.41 provides an overview.

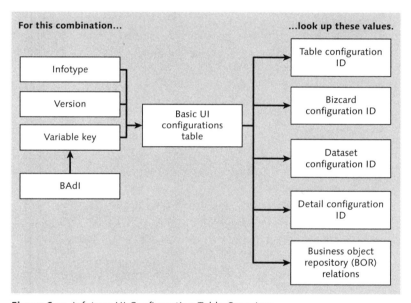

Figure 6.41 Infotype UI Configuration Table Overview

For the combination of infotype, version, and variable key, the table will identify the relevant component configurations. That component configuration specifies what the UI will look like. Finally, the BOR relations lets the UI talk to the backend.

Table 6.5 lists the fields in the table. We'll discuss each of the various view types and provide examples for each one shortly.

Field	Description
OBJECT TYPE	Basic object type (i.e., O, S, or P).
CONFIGURATION ID	Uses the format ITXXXX, where XXXX is the infotype number.
IT VERSION	Country (Molga) version for the infotype.
VARIABLE KEY	Used in conjunction with a BAdI, it allows you to further differentiate in cases in which infotype/screen version are not enough. The IMG step for the BAdI (BADI: UI LOGIC ENHANCEMENT) can be found in the same node as the UI configuration table.
DESCRIPTION	Description of the infotype.
BIZ CARD: WD CONFIG	Identity of the Web Dynpro configuration for the business card.
BIZ CARD: WD COMPONENT NAME	Web Dynpro component from which the component configuration originates. If this is left blank, the component configuration will default to `FPM_FORM_REPEATER_UIBB`.
BIZ CARD: WEB DYNPRO INTERFACE VIEW	Name of the interface view that is associated with the component configuration. If this is left blank, the interface view will default to `FORM_REPEATER_WINDOW`.
TABLE: WD CONFIG	The component configuration for the table view for the infotype.
TABLE: WD COMPONENT	Web Dynpro component from which the component configuration originates. If this is left blank, the component configuration will default to `FPM_LIST_UIBB_ATS`.
TABLE: WEB DYNPRO INTERFACE VIEW	Name of the interface view that is associated with the component configuration. If this is left blank, the interface view will default to `LIST_WINDOW`.
DATASET: WD CONFIG	The component configuration for the dataset view for the infotype.
DATASET: WD COMPONENT	Web Dynpro component from which the component configuration originates. If this is left blank, the component configuration will default to `FPM_FORM_REPEATER_UIBB`.
DATASET: WEB DYNPRO INTERFACE VIEW	Name of the interface view that is associated with the component configuration. If this is left blank, the interface view will default to `FORM_REPEATER_WINDOW`.
CONNECTOR TYPE	Either RELATION if the business object layer (BOL) is used or No CONNECTOR if BOL is not used.

Table 6.5 Component Configuration Elements

Field	Description
RELATION NAME	Name of the BOL model.
RELATION NAME 2	Used for specifying the secondary relation, required for country-specific BOL definitions.
DETAIL: WD CONFIG	The component configuration for the detail view for the infotype.
DETAIL: WD COMPONENT	Web Dynpro component from which the component configuration originates. If this is left blank, the component configuration will default to `FPM_FORM_UIBB_GL2`.
DETAIL: WEB DYNPRO INTERFACE VIEW	Name of the interface view that is associated with the component configuration. If this is left blank, the interface view will default to `FORM_WINDOW`.

Table 6.5 Component Configuration Elements (Cont.)

There are several new concepts in this table:

▸ **Bizcard view**

As explained previously, Bizcards are used in the Employee Profile in ESS. In HR Administrator, the Bizcard view is also used in the dataset view. In both cases, the application looks to the appropriate configuration table to determine the component configuration, which lists the fields that appear. Figure 6.42 shows the component configuration for the Infotype 2 (Personal Data) and what it looks like at runtime.

▸ **Table view**

The table view is one of two possible view options when the user accesses the infotype. In the table view, the infotype history is listed at the top, and the details are listed at the bottom, as shown in Figure 6.43.

Figure 6.42 Bizcard Component Configuration and Bizcard View

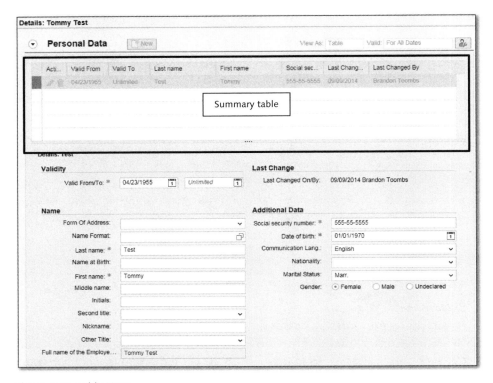

Figure 6.43 Table View

▶ **Dataset view**

The dataset view is the other view that is accessed when the user navigates to a specific infotype. This view gathers all of the Bizcards for all historical records for all subtypes and presents them as shown in Figure 6.44.

▶ **Detail view**

The detail view in Figure 6.45 shows all of the fields for the infotype; this view is where record updates occur.

We now know how we can influence the fields being displayed on the screen. Soon, we'll discuss stringing multiple screens (infotypes) together in succession via roadmap forms.

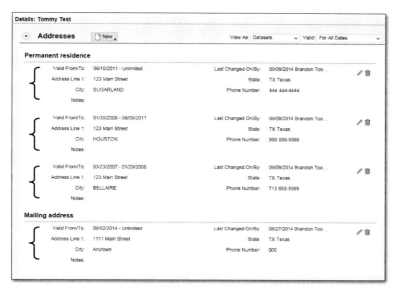

Figure 6.44 Dataset View

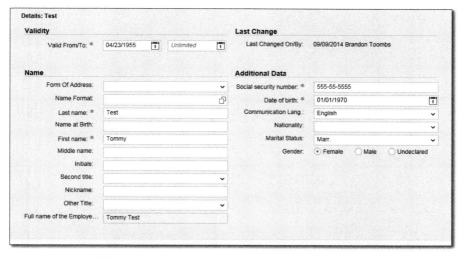

Figure 6.45 Detail View

▸ **Relation Name /Relation Name 2**
The relation name lets the BOL know what related object needs need to be contacted/updated.

243

The BOL is a very technical topic, the intricacies of which are beyond the scope of this book. However, because it is a key cog in the flow of information between the frontend and the infotypes, it probably warrants a brief overview. The BOL contains the "smarts" of the application. It serves as a broker between the frontend FPM configurations (such as for the detail view) and the backend infotypes.

We can see the structure of the HR view by going to Transaction GENIL_MODEL_BROWSER and looking at the HRPAD model. Let's take an example from the configuration table and trace it to the BOL model. Figure 6.46 shows the value from the basic UI configuration table for US Infotype 2.

Figure 6.46 BOL Entry from the Basic UI Configurations Table

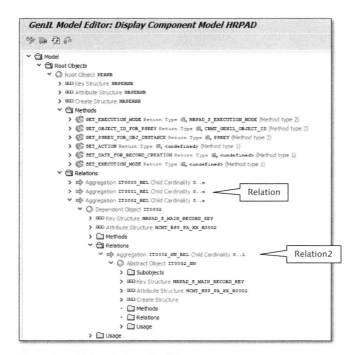

Figure 6.47 Values in BOL Model

RELATION NAME identifies the infotype, whereas the RELATION NAME 2 will contain an entry if there are country-specific infotype versions; otherwise, it is left blank. If we go to Transaction GENIL_MODEL_BROWSER, we can see these values as relations.

We have covered the briefest of explanations of the BOL model. The key takeaway for nontechnical resources is that the new infotype UI calls the BOL model and must be supplied with the proper relations. If more in-depth changes are required (such as adding new infotypes), then such changes will need to be completed by the technical team.

6.13   Using Forms

The configuration for HCM Processes and Forms (HCMPF) is designed around two main concepts: the process and the scenario (a subset of the process). In general, the process governs the overall workflow, whereas the scenario handles the processing and updating within SAP. It is at the scenario level that we decide what type of form we'll be working with: roadmap (Section 6.13.1), FPM (Section 6.13.3), or Adobe Interactive Form (which is the previous generation of HCMPF).

Additional Resources

The configuration of the HCM Processes and Forms toolset is too broad to cover in much depth here. Instead, we recommend another SAP PRESS book on the subject: *SAP ERP HCM Processes and Forms* by Justin Morgalis and Brandon Toombs (2013).

Therefore, in this book we will focus on only the key features and functions of HCMPF and its overall configuration. The one exception will be in the area of roadmap form configuration, which was not covered in the HCMPF book.

6.13.1   Roadmap Forms (HCMPF Lite)

Roadmap forms enable the organization of group activities that naturally belong together into a single transaction. For example, when an employee is transferred to another division within the company that is in another state several types of information need to be simultaneously updated: the position and organizational unit in which the person is working, the work tax jurisdiction, and probably a change in salary.

In classical model, this would be handled through Transaction PA40. In fact, it seems clear that SAP intends roadmap forms to be the web version of the PA40 actions. HCM Processes and Forms (HCMPF) is a specialized toolset for bringing Personnel Administration business processes online. The intent behind the roadmap forms version of HCMPF is to provide a coding-free way to set up online forms.

As you can see in Figure 6.48, the roadmap forms are structured with the menu of infotypes on the left-hand side. The user is taken step-by-step through the infotypes, starting with the general information screen, which mirrors the Infotype 0 (Actions) screen in PA30/PA40. After the user completes the infotype and clicks Next, he is taken sequentially to the next infotype. Alternatively, the user can select which specific infotype he or she wants to work on next from the left-hand pane.

When the roadmap has been completely processed, the user clicks the Check All button to trigger the form to perform error checking. If everything checks out, the user clicks Save, and the form either moves to the next step of the workflow or commits the change to SAP, depending on what was configured.

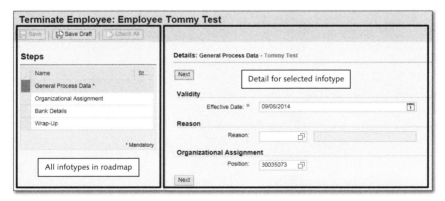

Figure 6.48 Roadmap Form Example

Compared to the classical PA40, roadmap forms offer a couple of significant improvements. The first is that the action does not save to the database until an error check has been completed on the entire list of infotypes that are part of the roadmap. Let's say that we are hiring someone, but unbeknownst to us when we start the hiring process, the pay grade for the job does not exist, so it will be impossible to complete the basic pay information. In the classical PA40 world, you might end up with a partially completed hire in the system. If left in the system, this can cause issues in areas such as outbound interfaces. In contrast, with roadmap form configuration you can specify what the minimum amount of data is that needs to be completed before the form can be committed to the database.

Another key improvement of roadmap forms when compared with PA40 is the ability to save a transaction as a draft and come back to it later. Let's go back to our example of missing pay grade data. In such a scenario, rather than abandoning all of the data that had been entered up to that point, the user can click the SAVE DRAFT button to save the contents of all fields and place the work item in the user's workflow inbox. A specific lane (Tasks, and more specifically, Tasks by Drafts) exists to display all draft work items for the user, as shown in Figure 6.49.

Figure 6.49 Tasks by Draft Lane

The final key improvement over PA40 is the ability to incorporate the entire transaction within a workflow. Using workflows, you can include approvals prior to committing a change to the database (Figure 6.50).

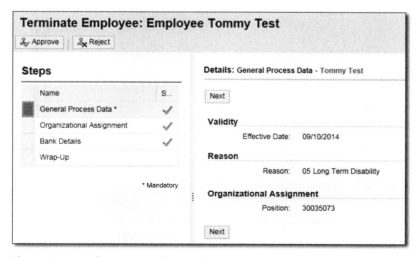

Figure 6.50 Roadmap Approval Example

Configuration Options

One of the key principles followed for the roadmap forms was to make the forms completely configuration based, meaning that HR administrators would be able to build out their HR transactions without any programming, which is essential for some companies that have scarce development resources.

However, because the roadmap forms don't have as much functionality (or configuration!) as full HCMPF, think of roadmap forms as "HCMPF lite." The configuration for HCMPF lite is all contained in a single integrated transaction called the HCM Forms Design Time Repository (DTR), accessible via Transaction HRASR_DT. The DTR has a left-side menu that includes all of the configuration settings, as you can see in Figure 6.51.

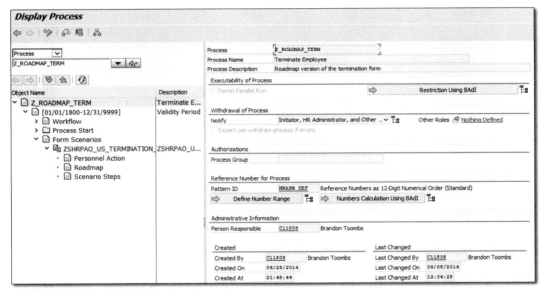

Figure 6.51 Design Time Repository

You can create a new roadmap process and scenario via the following steps:

1. In the dropdown menu in the upper left of the Transaction HRASR_DT screen, ensure that PROCESS is selected. For a new process, type in the name of the new process, and hit the down arrow, as shown in Figure 6.52.

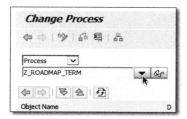

Figure 6.52 Create a Roadmap Process

2. Within your newly created process, click FORM SCENARIO, right-click, and choose CREATE FORM SCENARIO. The scenario is added to the process with the roadmap configuration steps, as you can see in Figure 6.53.

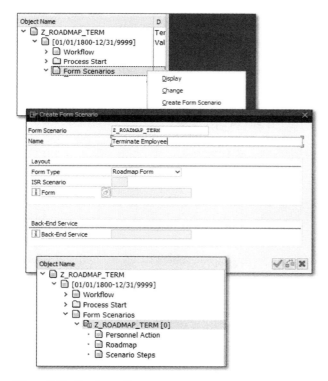

Figure 6.53 Roadmap Steps

Now that you've learned how to create a roadmap form scenario, let's look at the configuration steps that must be populated for the roadmap. The roadmap configuration is essentially a simplified version of the action and infogroup configuration from within SAP.

In the PERSONNEL ACTION section, the action type for the form is designated. You also have the ability to define a specific reason code and whether the reason code is editable or read-only.

The following fields are at the heart of the roadmap configuration:

▸ CONFIGURATION ID*: Uses the format ITXXXX, where XXXX is the infotype number.

▸ INFOTYPE VERSION*: Country (Molga) version for the infotype.

▸ SUBTYPE: Designated subtype for step.

▸ VARIABLE KEY*: In cases in which multiple configurations are required for the same infotype based on a specific business requirement, SAP provides this variable key.

▸ OPERATION: What type of database update should occur for the infotype: CREATE, CHANGE, COPY, DELIMIT, or DELETE.

▸ ATTRIBUTE: Whether the infotype must be completed in order for the form to commit to the database: REQUIRED or STANDARD (not required).

The three values with an asterisk serve as keys in the infotype UI configuration table that we discussed in Section 6.12.2. Using those keys, the appropriate UI configurations and backend relationships are determined for processing.

Finally, scenario steps are used in roadmap forms to perform two tasks:

▸ To provide details on the process' current business status for processes with approval enabled. For example, you might create a process with two approval steps: Department Director Approval and HR Director Approval. In the workflow, you will specify these step names for the approval steps (not pictured here). At the completion of the process (or even in the middle), you will see the step detail. Figure 6.54 shows the detail from HRASR_DT at the top of the figure. The bottom of the figure shows the names that appear in the Process Browser that the HR administrator or manager can access.

▸ To provide a confirmation text that is tailored to the particular step. The confirmation message can let the user know what will occur next in the process, as shown in Figure 6.55.

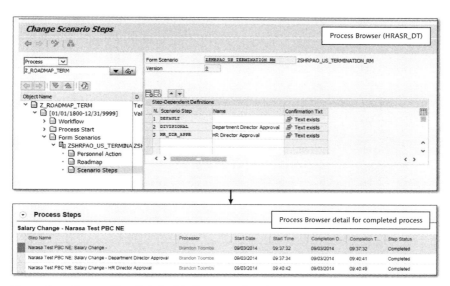

Figure 6.54 Process Step Detail with Corresponding Entry in Process Browser

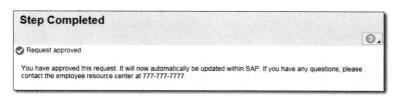

Figure 6.55 Confirmation Text

Setting up roadmap forms is fairly straightforward, but compared with the FPM forms they do have some significant functional limitations. We will review FPM forms in Section 6.13.3 and then compare and contrast FPM forms to the roadmap forms. However, first we need to cover another important recent development: dynamic processing rules (DPR). Dynamic processing rules are available for roadmap forms but not for FPM forms.

6.13.2 Dynamic Processing Rules

If roadmap forms can be thought of as a successor of PA40, you can think of DPRs as the next generation of dynamic actions. Using DPR, the roadmap form can react to the values that have been entered by the user and respond by adjusting the roadmap or even simply populating an infotype behind the scenes.

Let's look at an example DPR in which we are completing a new hire via a roadmap form. On the personal data, we enter all of the new employee's details. The marital status is set to MARR. (married), as shown in Figure 6.56.

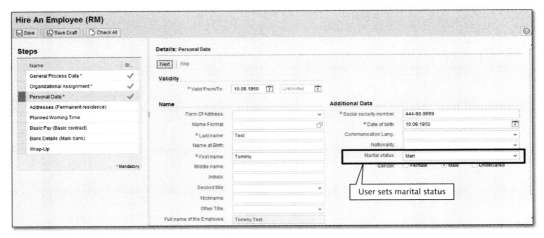

Figure 6.56 User Selects Marital Status

When the user clicks the NEXT button at the top of the screen in Figure 6.57, a new step is inserted into the roadmap so that the spouse's information can be entered in the Spouse subtype (1) of the Family Member infotype (21).

Figure 6.57 New Scenario Step via a Dynamic Processing Rule

DPRs apply both within roadmap forms and during direct infotype maintenance in POMDA. Figure 6.58 shows personal data being updated directly, with the marital status being changed to married.

When the user clicks SAVE, the screen refreshes, and we are suddenly in a roadmap process. PERSONAL DATA is the first step, and now FAMILY MEMBERS/DEPENDENTS (SPOUSE) is the second step in Figure 6.59.

Let's explore the configuration behind this wizardry.

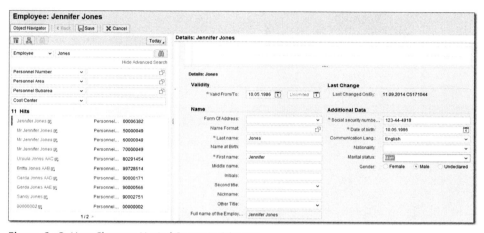

Figure 6.58 User Changes Marital Status in POMDA

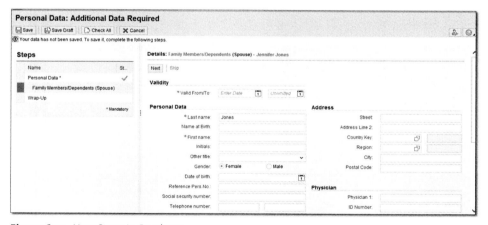

Figure 6.59 New Steps in Roadmap

Configuration Options

As you would expect, setting up a DPR is fairly straightforward. Readers familiar with dynamic actions will find similarities in DPR configuration, although DPR is more structured and therefore less likely to turn into a massive, unmanageable table the way that the dynamic actions have for some customers. The configuration can be accessed at PERSONNEL MANAGEMENT • PERSONNEL & ORGANIZATION • MASTER DATA APPLICATION • DYNAMIC PROCESSING RULES • DEFINE DYNAMIC PROCESSING RULES. The rule ID for our example is MAINTAIN_SPOUSE, as shown in Figure 6.60.

Configurati...	Rule	IT Version	IT Version T...	Subtype	Active	Create	Change	Delimit	Delete
IT0002	MAINTAIN_SPOUSE				☑	☑	☑	☐	☐

Figure 6.60 DPR Configuration Example

Setting up a DPR consists of setting conditions (when to do it) and operations (what to do). As Figure 6.61 shows, the transaction shows a folder hierarchy in the left-side pane, whereas the rules appear in the remainder of the page.

Change View "Dynamic Processing Rules": Overview

New Entries 🗋 🖺 🖘 🖺 🖺 🖺 Rule Manager

Dialog Structure
- Dynamic Processing Rule
  - Conditions
  - Operations
    - Default Values
  - Parameter Groups
    - Parameters
  - Rule Order

Dynamic Processing Rules

Configurati...	Rule	IT Version	IT Version T...	Subtype	Active	Create	Change	Delimit	Delete	Note
0002	MARITAL_STATUS_IT0241	34	Indonesia	FAMS	☐	☑	☑	☐	☐	Insert Record in 241 on Change of Marital Status
IT0000	COPY_IT0012_FISCAL_DATA	01	Germany		☑	☑	☑	☐	☐	
IT0001	COPY_IT0012_FISCAL_DATA	01	Germany		☑	☑	☑	☐	☐	
IT0001	PERFORM_RUECKW_WECHSEL	01	Germany		☑	☑	☑	☑	☐	
IT0001	Z_UPDATE_WORK_STATUS	10	USA		☑	☑	☑	☐	☐	
IT0002	MAINTAIN_CHILDREN				☑	☑	☑	☐	☐	
IT0002	MAINTAIN_SPOUSE				☑	☑	☑	☐	☐	
IT0002	MAINTAIN_SPOUSE	24	Saudi Arabia		☑	☑	☑	☐	☐	Maintain Spouse for KSA
IT0002	MAINTAIN_SPOUSE	AE	United Arab E..		☑	☑	☑	☐	☐	
IT0002	ZANZKD				☐	☐	☐	☐	☐	Will wils wissen
IT0002	Z_CHILD_DATA_ENTRY				☐	☑	☑	☐	☐	Shows screen to enter child data
IT0004	CREATE_IT0019_SEVERE_CHALLENGED				☑	☑	☑	☐	☐	
IT0006	Z_SIMONE_TEST				☐	☑	☐	☐	☐	Test Simone Roth
IT0008	UPDATE_IT0014_HOUSING_SA	24	Saudi Arabia		☑	☑	☑	☑	☐	Saudi Arabia: Change Housing Allowance
IT0008	ZRULE_03				☑	☑	☑	☐	☐	test
IT0008	ZSTRICT				☑	☐	☐	☐	☐	
IT0008	ZTEST_02				☑	☐	☐	☐	☐	
IT0008	Z_CHANGE_WORKING_HOURS	01	Germany		☑	☐	☑	☐	☐	Change in working hours triggers "Planned Worki
IT0013	CHANGE_IT0020_DEUEV	01	Germany		☑	☐	☑	☐	☐	

Figure 6.61 DPR Configuration Table

The configuration ID, subtype, and infotype version are the same concepts as in the roadmap forms and direct infotype updates via POMDA. One important thing to note is that if the IT VERSION field is left blank, as done in Figure 6.62, then it applies to all countries. CREATE, CHANGE, DELIMIT, and DELETE refer to which operations will trigger the DPR.

By accessing the CONDITIONS folder, we can see the exact changes to Infotype 2 that will trigger the DPR.

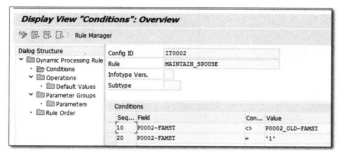

Figure 6.62 DPR Condition

Now that we have identified the infotype and the field-level conditions that should trigger the DPR, we need to tell it what to do by accessing the OPERATIONS folder on the left. Figure 6.63 shows our operation. Infotype 21 and Subtype 1 are created in the foreground.

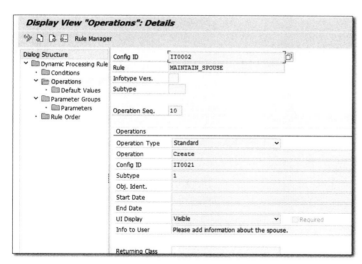

Figure 6.63 DPR Operation

Next, specify the start and end dates for the new record. Figure 6.64 shows that the begin date and end date for Infotype 2 will be used as defaults.

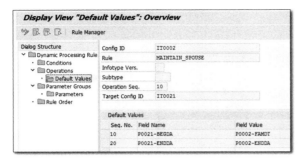

Figure 6.64 DPR Defaults

Finally, activate the status via the Rule Manager. Access the Rule Manager either by going to the RULE MANAGER step in the IMG (immediately after DYNAMIC PROCESSING RULES) or by simply clicking the RULE MANAGER button on the toolbar. Inside the Rule Manager, highlight the rule, and click the ACTIVATE SELECTED RULES button (the lit match in Figure 6.65) to change the customer status to ACTIVE.

R Config ID	O	Rule	IT	IT Version	Subt	Customer Status	Default Status	Type	C Content	Add. Attributes
IT0002	2	MAINTAIN_SPOUSE				Active	Inactive	Note		
								Trigger	Create, Change	
								Condition	P0002-FAMST <> P0002_OLD-FAMST	
								Condition	P0002-FAMST = '1'	
								Info to User	Please add information about the spouse.	
								Operation	Create IT0021, Subtype 1	
								Default Val	P0021-BEGDA = P0002-FAMDT	
								Default Val	P0021-ENDDA = P0002-ENDDA	

Rule Manager

Figure 6.65 DPR Activation via Rule Manager

For most DPRs, this is all of the effort that needs to be expended. However, SAP does provide a framework for custom code that can be used for either conditions or operations via something known as a *calculation class*, but working with calculation classes is beyond the scope of this book.

In summary, DPR is a welcome addition to the master data maintenance capabilities for the HR professional. For customers who relied heavily on PA30, the addition of DPR makes moving to the HR Professional role even more compelling. However, before you completely redo everything as a roadmap form, let's look at another part of the HCM UI portfolio: the FPM forms in HCM Processes and Forms. We'll then compare and contrast the two approaches to help you decide how these tools fit into the core HCM processing strategy at your organization.

6.13.3 HCM Processes and Forms (Full HCMPF)

HCMPF is a robust toolset that was created to allow customers to bring full SAP ERP HCM business processes online via the following functionality:

- Capturing the data from the source—even if the source is not a trained HR user.
- Validating the data during capture to ensure data quality.
- Providing the ability to route for editing and approval using workflows.
- Automatically updating SAP at the end of the process via standard infotype business logic.

There are two possible UIs for rendering the forms themselves: FPM and Adobe. Regardless of which one is chosen, the backend configuration, workflow, and processing are essentially the same. For purposes of simplicity, we will focus on the FPM frontend, because it is the most recent and is preferred by many customers.

The forms themselves have a similar look and feel to the DIRECT INFOTYPE UPDATE screens because they both use a similar technology for rendering. Figure 6.66 displays an example HCMPF form.

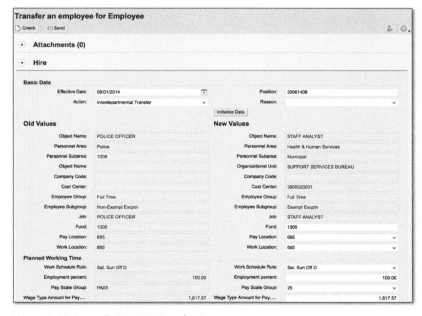

Figure 6.66 Example HCMPF Transfer Form

Key Features

Next, let's run through the highlights of HCMPF:

▶ **FPM Form Editor**

The Form Editor shown in Figure 6.67 provides great flexibility for designing forms. It is a WYSIWYG (what you see is what you get) editor that enables anyone to design forms by using a grid layout.

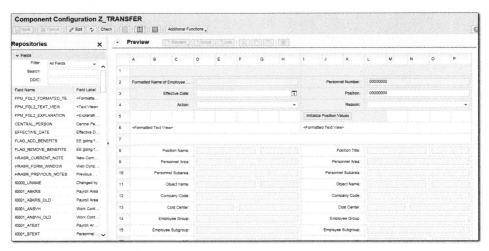

Figure 6.67 FPM Form Editor

▶ **Multiple entry points**

FPM forms can be started in the HR Professional, ESS, or MSS roles, which enables companies to follow the best practice of "capturing the change at the source." Otherwise, the HR administrator is almost always inputting the information based on a conversation, email, or even (gasp!) a sheet of paper. These secondhand methods are much less reliable.

▶ **Step-based field visibility**

Using FPM forms, you can vary which fields are presented or even required based on where you're at in the process. For example, imagine that your company has a complicated process for determining who is eligible for stock payments and that this is not currently calculated in SAP. When the manager initiates the transfer form, the STOCK OPTIONS field can be hidden, but when the form arrives at the HR department, the STOCK OPTIONS field could be available for input.

► **Manual search help and defaulting**
Let's say that a specific form should only use a subset of the reason codes. Several others are not to be used but are still retained in the system for historical purposes. With FPM forms, you can manually determine which search help options are available for a form. In addition, if the online form should always use a certain reason code, then this can be set manually as a default via configuration.

► **Attachments**
FPM forms also let you attach one or more documents as part of the process—and even can be configured to *require* that an attachment be included before the form can be submitted.

► **Modular workflows**
SAP delivers a number of predefined tasks that companies can plug in to a workflow in order to bring their business processes online, including the following:

  ► Approve form

  ► Edit form

  ► Forward to expert for further processing

  ► Read form values into the workflow to allow them to be used by the workflow for branching, etc.

  ► Delay the infotype updates processing in SAP if the employee is currently locked

► **Automatic update of SAP**
As with the roadmap forms, FPM forms automatically update SAP upon the completion of the approval process. They use a set of services named SAP_PA (for employee updates) or SAP_PD (for organizational/position updates). These services use the standard infotype logic to perform the validations and update SAP.

► **Message mapping**
In FPM forms, you can reword the standard SAP error and warning messages and, in the case of warning messages, suppress messages entirely. Figure 6.68 shows an example of message mapping. In the top section, MAP INDIVIDUAL MESSAGES, we see that when the message ID HRASR00_GENSERV, number 111 is received, an alternate message ID ZLSO, number 000 is used instead. In the

bottom section, MAP ALL MESSAGES IN ERROR CATEGORY, all warning messages in the INCONSIT error category are hidden.

▸ **Integration with digital personnel files**
Another key element of HCMPF is the ability to retain the completed form with the comments and attachments that were part of the process when the transaction was approved.

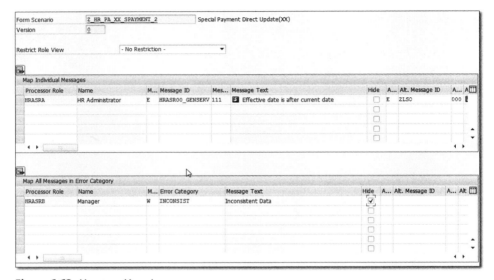

Figure 6.68 Message Mapping

All of these changes are possible without any code changes — but this is only part of the story. Let's look at your other options.

Development-Based Options

HCMPF includes a framework called Generic Services. Generic Services is a common, consistent method for manipulation that works across all HCMPF forms.

Once your development team is familiar with this framework, there are a whole host of possibilities for refining HCMPF forms to make them user-friendly enough for occasional users (e.g., managers and employees), including the following:

▸ **Make field B disappear or appear based on the input in field A.**

For example, on an LOA form you could make an Infotype 19 REMINDER DATE field appear automatically if a user selects a reason code of MATERNITY LEAVE.

▸ **Update the search help values in field B based on the input in field A.**

For example, on a transfer form you could populate the reason code based on the action type that the user chose.

▸ **Perform custom error checks.**

For example, add an error check that prevents users from entering a bonus amount of less than $1 to ensure data quality.

▸ **Calculate values based on a button click.**

For example, clicking a CALCULATE INCREASE button on a pay change form (see Figure 6.69) could cause a calculation of the percentage increase, which would be displayed on the form.

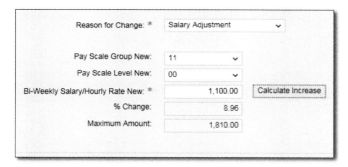

Figure 6.69 Calculation Button Example

Although some of these features are also available on roadmap forms, many are not. HCMPF functionality that is not available in roadmap forms includes the following elements:

▸ Customizable layout using the FPM Form Builder (roadmap forms use the infotype screens)

▸ Ability to initiate as an employee or a manager (roadmap forms are only available for HR admins)

▸ Attachments (roadmap forms do not allow attachments)

▸ Easy enhancement of validations, search helps, calculation buttons, dynamic hiding/unhiding, etc.

Of course, there are also aspects of the roadmap forms that HCMPF does not have. In the next section, we will provide a comparison of the two and then provide descriptions of when each option might make sense for your organization.

6.13.4 Comparing Roadmap and FPM Forms

Now that we have described each form type, let's lay out a comparison between the two in Table 6.6.

	Roadmap Forms	FPM Forms
Possible users	HR admins only possible initiators, although others can approve.	HR admins, managers, and employees can initiate or approve.
Level of configuration effort	Low—infotype screens are built, only need to select a given infotype and it gets added to the roadmap.	Medium—individual fields must be added one at a time to the form.
Level of design flexibility	Limited—can hide fields or make fields required, but otherwise you have one page per infotype, and the infotype layout cannot be changed.	Complete—can have old/new sections, include all field on one page, and add explanatory text using the FPM Form Designer.
Dynamic processing	Using DPR, you can dynamically make additional infotypes appear in the roadmap or even default in values in the background—all using configuration.	Can only trigger dynamically using programming—and even then it can only be done in the background.
Ability to revise or suppress standard error messages	None.	Using configuration.
Ability to attach documents during initiation or approval	None.	Using configuration.
Ability to dynamically change the form UI or search helps	None.	Using programming.

Table 6.6 Merits of Roadmap and FPM Forms

Which should you use? Most organizations would benefit from transitioning away from the old desktop-based transactions and to the new HR Professional role—in other words, away from transactions that were previously handled by PA30 or PA40 and toward those that constitute the HR Professional role. Rather than choosing roadmap over FPM forms or vice versa, we recommend that you consider both options as complementary solutions for your organization.

The potential of HCMPF is much broader. It can be used to bring entire business processes online in a maintainable, user-friendly solution. This enables organizations to eliminate informal processes or custom applications and replace them with efficient, audit-friendly, and sustainable solutions using HCMPF. Therefore, our recommendation for an ideal future state for most organizations would be to use HCMPF for high-frequency transactions that have a clear approval path. On the other hand, you'll want to use roadmap forms and direct infotype updates for the less frequently occurring situations that require more expertise to handle.

We are nearing the end of our coverage on HR Professional self-service. As we draw to a close, we need to address the topic of how to store and access the forms and attachments generated by HCMPF, which is accomplished through digital personnel files.

6.14   Digital Personnel Files

Digital personnel files can help organizations to get out of the business of storing paper in file cabinets. As documents are scanned in (such as physically signed documents), they need to be associated with the employee in question. In addition, at the end of a completed HCMPF process the completed form also can be stored in the DPF.

The DPF is accessed via the Actions menu for the employee, which means that it can be assigned to the HR administrator (HR Professional role) or manager (MSS role). Figure 6.70 shows that the DPF is divided into multiple folders; we'll look at how to organize these folders when we review the configuration.

Depending on the user's authorization and a parameter that is supplied, the DPF can be opened in update mode, which allows for uploads of documents to the DPF, or in view-only mode. This can be useful if the HR admin or manager receives documents for the employee that need to be scanned, such as completed

HCMPF forms (Figure 6.71). Not only are the forms themselves stored, but any documents that were attached to the process are also stored.

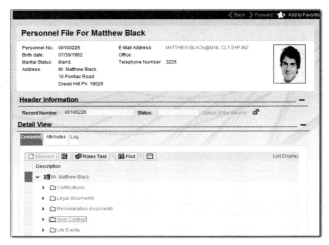

Figure 6.70 Digital Personnel File

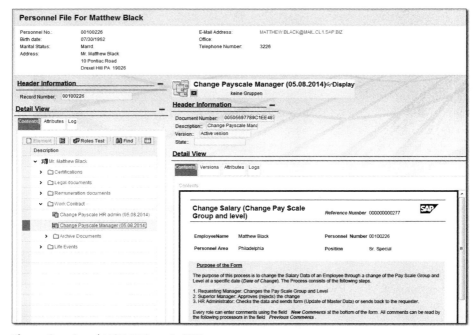

Figure 6.71 Saved HCMPF Form in DPF

For many organizations, DPF is the key link in the audit chain. DPF makes it possible to see the approval process and associated attachments that result in a data change in SAP.

It's important to note here that DPF is a broad conversation. DPF can be implemented with the documents managed within the SAP database, but this can cause potential size and performance constraints. For this reason, many companies will implement a separate content server. Going even further, many companies will elect to use a third-party tool such as XFT or OpenText to handle the employee file. These tools have richer functionality than the native SAP solution.

Now, let's discuss the configuration that produces the DPF.

Configuration Options

DPF is based on SAP Records Management, which provides a way to manage content across the SAP Business Suite. Taken from that perspective, the implementation of records management in support of DPF is very narrow; for our purposes we're only concerned with managing records for employees. You specify the model to be used in PERSONNEL MANAGEMENT • HR ADMINISTRATIVE SERVICES • DIGITAL PERSONNEL FILES. Because this is covered in the SAP PRESS book *SAP ERP HCM Processes and Forms*, we will not delve too deeply here. However, it's important to note that the folders in the DPF can be adjusted or renamed to meet your business requirements. You can assign a pointer called an anchor to your HCMPF process, and the anchor identifies for the process in which folder the completed form should be stored, as shown in Figure 6.72.

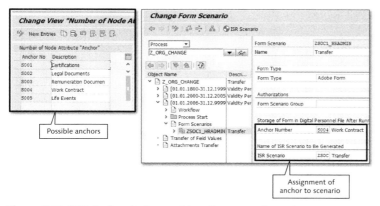

Figure 6.72 DPF Anchor Assignment to a Process or Scenario

Employee File Content

It should be mentioned here that if you employ a third-party product to manage the employee file content, you'll need to take additional configuration and connection steps. These will vary based on the vendor and will not be covered in this book.

6.15   Conclusion

We started this chapter by making the case for change from the traditional PA30 and PA40 model to the one offered in HR Renewal. We then covered the new lanes, the master data maintenance, and the options that exist for form-based processing. Hopefully, we've delivered on our promise of user interfaces that are more intuitive, have a shorter learning curve, and can engage more types of users through this process.

To this end, SAP has invested an immense amount of work in order to bring its UI up to par with the consumer-grade experiences we're all now used to throughout our lives. Perhaps you will be able to evaluate this and conclude, as we have, that the HR Professional role is an ambitious package that deserves a serious look as a tool to roll out to your HR administrators.

In a world teeming with smartphones and tablets, deploying successful self-service on mobile devices is increasingly important for companies both big and small. In this chapter, we tackle the challenges associated with making ESS and MSS services on mobile devices a reality.

7 Mobility for Self-Services

Mobility has long been an aspiration on many executives' minds, for whom the idea of an "always connected" workforce is intriguing. If employees have continuous access to their work, whether it's on a desktop, tablet, or smartphone, then an increase in productivity will inevitably occur. Meanwhile, many nonexecutives bemoan the whittling away of the "work–life" balance by continued and ubiquitous use of mobile devices in our lives. Either way, it's certainly an exciting time in the enterprise mobility space, especially for Human Resources.

In a world in which consumer applications such as Facebook, Instagram, and Twitter are setting the bar for user experience, businesses must react quickly or be faced with a dilemma. Without a solid mobile strategy and footprint in your organization, employees will not have opportunities to learn, contribute, and collaborate to the degree they are accustomed to with their consumer apps.

To set the context of how important mobility has become in the workforce, let's first take a brief look at the history of computing to remind ourselves of how far we have come (and where we are going!), beginning in the 1960s.

Table 7.1 lays out a diagram of the popular computing technology from the 1960s to the current day—that is, from mainframe, to the client–server model, to the age of the Internet, and now to mobile.

What's interesting is that we are almost back where we started. The mainframe concept of yesteryear was essentially a cloud-enabled environment, with a central hub linked to computers remotely wired in (e.g., an IBM mainframe engaging in so-called "timesharing"). In our current mobile Internet computing world, the cloud now works this same way—connecting remote devices (smartphones, tablets, etc.) to servers—but without the wires.

Era	Technology	Device	
1960s	Mainframe computing	Mainframes	Mainframe
1970s	Minicomputing	Minicomputers	Client–server
1980s	Personal computing	PCs/Macintosh	
1990s	Desktop Internet computing	PCs/Macs plus Internet	Internet
2000s	Mobile Internet computing	Smartphones and tablets	Mobile

Table 7.1 Computing Technology from the 1960s to the Present

Much of the current IT workforce has been employed for at least two of those decades. It's astonishing when you think about how much influence mobile has in our personal and professional lives today. When's the last time you left your house without your smartphone (and didn't go back for it)? How many participants *didn't* have smartphones or tablets with them at the last meeting you attended in person? Even on vacation, work travels with us; many employees now use their mobile devices to connect to the office even when they're "off the clock."

Whether or not we like it, mobile is here to stay and is only becoming increasingly popular as millennials enter the workforce. Consequently, HR organizations who want to remain attractive to employees need to stay on top of the implications for mobile access in the coming years. The ease with which employees can consume HR policies, procedures, and transactions via mobile devices will be an increasingly important topic for companies.

In some areas of the world, mobile devices are employees' only way to access company systems. More people own mobile devices than have electricity on the planet. In the developing world in particular, companies are increasingly looking to invest in applications delivered on mobile devices as a primary method of reach, versus technologies such as IVR and kiosks.

Although mobile innovations are at the forefront of technologists' minds now, the next stages of our computing age consist of even more intriguing possibilities:

▶ Wearable devices (glasses, watches or wristbands, and e-textiles)

▶ Avatars, surrogates, and robotics

▶ Universal translators

▶ Holography

These are subjects for entire (volumes of) books, so for now, suffice it to say that the future of innovative self-service will certainly not end with mobile and is sure to advance into these (and other) concepts. What will the impact on HR be in a global economy? The possibilities are certainly exciting. For example, in the recruiting field, could wearable glasses influence how you interview a candidate for a position? Perhaps the glasses could guide the interviewer through a matrix of questions. Could HR use holograms to interview candidates sitting in the conference room as a hologram, speaking another language that is being translated through a universal translator?

For now, we can only wonder and dissect important trends in mobile technology today. These trends will influence how you may deploy and roll out your self-service initiatives on a mobile device.

7.1   Important Trends in Mobility

Before talking about the specifics of SAP's mobile capability within a self-service context for HR, it's important to cover some important trends in mobility happening today. The following points will give us a better context for how we should consider deploying and using mobile technology within our HR systems:

- ▶ **Bring your own device**
  Bring your own device (BYOD) is the policy of permitting employees to bring personally owned mobile devices (laptops, tablets, phablets, and smartphones) to their workplace and to use those devices to access privileged company information and applications. BYOD policies are more popular than ever and will become increasingly popular if the current trend stays on pace. CIOs want to appear open-minded, modern, and trusting by allowing employees to bring their own devices to work. Employees want to feel that their workplace respects their preferences, and they feel that having their own devices at work lends them more freedom.

  BYOD is important when considering mobile in a few different aspects. On a technical layer, it can influence your deployment method (discussed in Section 7.2). The full implications of BYOD (allowing such a policy) is not within the scope of this book, but it is clearly a trend we should be aware of.

- ▶ **Mobile first**
  The phrase "mobile first" is by now cliché, but it is still considered to be an

important part of any software development philosophy. The idea is that applications should first be built with mobile in mind before other devices; the best practice is to develop first for phones, then for tablets, and finally for PCs or laptops. Because more and more users will consume HR services via mobile devices, it's of utmost importance that our software be built mobile friendly. Starting with a mobile first strategy in mind makes developers consider how to get something done in a simple way.

▶ **Device agnosticism**
Device agnosticism refers to the capability for software to be compatible with multiple devices, browsers, operating systems, and/or channels. Regardless of whether you are consuming a service via a tablet or a PC, on Safari or Internet Explorer, and so on, the experience of a web application should be intuitive and seamless for the end user.

▶ **Responsive design**
Responsive design is a concept that specifically caters the user experience of a user to the type of device. The main objective of responsive design is to optimize the viewing experience regardless of the device used. Responsive web design, then, goes hand in hand with device agnosticism.

Figure 7.1 shows an example of responsive design with the Leave Request service within the SAP Fiori suite of applications. The SAPUI5 screens dynamically render the screen layout based on the device being used. This means that different elements are shown onscreen if you're using a smartphone compared to a tablet or on a tablet compared to a laptop or PC.

Figure 7.1 Responsive Web Design with SAP Fiori

What's important here is that some HR applications (for example, leave request) are well-suited for mobile scenarios. We need to be aware of how we can take advantage of responsive design concepts in our self-service strategy.

7.2 Deployment Options and Why It Matters

How you deploy mobile solutions is a vital part of your strategy, because it impacts the user experience for your end users. An organization with a modern HR portal instead of a noticeably antiquated one will inevitably reflect positively on the company for its employees. Portals and self-service applications that are accessible via mobile devices are even better.

There are generally three methods available to deploy mobile solutions:

1. **Directly via a web page**
   This isn't really a formal strategy. Web pages, including a company's intranet and portal, can be accessed via a URL directly, constituting a typical "pinch and zoom" experience. Figure 7.2 shows a consumer example of a website deployed via a mobile device that has not been designed with mobile in mind.

2. **Via a mobile or native application**
   These applications are typically downloaded from a store or marketplace online (e.g., the Apple Store or Google Play). When using this method, the mobile application is deployed locally on the device, and access to the device's hardware functions (e.g., camera or contact list) is native. These applications do not use a web browser on the device.

   One example is the Twitter app, shown in Figure 7.3. From within the Twitter app, the user can take pictures with the smartphone's camera and send a tweet.

3. **Via a mobile web application**
   Accessed through your device's web browser, web pages are built and optimized for viewing on a mobile device. As shown in Figure 7.4, web pages conform to size of the device and feel like a native application, but the screen is not, in fact, being accessed through a native app.

   Typically, the browser URL is redirected. For example, a URL could be automatically changed from *www.company.com* to *m.company.com*. Yahoo's website becomes *m.yahoo.com* on a smartphone or *www.yahoo.com/tablet* on a tablet.

Figure 7.2 Absent Mobile Optimization

Figure 7.3 Twitter Mobile App

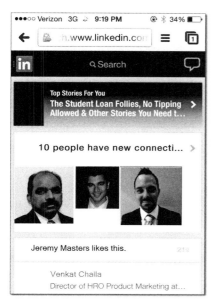

Figure 7.4 Mobile Web App for LinkedIn

Table 7.2 compares some of the important features, functions, and technologies that support both mobile apps and mobile web apps.

	Mobile Apps	Mobile Web Apps
Performance	Faster, more direct access to optimized OS modules and hardware features	(Generally) slower and dependent on the browser (Safari, Chrome, etc.)
User experience	Smoother, more polished, more integrated into the OS	Via Web browser, so the look and feel are relegated to browser capabilities
Maintenance	One application developed per OS (iOS, Android, Windows Phone, etc.) Updates/enhancements need to be coordinated and pushed to devices	The same application: WORA, write once, run anywhere Easier to deliver updates/enhancements

Table 7.2 Mobile Apps vs. Mobile Web Apps

273

	Mobile Apps	Mobile Web Apps
Main technologies	Objective C for iOS, Java for Android and BlackBerry, and .NET for Windows	HTML5, CSS3, JavaScript and web services programmed in Java, .NET, PHP, Perl, Python, Ruby, etc.
Example	Facebook app	Youtube.com on Chrome or Safari web browser

Table 7.2 Mobile Apps vs. Mobile Web Apps (Cont.)

Mobile applications are native to the operating system of the smartphone or tablet and therefore have more inherent hardware capabilities. Mobile web apps, by contrast, leverage the web browser and do not have as much device control but do make up for it in other areas. A major advantage of mobile web applications is on the support and maintenance side, because an enhancement can be implemented centrally and doesn't have to be downloaded as another release on a marketplace.

Now that we have seen the differences between the deployment and technology associated with native apps and mobile apps, we can dig into SAP's capabilities within the on-premise and cloud HCM platforms, beginning with the options available for customers who need self-service mobile capabilities for their on-premise SAP ERP HCM systems.

7.3   Self-Services on Mobile (On-Premise)

SAP offers a wide range of mobility offerings to support on-premise SAP ERP HCM processes. Table 7.3 lists the four primary ways to deploy mobile solutions for your SAP ERP HCM system.

Solution	Enabling Technologies	System
SAP Mobile Platform on-premise	SAP Afaria, SAP MEAP, etc.	SAP ERP
SAP Enterprise Portal mobile edition	SAP NetWeaver 7.3	SAP ERP
SAP Fiori	SAPUI5, SAP Gateway	SAP ERP
SAP Partner solutions	Web services, APIs, etc.	SAP ERP

Table 7.3 Mobile Platforms for On-Premise SAP ERP HCM

Let's first discuss SAP's hallmark mobile platform: the SAP Mobile Platform.

7.3.1 SAP Mobile Platform, On-Premise

The SAP Mobile Platform is SAP's on-premise offering for building, deploying, and managing mobile applications. SAP Mobile Platform offers an end-to-end solution for enabling mobility in the company, including full mobile device management (called SAP Afaria). SAP Mobile Platform is a *mobile enterprise application platform* (MEAP), which means that you can tweak purchased applications as necessary and even develop your own apps. It contains the functionality once provided by Sybase Unwired Platform.

Figure 7.5 shows the SAP Mobile Platform runtime architecture, including the four Cs:

- *Connect* to databases, web services, and applications.
- *Create* apps using the Eclipse platform.
- *Consume* services using the SAP-provided SDK for connecting to any device.
- *Control* devices via device and security management tools.

From a self-service perspective, several SAP Mobile Platform applications are available, but they're not free. You can make further enhancements using the SAP Mobile Platform development tools, such as AppBuilder, SMS Builder, and Agentry Editor, but you'll incur additional cost for services if these enhancements are performed by an external resource.

> **Additional Information**
>
> For detailed information on SAP's mobile platform and technology, refer to the SAP PRESS book *Mobilizing Your Enterprise with SAP* by Sanjeet Mall, Tzanko Stefanov, and Stanley Stadelman (2012). This book is not specific to Human Resources, but it does contain some good use cases that might be useful for HR professionals with a technical background.

Four mobile applications are available for employees within the SAP Mobile Platform:

- **SAP Employee Lookup**
  Provides a searchable directory of coworkers and their organizational details.

▶ **SAP Timesheet/SAP Timesheet Lite**
Allows employees to create, review, submit, and manage time entries.

▶ **SAP Leave Request/SAP Leave Request Lite**
Provides employees with a quick way to create and review leave requests on the go.

▶ **SAP Learning Assistant**
Provides on-demand, online training available anytime and anywhere so that users can access required classes to address compliance and job requirements.

Three mobile applications are available for managers within the SAP Mobile Platform:

▶ **SAP Manager Insight**
Access employee profiles and KPI reports—including headcount, diversity, and talent by location.

▶ **SAP HR Approvals**
View and respond to leave requests and timesheet entries. Check for incomplete timesheets, overbooking, and overlapping leave requests. Review team calendars and employees' time account balances to evaluate requests.

▶ **SAP Interview Assistant**
Display open requisitions, candidates, applications, and résumés or CVs, review candidates, schedule interviews, and evaluate candidates before, during, and after the interview.

All of these apps can be viewed and purchased on the SAP store by going to *store.sap.com*. The cost of these applications can be a challenge for some organizations to muster.

Additional Resources

For more information on mobile development in SAP, read the SAP PRESS book *Mobile Development for SAP* by Dave Haseman and Ross Hightower (2013). This book covers SAP Mobile Platform, Sybase Unwired Platform, Unwired Platform Runtime, Sybase Mobile SDK, Eclipse IDE, and the Hybrid Web Container.

HR resources are often called upon by Finance colleagues to assist in travel and expenses (T&E) projects, because there are strong links between these subjects. To that end, it's important for some of us to be aware of the mobility offerings available from SAP that focus on T&E:

▸ **SAP Travel Receipt Capture**
Users can capture receipt photos, and record voice notes for expenses.

  ▸ Create travel expense entries as they happen.

  ▸ Send expense entries and attachments to the back-office system.

▸ **SAP Travel Expense Report**
Users can record, organize, submit, and track expenses during a trip, direct from a mobile device.

  ▸ Create new expense reports.

  ▸ Capture photos of receipts with the phone's camera.

  ▸ Save expense reports, expense entries, and attachments to SAP.

  ▸ Enter expense line items.

  ▸ Send the expense report for approval.

▸ **SAP Travel Expense Approval**
Users can approve expense reports from a mobile device.

  ▸ Receive notification of travel expense reports awaiting approval.

  ▸ View policy violation details to ensure adherence to company policy.

  ▸ View a list of all travel expense approvals in a manager's workflow.

  ▸ Add comments and approve or reject travel expense reports.

In addition to the SAP Mobile Platform, SAP has invested in another standard offering, one that involves leveraging the SAP Enterprise Portal platform. We'll talk about the mobile edition of the SAP Enterprise Portal next.

7.3.2 SAP Enterprise Portal Mobile Edition

The SAP Enterprise Portal mobile edition is a role-based, multichannel portal that aggregates applications, documents, and content on multiple devices, providing a mobile-ready solution (without the SAP Mobile Platform infrastructure). You may hear about this solution as "SAP Portal on Device," which was its original product name.

Like other mobile solutions, the SAP Enterprise Portal mobile edition allows you to consume services across devices (tablets, smartphones, etc.). This is a key feature of the solution. The portal operates as an aggregator of various content, whether the content is a native SAP app, a non-SAP native app, or a web app.

Figure 7.5 shows the App Gallery, which is accessed from the launch menu. The App Gallery can be configured to launch both native web apps (such as the Price and Availability app seen in Figure 7.5) and browser-based apps, such as an SAP Fiori app (or any SAPUI5 app) for Timesheet Approvals. In this way, the portal becomes your multichannel gateway to disparate mobile technologies (if your landscape becomes this complex). You can also house links to SuccessFactors or other third-party applications here if you have some of your other processes in the cloud.

Figure 7.5 App Gallery

Additional Resources

If you decide to implement the SAP Enterprise Portal mobile edition as your mobile solution, then you should review some of the known limitations and issues associated with the solution in SAP Note 1705067 (Known Issues for Portal on Device).

7.3.3 Various Partner Solutions

Some SAP partners offer third-party alternatives for mobile solutions, built with various technologies. Some vendors have developed applications on the SAP Mobile Platform, whereas others have looked for more "lightweight" alternatives.

There are three general methods for delivering mobile technologies employed by SAP partners:

▸ **SAP Mobile Platform based**
Partners have developed mobile applications using the MEAP and *mobile device management* (MDM) within the SAP Mobile Platform.

▸ **Web-services based**
Expose web services through a broker system (such as SAP Gateway), using OData or other open protocols, such as *remote function calls* (RFC) and enterprise services (i.e., web services).

▸ **Portal based**
Use SAP's existing portal as a service connectivity layer to access SAP ERP business logic and data.

Consider these solutions. They can often be cost-effective, can solve a specific organizational need, and offer a lightweight alternative to SAP's more ambitious offerings. For example, if your company only needs a way to approve simple work items, then purchasing the full SAP Mobile Platform is likely overkill. Instead, implementing a partner solution or leveraging the Work Item app in SAP Fiori might be the more streamlined option.

Now that we have reviewed the available solutions for mobile on-premise, let's turn to the mobile cloud solutions in HR.

7.4 Self-Services on Mobile (Cloud)

Table 7.4 lists two major ways to enable mobility by using cloud technologies.

Solution	Enabling Technologies	System
SAP HANA Cloud Platform mobile services	SAP MEAP and SAP Afaria	SAP ERP
SuccessFactors Mobile	Native app on Apple, Android, and Blackberry devices	SuccessFactors

Table 7.4 Mobile Technologies for Self-Services

The main difference between SAP HANA Cloud Platform mobile services and Suc-cessFactors Mobile is the backend system. Because many companies having gone (or are going) hybrid, it's important to understand how we can bridge the cloud and on-premise SAP ERP HCM systems. This has become a pain point for many customers for which data exists in two (or more) disparate systems, such as SAP ERP and SuccessFactors. The vision is of an integrated platform in which the end user of the mobile application is unaware of which system he or she is using. A seamless user experience doesn't exist yet, but SAP and its partners are moving quickly to try to overcome this gap.

7.4.1 SAP HANA Cloud Platform Mobile Services

SAP HANA Cloud Platform mobile services is a cloud subscription service that offers a more lightweight option for customers who want the extensibility of the SAP Mobile Platform solution but don't want to maintain the infrastructure.

Also referred to as "SAP Mobile Platform on SAP HANA Cloud" and "mobile as a service" (MaaS), SAP HANA Cloud Platform mobile services allow you to connect mobile solutions hosted in the cloud with SAP ERP data (via the SAP Gateway), SAP HANA applications (via the Concept Gateway), or SAP BusinessObjects BI. Figure 7.6 illustrates this concept.

The architecture behind the SAP HANA Cloud Platform mobile services is based on a three-tiered delivery mechanism organized into the concepts of connect, configure, and try/buy:

- Connect to an SAP or non-SAP system via open protocols, such as OData and Open HTTPS,
- Configure the SAP Mobile Platform to manage application security, notification management, application lifecycle, and other important aspects of mobility.
- Try and (potentially) buy applications built either natively or with third-party frameworks, such as HTML5.

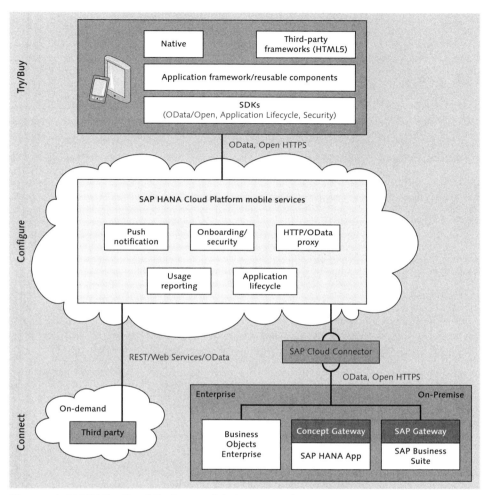

Figure 7.6 SAP HANA Cloud Platform Mobile Services Architecture

7.4.2 SuccessFactors Mobile

The SuccessFactors Mobile offering is only available for users who have some or all of their applications in a SuccessFactors subscription (in the cloud). Like SAP Fiori for on-premise HCM, the mobile application is part of the overall product cost (for SuccessFactors, this is the subscription).

The following mobile applications are available from SuccessFactors:

▶ **To Dos**
Use work item to dos, such as job change, LOA, and so on.

▶ **Touchbase**
Set the right priorities and make one-on-one meetings more efficient.

▶ **Jam**
Stay on top of projects, find experts and content, and contribute new videos and photos.

▶ **Org Chart**
Find people in your company fast, and then connect via email, phone, or a text.

▶ **Candidate Assessment**
View and assess candidates as part of the SuccessFactors recruitment module.

▶ **Job Requisition Approvals**
Approve or decline job requisitions as part of the SuccessFactors recruitment module.

▶ **Learning**
Sign up for courses, connect with experts, and even complete entire classes while on the go; instructors can manage their classes and enrollment.

▶ **Goals**
Allows employees and managers the ability to track and update goals.

▶ **Time Off**
Employees can request and cancel time off via a mobile device. Managers can approve the time off requests. HR admin maintains each employee's accounts and absences.

▶ **Headlines**
View analytics for key metrics within the organization.

In contrast to the SAP Mobile Platform offerings from SAP, the SuccessFactors Mobile functionality is encapsulated into one mobile application (see Figure 7.7). There are native mobile applications available for iPhone, Android, and Blackberry devices (but not yet Windows, as of fall 2014). There is no current HTML5 version of the mobile version of SuccessFactors, but the use of SAP Fiori as an umbrella technology to fuse on-premise and cloud-based HR applications is a promising area to watch.

Figure 7.7 Homepage of the SuccessFactors Mobile (iPad)

The iPhone application also recently refreshed its look, and it now matches the user experience in the iPad.

7.5 Summary

Deploying self-service solutions on a mobile device is a robust way to empower the employees, managers, and HR professionals within your organization. Knowing the various technologies and deployment methods available is critical to the success of any company's mobile strategy. Now more than ever, employees—who carry high expectations of mobile apps into work from the outside world—expect their self-service functionalities on mobile devices to be intuitive and consumer-grade.

The next chapter reviews the offerings available with SAP Fiori, which is one of SAP's latest offerings of self-service for the casual user. As we will explain—and regardless of its original intent—it's important to understand the functionality offered and the importance it has within the current SAP ecosystem.

An important solution offered by SAP is SAP Fiori, which contains HR-specific employee and manager self-services apps. In this chapter, we introduce SAP Fiori, the SAP Fiori Launchpad, and its applications, and we contextualize its launch in the current SAP solution landscape.

8   SAP Fiori

A relative newcomer in the SAP technology space, SAP Fiori already has a much-storied history. Announced at the annual SAPPHIRENOW conference in 2013, SAP Fiori caused much fury as customers came to understand what it was (and what it was not). Touted as the next-generation user interface for SAP, it also originally came with an additional license fee, which many customers considered unjust. After pushback from customers, analysts, and the greater SAP ERP HCM community, SAP announced at the 2014 conference that the solution was now included as part of the SAP Business Suite maintenance cost.

The origins of SAP Fiori (Italian for "flowers") were in a project in which SAP partnered with Google to come up with a "simplified user experience" for common applications. As of the time of writing (fall 2014), there are over 360 applications included in the SAP Fiori catalog, but only seven of them are specific to HR.

SAP Fiori Versatility

SAP Fiori is not only an option for mobility; it is also another way to access services in SAP using SAPUI5 technology. Many professionals (including consultants) find this confusing, because SAP Fiori is often associated with mobile access (due to its mobile-friendly technology).

SAP Fiori offers responsive design and device agnosticism. Put another way, SAP Fiori can be accessed by any device (PC, tablet, smartphone, etc.) and via any browser (Chrome, Safari, etc.), but the look and feel will always be optimized for an end user's perspective. Recall from Chapter 7 that this is consistent with consumer applications as well; when you shop on Amazon's website via your tablet, for example, the experience is different than when shopping via your laptop.

Because employees have high expectations for mobile experiences based on their consumer experiences, enterprise applications need to leapfrog ahead and cannot be content to simply achieve the standard in mobility. Historically, many SAP customers have struggled with delivering robust HR apps, but the race is on now to deliver powerful applications to employees, managers, HR professionals, and executives, and this is where SAP Fiori comes into play. SAP Fiori has been created to deliver a powerful set of applications with simplicity at the forefront of its design.

Let's talk now about how we typically access SAP Fiori applications—via the SAP Fiori Launchpad.

8.1   SAP Fiori Launchpad

SAP offers its own entry point to access SAP Fiori applications. The SAP Fiori Launchpad was designed specifically for the SAP Fiori user experience.

Figure 8.1 shows the login screen for the SAP Fiori Launchpad. You can choose to either prompt the user for a password or set up single sign-on (SSO) within your environment (the route most companies choose). The following authentication and SSO mechanisms are supported for SAP Fiori apps:

▶ Kerberos/SPNego

▶ X.509 Certificates

▶ SAML 2.0

▶ Logon tickets

For more information about authentication, visit SAP Help at *help.sap.com/fiori* and navigate to the SETUP OF SAP FIORI SYSTEM LANDSCAPE section.

Once logged in, the user is presented with one or more tiles. These tiles represent the link or entry point to an application. The tiles usually show the number of items that require attention from the employee and/or manager. Both the look and feel of the application (called the *theme*) and the placement of tiles and associated icons (shown in Figure 8.2) are configurable.

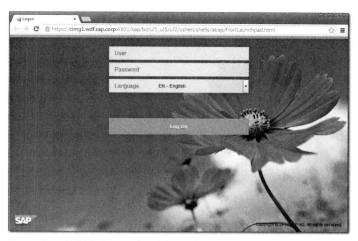

Figure 8.1 SAP Fiori Launchpad Login Screen

Figure 8.2 shows the SAP Fiori Launchpad and the available Employee Self-Service applications. There is also a set of applications available for managers. In most implementations, these manager tiles would be on the same landing page but in another group. In Figure 8.3, there are two groups available: MANAGER, which contains two tiles, and MANAGER (TRAVEL), which contains one tile.

Figure 8.2 SAP Fiori Launchpad Page with ESS Applications

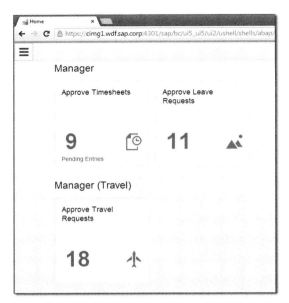

Figure 8.3 SAP Fiori Launchpad Page with MSS Applications

Now that we've seen what the launchpad looks like, let's examine the available SAP Fiori applications for HR.

8.2 HR Applications for SAP Fiori

Table 8.1 lists the applications available via SAP Fiori as of fall 2014. The third column, ROLE, indicates whether the application is designed for the employee or manager. Currently, there are no services in SAP Fiori available for the HR Professional role.

Application	Description	Role
My Leave Requests	Enables employees to create and submit leave requests quickly and flexibly, using their desktops or mobile devices. The app also allows employees to track the status of their requests and view their current leave balances.	Employee

Table 8.1 SAP Fiori Applications by Role

Application	Description	Role
My Benefits	Provides an overview of the benefit plans in which an employee is enrolled.	Employee
My Paystubs	Enables employees to check and manage a digital version of all their paystubs issued by the company for each payroll period.	Employee
My Timesheets	Enables employees to manage their time entries.	Employee
Approve Timesheets	Enables managers to see all pending approvals for their reports, enabling them to easily approve timesheets.	Manager
Approve Leave Requests	Enables managers to approve or reject leave requests for their direct reports.	Manager

Table 8.1 SAP Fiori Applications by Role (Cont.)

Let's review the ESS applications first.

8.2.1 Apps for Employees

The My Leave Requests application shown in Figure 8.4 allows the employee to perform the following actions:

- Create leave requests, including partial day leave
- Select a leave period using an integrated calendar that shows nonworking days, holidays, booked leaves, and leaves pending approval
- Add a note for the approver
- Display a summary of leave entitlement, leave taken so far, and available balance
- Display leave requests and check requests' approval status
- Withdraw or change leave requests

The technical software name of this app is UIX01HCM 100 and its SAPUI5 application is HCM_LR_CRE.

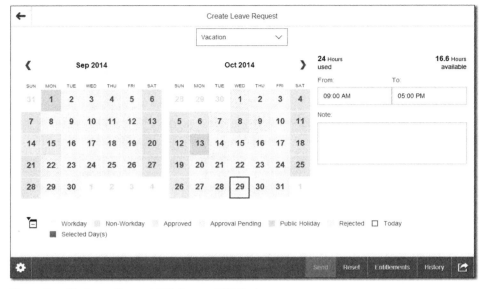

Figure 8.4 My Leave Request ESS App on SAP Fiori

The second service available for employees is to view benefits information. The My Benefits application in Figure 8.5 allows you to perform the following tasks:

▶ Display the benefit plans in which you are enrolled by plan categories

▶ Display eligible benefit plans for which you have not yet enrolled

▶ Display plan details of a selected benefit plan (coverage level and pre- or post-tax costs)

▶ View the benefits overview or detailed information for any given date

▶ Access links to benefit plan documents to find information on the definition of benefit plans

▶ Open the benefits summary statement as a PDF that can be downloaded and saved locally

The technical software name of this app is UIX01HCM 100 and its SAPUI5 application is HCM_BEN_MON.

Figure 8.5 My Benefits ESS App on SAP Fiori

The third ESS application available on SAP Fiori is the My Paystubs service, which you'd only use to distribute paystubs from your SAP system. (If you are distributing pay statements from a third party, then you would likely use that vendor's own portal to retrieve your pay stubs.) Figure 8.6 shows the application, with the pay statements on the left and the wage details (gross to net calculations) in the main panel of the screen. Within this service, the employee can perform the following tasks:

▶ View a list of paystubs

▶ Check the details of a paystub

▶ Download and store a PDF version of a paystub

The technical software name of this app is UIX01HCM 100 and its SAPUI5 application is HCM_PS_MON.

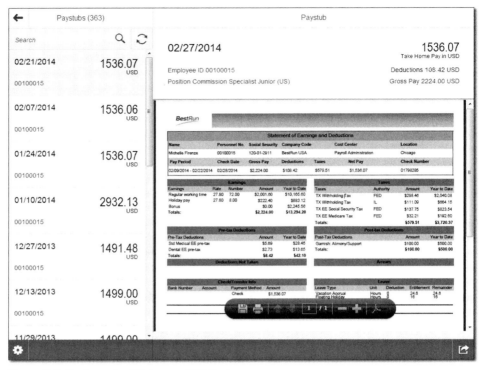

Figure 8.6 My Paystubs ESS App on SAP Fiori

The last Employee Self-Service application available in SAP Fiori is for time recording via the My Timesheet service in Figure 8.7. Within this application, the employee can perform the following tasks:

▶ Enter time for a week, for a month, or for all missing time entries

▶ View the time entry status overview for a month

▶ View weekly time entry details with one-step release or delete

▶ Create time entries for a single day or multiple days in a single step

▶ Review and modify existing timesheet entries

The technical software name of this app is UIX01HCM 100 and its SAPUI5 application is HCM_TS_CRE.

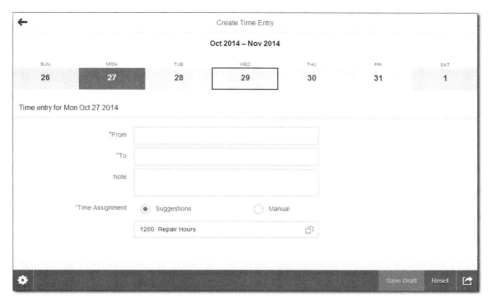

Figure 8.7 My Timesheet ESS App on SAP Fiori

8.2.2 Apps for Managers

On the manager side, only two applications within SAP Fiori are available (as of fall 2014).

First, managers can use Approve Timesheets (see Figure 8.8) for handling the timesheets for members of their team. With this service, a manager can perform the following tasks:

▶ Review timesheets for all employees and view time entry compliance

▶ View time entry details by project and cost object

▶ View a weekly summary of time entries, per employee, project, or cost object and with an option to view time entry details

▶ Approve or reject time entries at both the timesheet and time entry levels

Figure 8.8 Approve Timesheets MSS App on SAP Fiori

The technical software name of this app is UIX01HCM 100 and its SAPUI5 application is HCM_TS_APV.

Second, the following tasks can be performed by the manager when using the Approve Leave Requests application in Figure 8.9:

▸ Browse requests submitted for approval in a personalized workflow inbox

▸ View details for specific requests, including the leave requested, the available balance, and any comments related to the request

▸ View a team calendar that shows overlapping leave requests if there are leave conflicts

▸ Approve or reject requests (with an optional note to the requester)

The technical software name of this app is UIX01HCM 100 and its SAPUI5 application is HCM_LR_APV.

Approve Requests

Another important service, Approve Requests, is actually not an HR-specific app but rather is categorized as an SAP Fiori "cross app", meaning it is used across multiple functional areas (and not just HR). This is a popular application to deploy, because it is essentially the equivalent of your workflow inbox. The technical software name of this app is UIX01CA1: Fiori Approve Requests X1 1.0.

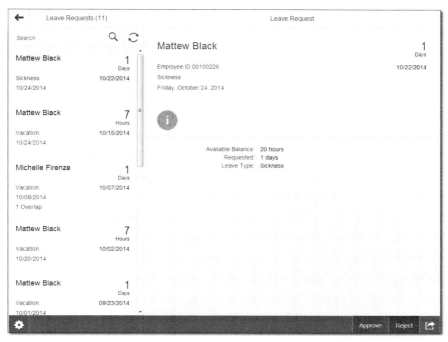

Figure 8.9 Approve Leave Requests MSS App on SAP Fiori

Like the SAPUI5 applications available within HR Renewal, the SAP Fiori framework is supported by SAP Gateway, either as a central hub deployment or an embedded deployment of the SAP Gateway. With the central hub deployment, the SAP Gateway components will be deployed on a standalone system (either behind or in front of the corporate firewall). With the embedded deployment, the components of SAP Gateway are deployed together in the SAP ERP backend system.

Recall from Chapter 3 that OData is the data access protocol used to fetch and update data to and from the SAP ERP system. In previous self-service frameworks from SAP, communications between the frontend and backend systems were achieved through business APIs (BAPIs) or RFCs. However, there are ways to leverage previously exposed RFCs and consume these services through the SAP Gateway as OData services. For more information about this subject, we again recommend the SAP PRESS book *OData and SAP NetWeaver Gateway*, by Carsten Bönnen, Volker Drees, André Fischer, Ludwig Heinz, and Karsten Strothmann (2014).

8.3   Rationale for SAP Fiori

Why would SAP provide multiple technologies for accessing the same (or similar) functionality in HR (and other modules, for that matter)? For example, the SAP Mobile Platform, SAP Enterprise Portal mobile edition, and SAP Fiori all have the manager task inbox for workflow management. Often referred to as the "enterprise's second killer app" (behind email), the Workflow Inbox is a key business requirement for many mobile projects in HR and other areas.

This question is not an easy one to answer, because we need to understand a bit of history first. The SAP Mobile Platform grew out of SAP's purchase of Sybase in 2010, whereas the SAP Enterprise Portal mobile edition was a natural extension of the existing SAP Enterprise Portal platform that many customers already owned. In this context, SAP Fiori is the newest platform and SAP's latest attempt at simplification; it addresses customers' concerns about needing a lightweight option for mobile solutions that use modern technologies (e.g., SAPUI5 and CSS3). Because Web Dynpro for ABAP services are not mobile friendly (and even contain some Adobe Flash Island technology, which does not even work on iPads), SAPUI5 was needed to quickly answer the demands of the modern mobile world.

8.4   Summary

Deploying self-service solutions with SAP Fiori can be a robust way of empowering the employee and manager (and later, perhaps the HR professional) within your organization. Knowing the various technologies and deployment methods available is critical to the success of any company's self-service strategy. Employees expect their self-service functionalities on desktops and on mobile devices to be intuitive and consumer grade more now than ever before.

In the next chapter, we provide information on the resources available to you in the marketplace. The good news to always keep in mind is that you are never alone in your SAP self-services journey. Oodles of information exists within the SAP ecosystem to assist you, and plenty of HR and IT professionals are ready to help and share knowledge.

This chapter inventories best practices and essential resources available to assist you before, during, and after your implementation.

9   Best Practices and Additional Resources

From making use of other practitioners' lessons learned and knowing where to find more information, resourcefulness is crucial in planning and executing self-service implementations. In this chapter, we offer tips for implementing self-services functionality and share helpful resources for consulting with other users and consultants who are working with HR Renewal and the new self-services within SAP.

9.1   Best Practices

These principles apply universally to successful implementations regardless of size, so whether you are part of a large, multinational company or a small organization, we offer the following tips, derived from lessons learned while delivering self-services projects during the past fifteen years within the SAP eco-system.

Roll out self-services in multiple phases.

Organizations that introduce self-services for the first time tackle the functionality in a variety of ways. For example, some companies first implement MSS by introducing functionality around a particular process, such as performance management or compensation management. This approach works well, because it often displaces existing functionality with an already-defined process.

Another route (introducing employee transactions and employee data via HCM Processes and Forms) has not been as successful, especially when managers, for example, have not been accustomed to having responsibility for initiating HR transactions online. You may encounter pushback and hear from managers that feel they are "doing HR's job." There may be a perception within the organization that MSS will add additional administrative work to the manager with little or no direct benefit. Although this is not the case, it can negatively impact the ease of implementation and the rate of adoption. Proper change management can address these important issues.

One of the ways we have been able to overcome these issues is to plan self-service projects in (at least) two phases. For MSS, that may look like the following:

▶ The first phase targets the delivery of information about employees and the organization. This approach gives managers easy access to robust information (such as compensation and work history, career information, etc.) that has typically been hard to obtain without HR manager involvement. This approach engages and excites managers and gets them accustomed to using these tools online.

▶ Once the first phase is completed and managers have adopted the portal and its offerings, you can launch more process-oriented transactions, such as Performance Management, Compensation Management, or forms. Future phases can built on the functionality of this second phase, based on feedback from previous phases.

Using this approach will not only increase manager acceptance of the portal but will also decrease the learning curve by allowing managers to focus on subsets of functionality instead of overwhelming them with many self-service applications all at once.

Simplify transactions and avoid multiple layers of approval.

A common issue that we have encountered while designing and implementing self-service applications is the desire to "overengineer" a process, especially with regards to manager-initiated transactions for their employees. It is common to want to capture every possible variation of a transaction in order to improve productivity and deliver a more robust system; however, doing so often leads to a very complex process that managers and HR do not understand and that IT cannot support effectively.

This same principle applies to workflow approvals. The unlimited capability of SAP's workflow engine enables many designs to become overly complicated, with multiple approval steps and notifications that often prove to reduce the efficiency of the system and overall process. Also, such a complicated design will almost certainly frustrate users and distract them from their daily activities.

Having inboxes inundated with emails from transactions spawning from SAP processes is a recipe for an irritable staff.

Let's first revisit the topic of forms. As a general rule, these forms should be limited to no more than two pages, and most transactions should be under one page. Transactions should have clear titles and be limited in scope to make them easy to understand and simple to complete (the new FPM functionality goes a long way in providing that capability). If there are decisions to be made that are outside the knowledge of the manager, it may be best to move that work on to the appropriate subject matter expert. Guessing whether an employee move should be coded as a promotion or lateral could be outside of managers' realm of HR knowledge. Educating managers on the process or driving the transaction to incorporate the subject matter expert in the workflow later in the process may be a better option, depending on your corporate philosophy.

Workflow is another often nebulous concept for many SAP professionals. Although workflow is one of the most robust functionalities within SAP, workflow and its inherent approval processes should be designed with the utmost basic process in mind. When possible, manager transactions that need approval should have a flow that consists of one-up manager approval and an escalation path to the next level after three to five days of inaction. These escalation procedures should be included in your workflow rules through the use of SAP's deadline monitoring concept.

Exception cases should be examined and dealt with offline. Designing approval processes with these exception cases in mind could be dangerous and cost prohibitive. Try to apply the "80/20" rule to your online workflow processes. In many organizations, these exceptions are the first to change from year to year, so baking them into your approval process may be a waste of effort.

We are not suggesting that complex approval processes cannot be handled by SAP. However, you should design approval processes that are more complex with care, and monitor them for impacts to productivity. Complex routing rules based on relationships established in the SAP system is achievable and sometimes necessary but should be architected with a future state in mind. You can do some amazing things with workflow, but the questions you should ask yourself are these: What is the business need for the workflow's complexity? Are there ways to simplify the process such that the technology can more effectively support the business requirement?

Determine whether delegation is required, and implement a solution that is both functional and intuitive.

A common requirement requested in many Manager Self-Service implementations is the ability to delegate transactional and/or approval authority to a peer or administrative assistant.

In the absence of this functionality, a manager often gives administrative assistants or peers his or her own portal username and password so that the assistants can login and act on the manager's behalf. However, this bad habit endangers the security of the system and introduces huge liabilities for data leakage, particularly with sensitive employee information, such as *personally identifiable information* (PII). Exposing PII, such as employees' national identifications, addresses, and credit card data, can lead to grave consequences. It is critical to determine if this is an issue in your organization and to provide an intuitive solution that safeguards the system.

Providing delegation capability within the SAP environment is not a trivial task, but it is feasible to implement. We have implemented delegation functionality many times over on the SAP Enterprise Portal and believe it is a viable and important option to offer the organization via the following steps:

▶ Implement a delegate portal role and a backend SAP role to enable managers (and non-managers, such as administrative assistants) to have delegation-relevant access to Manager Self-Service functionality. Both roles will be needed in order to provide delegate functionality on the SAP Enterprise Portal.

▶ Create custom relationships using SAP ERP HCM Organizational Management objects in order to manage the delegation of responsibilities from a transaction perspective. Like all organizational management objects and relationships, the effective dates of the relationships can limit the duration of the delegate relationship.

▶ Optionally, you can provide a workflow that enables the delegate to approve the responsibility. The workflow process provides a robust audit trail. The workflow will allow the delegate to approve the request in the portal's universal worklist and will inform the manager via an email once the responsibility has been accepted.

▶ Automate the assignment of the required SAP roles once the delegate has approved the request. A custom program can be created that can assign the appropriate roles to the delegate for the period of time for which the delegation relationship is required.

▶ Conduct usability labs as early as possible with a representative set of users.

Having the best user experience possible is one of the most important components of a successful project. Providing end users with an intuitive flow, look and feel, and layout within self-service applications enables efficiencies within the service delivery that are unparalleled elsewhere. Avoiding experiences that cause confusion and frustration for your users will go a long way toward securing self-service as a viable and effective means of delivery in the future.

During the realization phase of the project, we suggest that you identify a time in which your self-service applications are working as expected (or close to as expected). During that time, create a user group that can test the application(s). Conduct individual sessions in which you provide the user with a scenario and ask him or her to complete that part of the process. Do not provide the user with much instruction on how to complete the transaction. Observe where he or she gets stuck. If the user is at a dead end and can no longer navigate, ask him or her to explain what did not make sense on the screen and what he or she would expect in order to continue.

Once all the users have completed the usability lab, collect the results and isolate the common issues. It is best to address these issues before rolling out the process in order to gain the maximum acceptance and adoption of the new functionality. Depending on the quantity of the changes, you may need to get creative with timelines, depending on where you are in the build or testing of the application.

You may be surprised at how consistent the responses are. The challenge will be in deciding which changes can be (or should be) incorporated, given the timeframe of the project. In some cases, changes that are rejected or delayed until a later phase can, at minimum, be incorporated into the training materials.

Communicate terms that may not be self-evident to employees and managers.

A common challenge that is encountered when rolling out self-service information and transactions is the language that the underlying system imposes. Many of us have heard of "SAPanese" and other cute terms to describe the language and semantics used within the SAP system and portal. It is common for users to be unfamiliar with the new terminology.

Many companies roll out self-service and then spend time answering questions about the data that is presented. For example, managers may not understand what "personnel area" means. In addition, if this is the first venture into self-service for your organization, then managers and employees may not be familiar with concepts such as organizational units, positions, and jobs or how they inter-relate.

One approach to mitigate the impact is to introduce the unfamiliar terminology with a frequently asked questions (FAQ) document that is readily accessible on the portal for users to access during the transaction. Educating users on new ter-minology helps to remove the apprehension associated with the new technology or products you are implementing.

Another more costly approach is to do some level of translation for the manager on the actual portal screens. Labels within services, lanes, and employee cards could be updated to reflect the business-appropriate term for your company. For example, the term "Position Title" could be re-labeled "Job Title" to properly reflect the "business card" title of the employee. "Pay Scale Group" could be changed to read "Salary Grade."

These are just a few examples, but as you can see attempting to implement these changes portal-wide comes with challenges, especially if keeping to standard SAP is desired. In some cases, this verbiage can be changed via standard configuration, but in other cases an enhancement to the application is needed. Whether to make these changes or not should be an informed decision from the appropriate HR and IT stakeholders.

Limit the number of automated emails that are generated from the system.

Automated, system-generated communication can sound like a great idea during blueprinting, but we advise that email automation be kept to a minimum in your self-service design. Emails work well to kick off a process, but they can quickly become overwhelming if they are used to notify employees and managers too often. Frequently, these emails become ignored and deleted by the recipient.

However, you can leverage SAP's workflow functionality for approval processes and notifications. Some of these notifications are portal based. In other words, out-of-the-box notifications will come to the user's inbox on the portal and not to their corporate email client (Microsoft Outlook, Lotus Notes, etc.). Companies have been reluctant to drive notification to the portal; the concern is that users won't check their portal inbox as frequently as they check their corporate email (clearly a valid concern). However, this doesn't necessarily warrant a flux of processes that introduce additional emails to the corporate email, because employees and managers today are already flooded with unread emails. Portal inbox notifications should be considered and used whenever it makes good business sense. Over time, behaviors will change, and employees and managers will start checking their portal inboxes if they realize that there is value in doing so. This change does not happen overnight, but with the right campaign and communication users will start to adopt the portal as an information cockpit.

Another alternative is to manage certain notifications centrally from HR. In some companies, this is not a change. Emails have always been distributed manually. Many HR folks are eager to look at the system to assist them with these administrative tasks. It is important, though, to understand that SAP is not meant to be an email system. Whether an email should be auto-generated by the system depends on the process and circumstances of notification. For example, with one-off approvals (such as promotions and other pay changes) a system-generated email notification may make good business sense in order to facilitate and expedite the approvals of the request. However, during your annual compensation planning time it is probably a good idea to manually manage communication from the compensation department and/or HR, because this is a condensed period of time in which system-generated emails could prove overwhelming for your users.

At the end of the blueprinting phase, it is important to review the various communications that employees and managers will receive throughout the process to ensure that they will not be confused by repeated messages. Look at alternatives, such as using portal work items (via the universal worklist) or managing notifications in bulk centrally from HR and/or from the appropriate business function.

Review any changes to online forms, transactions, and processes with the affected business units and functions.

Don't do process reengineering in a vacuum, especially when it impacts the entire organization. For example, migrating PCR forms from a paper-based process to an online, workflow-enabled process should prompt the review from other areas in the company that may have critical dependencies or feedback about the how the new forms and processes will impact them. We have seen project teams complete their blueprints and then soon delay the projects themselves because they could not obtain the required signoff when other functions did not agree with a redesigned process. Making processes and forms too complicated may prevent you from using them company-wide if business rules and user interfaces cannot be reconciled and/or standardized between the groups.

Exposing the SAP Enterprise Portal and self-service functionality over the Internet can enable users to gain access from remote locations.

Many corporate portals are designed to be accessible while the employee is in the workplace or through the use of a virtual private network (VPN) on company-supplied computers. This approach limits employees that want to access their personal information and enterprise applications from home or remote locations, because some employees do not have laptops or are not using company computers. Providing self-service access from the Internet allows employees and managers to have the tools, transactions, and content they need, even when they are not in the office.

Today, the SAP Enterprise Portal and the applications that it hosts are becoming fundamental to service delivery. From an employee's perspective, certain information and transactions that relate to life events and/or life decisions are best viewed at home with a spouse, partner, or loved one. This is especially true when most of the information that was sent to employees' homes is now contained within the portal, such as pay stubs and benefits statements. The best example of a process that needs remote access is annual benefits enrollment, which is often a decision made between the employee and his or her spouse or domestic partner.

With the advanced security inherent in the latest SAP NetWeaver platform, it is feasible to deliver portions or all of the functionality contained within the portal to users over the Internet. Our experience has shown that the SAP Enterprise Portal becomes a more viable and well-adopted tool for employees and managers if it is available over the Internet, because Internet availability dramatically increases the ability to deliver information and transactions to all employees, regardless of where they are physically.

Conduct performance tests that take into account peak periods in processes such as compensation planning, in which managers typically attempt to complete the process in a compressed period of time.

The performance of your applications is a major contributor to the rate of adoption and user experience. Applications that respond quickly are more likely to be adopted by users. Self-service applications add another dimension, because the overall process depends on a user being able to access the system and complete the work in a timely manner. In several implementations, we have observed that a slow and unresponsive SAP Enterprise Portal has contributed to delays in the overall process. In such a situation, HR would need to continually extend dates for employees to complete the process.

Considering that some processes, such as performance management and compensation management, affect large user populations, delays in the process cost a company a considerable amount of money.

Performance testing (sometimes called stress testing) is not a new concept, and most companies conduct performance tests prior to rolling out any Internet or intranet application to assess how the application will behave under a heavy load. The challenge is to run performance tests indicative of the peak usage that the applications will be subjected to and to determine an acceptable response time. Some strongly believe that an acceptable response time should be one or two seconds between clicks, whereas others do not hold such high standards.

An effective way to approach performance testing is to use existing data from legacy applications that perform similar functionality. If this data does not exist in your system, then you need to step back and look at the key processes that are being rolled out and the behavior of the user population. For example, we have observed that over 60 percent of employees complete benefits enrollment in the last week of the open enrollment period. It is human nature that your employee base (as well as managers) will procrastinate.

When you consider processes like benefits enrollment and the dynamics of how users complete this process, you can design appropriate performance tests that can reveal potential issues in your implementation. There are several testing software tools in the marketplace to assist you in automating this process.

Your performance tests might produce the following outcomes:

▶ Verify that you have a proper environment/landscape on which to roll out your functionality

▶ Cause you to make tweaks within the SAP ERP backend and SAP Enterprise Portal configuration to enhance performance

▶ Force a second look at how the system landscape and components are set up

The first two outcomes can be expected, but if the last outcome is reached, then you may need to reevaluate your deployment plan.

Enforce a security and data privacy stance prior to rolling out self-service functionality.

Security has become a major concern for many organizations in the past few years. Many high-profile companies have had security breaches that have generated system down time, loss of confidential information, and eventual loss of revenue.

Self-service applications are designed to enable employees and managers to gain access to key HR information that is highly sensitive and can easily be used to cause damage to employees and/or the enterprise. It is advised that security policies be reviewed when releasing self-service for the first time. Your IT security team—as well as legal and compliance teams—should be involved in and aware of your project. Specific policies that govern the length and complexity of passwords, when passwords should be changed, the sharing of passwords, and access controls should be reviewed and reinforced by your IT security organization.

Data privacy is also of chief concern to many users in Europe and other areas. Data origins and the viewing of data across borders are of principal concern, because many companies with offices in Europe need to conform to local work councils and regulatory laws. If your implementation is global in nature, then be sure to involve your legal and compliance organizations when you localize your self-service applications.

Automate the hiring process to include creating a user and assigning the appropriate security roles.

Depending on the size of your organization, you may want to analyze the effort required in administering security and access controls. Larger organizations invest considerable resources to this effort. Both the SAP Enterprise Portal and the backend SAP ERP system provide all the necessary information and controls to administer security and access controls without needing to introduce new processes and additional resources. In many of our implementations, we have opted to automate the process of administering security by embedding it into the user lifecycle.

The security and maintenance associated with granting access for a new hire can be expedited by implementing an automated process, like the one in the following example:

▶ An employee is hired into the organization. After the hiring action is complete, a background process is started that creates the user ID. After the user ID is created, it is then linked to the employee's Infotype 105 record (Subtype 1, SY-UNAME) and, based on the position that the employee is hired into, additional roles are assigned to the user. User creation, user assignment, and authorization assignments are now complete in SAP ERP.

▶ Once this process is complete, the information is synchronized with the company's LDAP server, which your portal (most likely) uses for authentication and authorization. (You will have to work with your portal and networking group if these concepts are not familiar to you.)

In this example, little to no manual intervention is required for the administration of security. The employee was hired into the system, and basic access was available (in near real time) after the hiring action was completed. We have created many of these extensions to the employee lifecycle — automating everything from the initial creation of the user to the final deactivation of the account upon employee termination. The result has been extensive cost savings and a reliable process that provides (or removes) access in a timely manner.

Test your self-service solution with multiple browsers.

With the SAP Enterprise Portal supporting more and more browsers and the trend to allow employees to have access from home, it becomes critical to test the various browsers during the testing phase of the project. It is more and more common that browsers such as Chrome and Firefox are used to access the Internet. We have seen many companies set the standard to Internet Explorer.

It is also important to understand the Adobe Acrobat versions that you use within your company, especially if the Adobe form technology is being used for change requests. Regardless of the version of your Adobe software, testing should be performed on the version(s) supported.

Implement a testing strategy that takes self-service into consideration.

Testing integrated systems can sometimes be challenging, because it requires comprehensive data to be created in support of the various business scenarios. Self-service applications can also add an additional layer of complexity, because they introduce the SAP Enterprise Portal as their frontend. A portal layer adds complexity and makes the testing effort more challenging.

Table 9.1 lists some of the most common testing issues that we have faced in SAP self-service implementations. Next to each issue, we list the approach we have used to handle this issue in the past.

Issue	Solution
Self-service applications require an extensive set of data, with many employees set to a particular state. As you cycle through each test case, new employees are needed. For example, if you are terminating employees as a manager, you will need other employees that are not terminated to continue to test.	▸ Create a "build up" and "tear down" approach to testing based on what components you are implementing. You can create scenarios that hire employees as part of the test script and then use those employees to complete an entire lifecycle that tests every self-service component. ▸ Consider moving your production master data to your staging system, and decide which organizations you will use for your test data. ▸ Separate your test data from your testing scripts so that the testing scripts can be reused to accommodate different employees within different business scenarios. ▸ Some customers opt to conduct client refreshes to "reset" employee data for the test cycles. This will return the testing environment data to a previous snapshot, which can prove valuable before each cycle of testing.

Table 9.1 Common Testing Issues and Approaches for Mitigation

Issue	Solution
You may not have enough portal users to complete test scenarios. Also, a complicated set of users with varying passwords slows progress.	► When selecting an organization and employees, request that the SAP Basis team (your SAP system administrators) create user IDs based on what is assigned within Infotype 0105. Request that every user have a common password to limit confusion when testing. ► However, be sure that your HR master data is scrambled if there is sensitive information (i.e., birth date, salary and benefits data). There are programs that can be created or software for purchase that can perform this task.
Workflow notifications and system emails are being sent to active employees.	► Testing system notifications, such as emails, can be an issue and could expose the wrong people to HR data that they should not have access to. ► Request that a script be created by SAP Basis that will set all user email addresses to a group email box that the testing team can access. Using this approach will make it easier to test system notifications and will reduce the possibility that data in emails is sent to the wrong email address. ► Queuing emails in Transaction SOST and manually sending requests is one approach, but it could be dangerous if an email is sent to a production user by accident.
Many self-service transactions can affect payroll processing. Lack of payroll testing could result in project delays and/or issues with completing testing.	► If SAP Payroll is performed in-house, then allocate a payroll resource to your testing cycles that can run payroll for a specified period. Payroll should be run at the end of a testing cycle and verified against the business scenarios that are being tested. ► Ensure that all payroll-related Employee Self-Service transactions get tested and approved by the payroll department. Services such as online pay stubs, bank information, and W4 should be tested by a subject matter expert in the payroll group.

Table 9.1 Common Testing Issues and Approaches for Mitigation (Cont.)

Leverage testing cycles to train service center personnel and the HRIS team.

Testing a system and being able to experience the resolution of issues has proven to be a powerful mechanism for getting the HRIS team trained and prepared to support the system after go-live. We have also found that if you allow the service center personnel (or appropriate HR support organization) to participate in the testing cycles you may be able to reduce training time by more than fifty percent. There's nothing quite like on the job training, and by participating in the testing test cycles your support teams will experience "a day in the life" scenarios that will soon become second nature to them.

Form a steering committee to review project progress and resolve project-level issues.

It is important to note that a steering committee should be formed during the project to review program status and to provide advice on key, outstanding issues. Typically, this committee is comprised of senior-level management and other key stakeholders of the process. The project sponsor or his or her representative is usually on the committee as well. It is not uncommon to have VP and even C-level involvement at this level. HR and IT representation is normal, because self-service functionally affects stakeholders in both functions of the organization.

The frequency of these meetings will depend on the group's availability, but the project's timeline and status also should be considered. As the project ramps into the deployment phase, it may be necessary to hold more meetings to ensure a smooth transition. Also, if a project reaches a critical point at any time during the implementation it may be necessary to increase the number of meetings or call impromptu meetings to resolve issues and remove any roadblocks along the way.

In an average project, it is not uncommon for the steering committee to meet biweekly. For these meetings, it is important that your project leaders are in attendance to provide direct feedback to senior leaders and raise issues if needed. A steering committee must be able to make quick decisions when necessary in order not to impede the progress of the project.

The steering committee also can exist after go-live. It then moves into an advisory role on operational issues and future enhancements rather than an advisory in a typical project implementation. This is not as common, but we have seen many companies implement a post-go-live committee or review board in order to provide some continuity between the project and operations associated with it post-implementation.

These best practices are great, but there are also some other tangible resources available at your disposal. We discuss those now.

9.2   Additional Resources

In this next section, we list recommended websites, information repositories, user communities, and industry conferences that will help you gain a better understanding of SAP's self-service offerings. It comprises a thorough inventory of resources you can leverage before, during, and after your implementation. Although this is not a complete listing of where to get all information, it does cover the major resources that are typically tapped into during Employee, Manager, and HR Professional self-service projects.

9.2.1   SAP Service Marketplace

Solution documentation for self-service is available on the SAP Service Marketplace website for registered users. If you do not have SAP Service Marketplace access, ask one of your project team leaders and/or SAP Basis resources how to obtain a username and password for the SAP Service Marketplace.

> **Single Sign-On**
>
> In addition to logging in to the SAP Service Marketplace, you can also apply for a "passport" with your SAP username to enable single sign-on. Once logged in, look under your user profile for the MAINTAIN MY SINGLE SIGN-ON CERTIFICATE option.

To peruse and download product documentation, go to *http://service.sap.com/erp-hcm* in your web browser. Log in with your SAP Service Marketplace username and password. In the left navigation panel, follow one of these paths:

▶ SAP ERP • SAP ERP HUMAN CAPITAL MANAGEMENT • CORE HR & PAYROLL • EMPLOYEE SELF-SERVICE (ESS) for employee self-service information

▶ SAP ERP • SAP ERP HUMAN CAPITAL MANAGEMENT • CORE HR & PAYROLL • EMPLOYEE SELF-SERVICE (ESS) for manager self-service information

▶ SAP ERP • SAP ERP HUMAN CAPITAL MANAGEMENT • CORE HR & PAYROLL • HCM PROCESSES & FORMS for forms information

▶ SAP ERP • SAP ERP HUMAN CAPITAL MANAGEMENT • CORE HR & PAYROLL • HCM PROCESSES & FORMS for information on SAP FIORI

Under each section, you can click on RESOURCES for access to documents such as the following:

▶ Collateral, such as solution brochures

▶ Documentation, such as how-to guides

▶ Detailed and brief overview presentations on functionality

▶ Links to the most relevant blog posts on HR Renewal

▶ Customer success stories

▶ Solution videos posted on YouTube

Figure 9.1 shows the homepage for the Manager Self-Service section of the SAP Service Marketplace. Be sure to check out the information in the right column in addition to exploring the RESOURCES section in the left panel.

The SAP NOTES section of the SAP Service Marketplace is typically where SAP customers go when they need to troubleshoot an issue. This site, previously called OSS (for Online Service System), provides important bug fixes for SAP customers and consultative advice on workarounds for known product issues. It is a lifeline for many project implementations.

The SAP NOTES section of the SAP Service Marketplace can be accessed directly by going to *http://service.sap.com/notes*. You will be prompted for a username and password, and you will need to be a registered user.

SAP Notes for ESS are categorized under the following application areas:

▶ CA-ESS-ITS (ESS Internet Transaction Server [ITS])

▶ CA-ESS-WD (ESS Web Dynpro)

▶ PA-ESS-XSS (ESS—Common Parts)

SAP Notes for MSS are categorized under the following application areas:

▶ CA-MSS-APL (Manager Self-Service—Application)

▶ CA-MSS-HCM (Manager Self-Service—HR)

▶ CA-MSS-OVR (Manager Self-Service—Workset Work Overview)

▶ CA-MSS-RPT (Manager Self-Service—Reports)

▶ CA-MSS-TEC (Manager Self-Service—Technical)

▶ CA-MSS-TEM (Manager Self-Service—Workset Team)

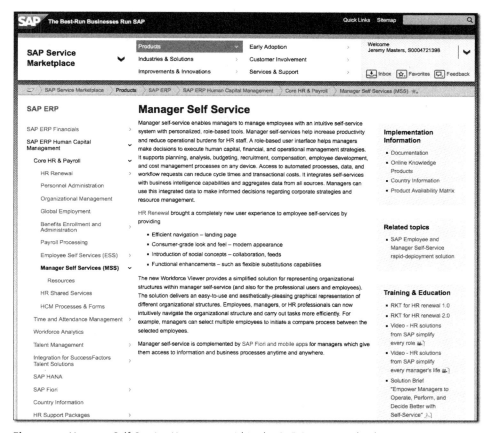

Figure 9.1 Manager Self-Service Homepage within the SAP Service Marketplace

At the time of writing (fall 2014), there are over 1,000 SAP Notes available in the SAP Service Marketplace concerning self-service in HR. We won't mention all of them, but we do recommend that you reference some of them, including the following:

▶ **SAP Note 1965692 (HR Renewal 2.0: Release Information Note)**
This note contains important SAP Business Suite release information for HR Renewal 2.0, including Manager Self-Services.

▶ **SAP Note 2010994 (SAP's Rapid Deployment Solution (RDS) for ESS and MSS)**
This note includes an attachment, "Quick Guide to Implementing the SAP Employee and Manager Self-Service rapid-deployment solution."

▶ **SAP Note 1881006 (Release Strategy for the ABAP Add-On HR Renewal)**
This note contains information about planning the installation or an upgrade of the ABAP add-on for HR renewal.

▶ **SAP Note 1701634 (HR Renewal 1.0: Release Information Note)**
This note contains important SAP Business Suite release information for HR Renewal 1.0.

▶ **SAP Note 1876899 (Browser Information for HR Renewal 1.0)**
This note contains important information about browser support and compatibility when using HR Renewal 1.0.

▶ **SAP Note 1691231 (Release Strategy for the ABAP Add-on SAP HR Renewal 1.0)**
This note contains information about planning the installation and upgrade of the ABAP add-on for HR Renewal 1.0.

Searches for these and other SAP Notes are performed through the website. Figure 9.2 shows the website's main search screen. For frequent searches, you can maintain a "template," which can hold prefilled parameters.

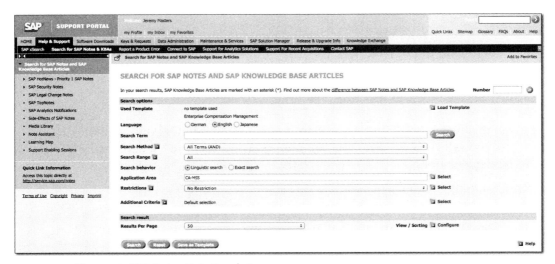

Figure 9.2 SAP Notes Main Search Page

9.2.2 SAP Help

SAP's online help is often overlooked as a great resource for documentation. It is always helpful to ground yourself with the standard documentation from SAP. SAP posts the latest, revised help documentation online to the help website. To read the documentation on the help website, perform the following steps:

1. Go to *http://help.sap.com* in your web browser.

2. In the top header section, click SAP BUSINESS SUITE.

3. In the left navigation, click SAP ERP. This will expand to show the latest versions of SAP (EHP 6, EHP 7, etc.).

4. Select the version of the software that you are interested in learning more about.

For the latest information about HR Renewal specifically, you will find the HR Renewal links under SAP ERP ADD-ONS in the left navigation panel. HR Renewal 1.0 and HR Renewal 2.0 are listed separately and organized by initial shipment as well as feature packs.

Within each section, you will find information about the topic in general, what new features are available, installation and upgrades, business functions, configuration and deployment, applications, and roles and security. The APPLICATION HELP section is particularly popular, because it speaks to the latest features and functionality that many practitioners are interested in.

9.2.3 SAP Community Network

SAP Community Network (SCN) is a free online community and network of SAP practitioners—that is, developers, configurators, and project team members. Members can post, respond to, and view questions found in this popular forum at *http://scn.sap.com*. The blogs on SCN have become extremely popular in recent years. If you can filter out the marketing shine, some blogs can be valuable to your implementation.

To this end, the SAP Support Knowledgebase search engine (SAP xSearch) searches different repositories, including Support Documents, SAP Solutions, SCN Discussion/Blogs/Wikis, and SAP Notes.

9.2.4   HR Expert

Wellesley Information Services publishes HR Expert—an online magazine that covers essential SAP ERP HCM concepts, tips, and best practices. There is a focus on case studies and "real-world" experiences in the magazine's articles, videos, blogs, and podcasts. You can find a lot of good material at *http://sapexperts.wispubs.com/HR*. Membership requires a paid subscription. Figure 9.3 shows a screenshot of a video recorded at a conference.

Figure 9.3 Video about HR Renewal on HR Expert Website

9.2.5   Annual Conferences

Several annual conferences are popular among SAP ERP HCM practitioners. Conferences are a great way to meet with others in your field and get insights into other implementations (both project successes and war stories). The following list describes some of these useful conferences:

▶ Every year, Wellesley Information Services produces the SAPInsider conferences (*http://sapinsider.wispubs.com*), which SAP partners, exhibitors, and customers attend to listen to speakers, share best practices, and see what new functionality is becoming available. The conferences are a great opportunity to network, hear what others are doing, and have fun. There are usually three conferences per year: one in the United States, one in Europe, and one in Asia. From the conference page, select the EVENTS option to see all upcoming events.

▶ The Eventful Group (*www.masteringsap.com/sap*) produces a Mastering SAP HR & Payroll event in South Africa and Australia. This event is a more intimate atmosphere with great content. They also produce more targeted seminars, which can be beneficial for learning about specialized topics within SAP ERP HCM.

▶ SAP annually hosts a combined ASUG/SAPPHIRE event (*www.sapsapphire.com*) that is geared for both current and prospective clients. It is an opportunity for SAP to show its cutting-edge solutions to its customer base. As you might expect, the ASUG/SAPPHIRE event includes speaker presentations, demos, and an exhibitor area.

▶ The HR Technology conference (*www.hrtechnologyconference.com*) is also worth attending for a broader view of what other vendors offer for self-services and what other companies are using for their software (aside from SAP).

9.2.6 User Communities and Networks

Two SAP ERP HCM user communities are popular for networking events, knowledge sharing/harvesting, and round-table discussions:

▶ Americas' SAP Users' Group, known as ASUG (*www.asug.com*), is a customer-driven community of SAP professionals and partners. There are more than 140,000 individuals and 3,700 companies represented within the community. ASUG provides a great opportunity for networking. Other areas of the world have strong SAP user groups as well. Check out your local SAP user group community, and join in!

▶ The Society for Human Resource Management (SHRM; *www.shrm.org*) is the world's largest association devoted to human resource management. Founded in 1948 and representing more than 275,000 individual members, SHRM currently has more than 575 affiliated chapters and members in more than 160 countries.

LinkedIn can also be a valuable resource. LinkedIn (*www.linkedin.com*) is the popular business-oriented social networking site launched in May of 2003 and mainly used for professional networking. The site has some excellent groups to subscribe to for registered users. Membership is free. LinkedIn has also started to become a great place for posting and reading content.

9.3   Summary

In conclusion, there are many best practices and resources you can embrace to research answers to your self-service questions. We have covered several important best practices during our 50-plus years of collective experience implementing self-services. We have also listed some valuable resources, such as the SAP Community Network (SCN) and the SAP Service Marketplace, which are absolutely free yet provide a wealth of information at your fingertips. Just remember two things. First, remember where information comes from and take that factor into account when evaluating the validity of a piece of information. Second, if you are stuck on something there are probably fellow SAP ERP HCM practitioners who are struggling or have struggled with the same or a similar challenge. Go out there, and take advantage of all the resources at your disposal!

Let's close by bringing everything back together. We will focus on the high points of what we covered in each chapter as we guide this book to its natural conclusion.

10   Summary

Imagine you are sitting in your kitchen, holding that first cup of coffee (or tea) in the morning. Everything is quiet, and you are the master of your domain. The stillness of the morning reminds your inner nerd that, even though everything is calm in your kitchen, you are actually spinning on the surface of the Earth at over 1,000 mph, traveling around the sun at around 67,000 mph, and orbiting the galaxy at a mere 514,000 mph or so. The whole process yields some crazy, quasihelical motion at incomprehensible speeds that would look insane if you tried to picture it. It's enough to make you feel small and completely out of control. Yet, when you reel your mind back in you realize that, although everything about this astrophysical portrait you've painted is true, you are still very much in control of your kitchen. Things are still calm and quiet, and you know exactly what's happening in your little patch of the galaxy.

We liken this book to that little thought experiment. We have introduced you, the reader, to an enormous amount of new content. As you step back and view SAP's self-service landscape, you see how fast it is moving and in how many directions. How can anyone possibly keep up with all those moving parts? How can anyone find his or her place in this impossibly large and dynamic landscape?

The answer to that question is similar to how our early morning astronaut regained composure: it's all about your point of view. Although we have seen how SAP's self-service landscape is rapidly evolving and taking new and bold directions—and not waiting around for anyone to catch up while doing it—you are still in control of you and your enterprise, and you still know your little patch of the galaxy the best. You are still the master of your domain. With that knowledge and the information we have given you in this book, it is our sincere hope that you will feel well equipped to make intelligent SAP ERP HCM self-service decisions on behalf of your enterprise or at least be able to confidently advise those who do.

With that in mind, let's take a quick look back at the content we have covered in this book, chapter by chapter.

The Changing Landscape of Self-Service

In Chapter 1, we talked about how the technological landscape is changing, which is requiring SAP to adapt. The major changes revolve around cloud-based applications and mobility. The impact of the cloud is that applications can improve faster, which means that in order to keep up, on-premise HR functionality must become more agile. The impact of mobile is that customers have higher standards for what they expect from applications.

We then talked about how SAP has responded to these changes with an initiative called HR Renewal, which modernizes the user interface (UI) via SAPUI5 and Web Dynpro for ABAP. SAPUI5 is sleek, modern, and mobile capable, whereas Web Dynpro for ABAP is a robust, but mobile unfriendly, workhorse. SAP Fiori is a specialized SAPUI5 look and feel that is currently being adopted across all of SAP and itself includes some HR applications.

Deployment Options

In Chapter 2, we set out to discuss the various deployment options available to a customer looking to implement SAP ERP HCM self-services in the current environment. We took a look at the venerable SAP GUI and how its usefulness for self-services has passed. We then spent some time talking about the SAP Enterprise Portal. We talked about its most recent innovations and the fact that it is as relevant as ever as a deployment option. We briefly brought the Ajax Framework Page into our SAP Enterprise Portal discussion as well. We also talked about the SAP Enterprise Portal mobile edition and its ability to stand alongside the SAP Enterprise Portal and serve content to mobile devices.

Next, we talked about the capabilities of SAP to support third-party portals as a deployment option. Then, we talked about the SAP NetWeaver Business Client and its various flavors and strengths. We wrapped up by talking about the SAP HANA Cloud Portal and how it allows you to extend SAP's cloud offerings in a seamless way.

Refreshing the UI

In Chapter 3, we focused on SAP's move from a traditional UI to a user experience (UX). This is in response to the marketplace demanding a more consumer-grade experience from enterprise software. SAP responded to this pressure by introducing its UX strategy and laying out its plan to use new and existing technologies to build—and allow its customers to build—a consumer-grade experience for users.

SAP's UX strategy revolved around three words: New, Renew, and Enable. New means that SAP uses new technologies, such as SAP Fiori, SAPUI5, and SAP Gateway and OData, going forward to create new applications. Renew focuses on using these same technologies, along with Web Dynpro for ABAP with Floorplan Manager, to refresh the look and feel as well as the functionality of SAP. Finally, Enable centers on the idea of SAP making a series of tools and resources available to allow customers to build their own custom applications in the image of the new UX strategy.

We next showed how SAP Fiori, the new UX for SAP enterprise applications, and its design principles are so key to SAP's UX revolution. Five terms sum up SAP Fiori's design principles: role based, responsive, simple, coherent, and delightful. These principles are envisioned to make SAP Fiori easy to use and intuitive for you specifically, to make your job easier.

We then introduced the technologies that form the backbone of the new UX strategy: SAPUI5 and SAP Gateway and OData. We described what SAPUI5 was and its key benefits. We also looked at how development happens in SAPUI5, showing Eclipse and introducing SAP Web IDE, the new browser-based development environment for SAPUI5 applications. We wrapped up by talking about how SAP Gateway and OData interact and why they are important to the new UX SAP is seeking to build.

Employee Self-Service in SAP ERP HCM

In Chapter 4, we started off by introducing many of the new concepts SAP has introduced into ESS with HR Renewal. For example, we looked at landing pages, the new timesheet and leave request, and the paystub conversion. We then laid the groundwork for our discussion of the finer-grained details of ESS by talking about the software components, business functions, and services needed for ESS. We then briefly touched on SAP Gateway and OData setup and configuration.

Next, we delved a little deeper into the landing page concept and configuration. We talked about the personalization options available to the ESS user before talking about how to administer Suite Page Builder.

Then, we took a look at the specific functionality within the ESS role. We broke this functionality up into its lanes, starting with the My Info lane. Within My Info, we talked about the Employee Profile, the Talent Profile, Leave Request, Paystub, and the Organization Chart. The next lane we discussed was My Services, which is broken up into many service groupings. We started with the Overview and its view into active applications and processes, team and corporate information, and related links. Next, we discussed the Working Time service group and the Benefits and Payment service group. We continued with the Personal Information service group before talking about Career Development and Learning. We wrapped up our discussion of My Services by discussing the Travel and Expense service group.

Next, we analyzed the new My Time lane with its new SAPUI5 timesheet. Then, we looked at My Learnings and its integration into SAP's LSO. We continued with a look into My Work Feeds before talking about the Search component of the new landing page.

We wrapped up our discussion of ESS by talking about authorizations and roles in ESS.

Manager Self-Service in SAP ERP HCM

Chapter 5 follows a similar format as that of Chapter 4. We started off with a review of the important application areas, deployment options, business functions, and services that must be activated before starting an MSS initiative. We then moved to a discussion of the MSS landing page, including the delivered CHIPs. Next came a review of the following components of the new MSS: My Team, My Team Services, Approvals and Substitution, My Reports, My KPIs, KPI Monitor, and Work Feeds.

Then, we took a look at the new Workforce Viewer for managers, from features and functionality to configuration. After that, we spent some time covering launchpad customizing. We discussed SAP authorization for MSS, including roles, structural authorizations in MSS, and the use of the personalization keys that correspond to the launchpad role and menu.

Next, we reviewed manager reports, including the new Employee List based on the new Operational Reports Provisioning (OPD) framework. We then reviewed the new transactional substitution functionality available for managers with HR Renewal 2.0, initial shipment. Then we looked at highlights from the new search and Work Feeds functionality. Finally, we focused on available enhancement spots within MSS, with a focus on the `HRMSS_UI5_EMP_PROFILE` BAdI.

HR Professional Self-Service in SAP ERP HCM

In Chapter 6, we answered the question of why SAP is investing so much in changing HR administrator applications. We then went through the new swim lanes, master data maintenance via POMDA, and the options that exist for form-based processing.

The immense amount of work that SAP has invested in order to bring its UX on par with the consumer-grade experiences we're all now used to throughout our lives is plain to see. Perhaps you will be able to evaluate this and conclude, as we have, that the HR Professional role is an ambitious package that deserves a serious look as a tool to roll out to your HR administrators.

Mobility in ESS and MSS

In Chapter 7, we started by recognizing the important trends and concepts at the intersection of society and technology that influence mobility, including the BYOD phenomenon, mobile-first development, device agnosticism, and responsive design. It is important to understand the deployment methods for mobile via either mobile apps or mobile web applications, including the pros and cons for each. Next, we talked about the options for customers for technology platforms on-premise versus on the cloud.

Our next topic was a mobile application review for each offering (SAP Mobile Platform on-premise, SAP Enterprise Portal mobile edition, SAP Fiori, SuccessFactors, and SAP HANA Cloud Platform mobile services). Given all those options, we also wanted to talk about some partner solutions that use alternative, more lightweight technologies.

SAP Fiori

Chapter 8 offered a more detailed look at SAP Fiori. SAP Fiori is referred to as a set of applications for business technology and also as the general direction SAP is taking in terms of moving from a focus on the UI to a focus on the UX.

Our objective in this chapter was to look at it as a platform for self-services instead of simply the inspiration behind HR Renewal changes. To that end, we examined the various applications that SAP offers via SAP Fiori that relate to self-services for employees and managers. SAP hasn't yet developed this space for HR professionals, but such development could be on the way.

Best Practices and Additional Resources

Finally, we wrapped up this book with some best practices and helpful resources to assist you in your future self-service implementations.

We wish you the best of luck and hope that we have been able to provide some help with your next self-service implementation. Self-service is a powerful toolset that is growing more powerful by the iteration.

A Business Functions and Applications

This appendix contains lists that are useful references any time during your planning or deployment of self-services. We cover business functions available for self-service (Table A.1); available Web Dynpro for ABAP applications for ESS (Table A.2), MSS (Table A.3), and HR Professional Self-Service (Table A.4); available SAPUI5 applications and their respective OData services (Table A.5); a list of all SAP Fiori applications available (Table A.6); standard composite SAP roles (Table A.7); and all SAP HR mobile applications, divided into lists of ESS (Table A.8) and MSS (Table A.9) services and applications included in the latest enhancement packages. For the last two lists, please note that they are not exhaustive lists of partner solutions.

Versions
All information in this chapter is based on the latest available versions of SAP applications at the time of writing (SAP ERP 6.0, EHP 7).

Business Function	Name	Business Function Prerequisites
CA_HAP_CI_1	CA, Evaluations, Appraisals, and Surveys 01	
FIN_TRAVEL_1	Travel Management	
FIN_TRAVEL_2	Travel Management	FIN_TRAVEL_1
FIN_TRAVEL_3	Travel Management	FIN_TRAVEL_2
HCM_ASR_CI_1	HCM, Administrative Services 01 (EhP2)	
HCM_ASR_CI_2	HCM, Administrative Services 02 (EhP4)	HCM_ASR_CI_1
HCM_ASR_CI_3	HCM, Administrative Services 03 (EhP5)	HCM_ASR_CI_2
HCM_ASR_CI_4	HCM, Administrative Services 04 (Reversible)	HCM_ASR_CI_3
HCM_ASR_CI_5	HCM, Administrative Services 05 (Reversible)	HCM_ASR_CI_4
HCM_ECM_CI_1	HCM, Enterprise Compensation Management 01	

Table A.1 Business Functions Relevant for Self-Service

Business Function	Name	Business Function Prerequisites
HCM_ECM_CI_2	HCM, Enterprise Compensation Management 02	HCM_ECM_CI_1
HCM_ERC_CI_1	HCM, SAP E-Recruiting 1	
HCM_ERC_CI_2	HCM, SAP E-Recruiting 2	HCM_ERC_CI_1
HCM_ERC_CI_3	HCM, SAP E-Recruiting 3	HCM_ERC_CI_2
HCM_ERC_CI_4	HCM, SAP E-Recruiting 4	HCM_ERC_CI_3
HCM_ERC_SES_1	HCM, SAP E-Recruiting Search Functions 1	
HCM_ESS_CI_1	HCM, ESS for Personal Information	
HCM_ESS_WDA_1	Employee Self Services on Web Dynpro for ABAP	
HCM_ESS_WDA_2	HCM, ESS on Web Dynpro ABAP 2	HCM_ESS_WDA_1
HCM_ESS_WDA_3	HCM, Employee Self-Services on Web Dynpro for ABAP 3	HCM_ESS_WDA_2
HCM_HIRE_INT_CI_1	HCM, Hire Integration 1 (optional)	
HCM_MSS_ERC_CI_1	HCM, MSS for SAP E-Recruiting	
HCM_NWBC_ROLES	HCM, Roles for SAP NetWeaver Business Client (Reversible)	
HCM_OSA_CI_1	HCM, Performance Management 01	
HCM_OSA_CI_2	HCM, Performance Management 02	HCM_OSA_CI_1
HCM_OSA_CI_3	HCM, Performance Management 03	HCM_OSA_CI_2
HCM_TMC_CI_1	HCM, Core Processes in Talent Management	
HCM_TMC_CI_2	HCM, Core Processes in Talent Management 02	HCM_TMC_CI_1
HCM_ANALYTICS_1	HCM, Cross Analytics 1	
HCM_ANALYTICS_2	HCM, Operational Data Provisioning for Analytics (Reversible)	
HCM_ANALYTICS_3	HCM, Analytics for Manager	FND_ANALYTICS_TOOLS
HCM_ESS_UI5_1	HCM, Employee Self-Service on SAP UI5	
HCM_MSS_WDA_1	HCM, MSS on Web Dynpro ABAP	

Table A.1 Business Functions Relevant for Self-Service (Cont.)

Business Function	Name	Business Function Prerequisites
HCM_MSS_WDA_2	HCM, MSS on Web Dynpro ABAP 2	HCM_MSS_WDA_1
HCM_MSS_UI5_1	HCM, Manager Self Service on SAP UI5	HCM_MSS_WDA_2
HCM_MSS_UI5_2	HCM, Manager Self Service on SAP UI5 2	HCM_ESS_UI5_1 HCM_MSS_UI5_1
HCM_PD_ORGVIS_1	HCM, Workforce Viewer 01	HCM_ESS_UI5_1 HCM_MSS_UI5_1 HCM_PAO_CI_3
HCM_LSO_CI_1	HCM, Learning Solution 01	
HCM_LSO_CI_2	HCM, Learning Solution 02	HCM_LSO_CI_1
HCM_LSO_CI_3	HCM, Learning Solution 03	HCM_LSO_CI_2
HCM_MSS_OADP_1	HCM, Manager Self-Service Performance Optimization with OADP	HCM_MSS_WDA_2
HCM_PD_UI_1	HCM, PD UI Visualization 01 Technical	
HCM_PD_UI_2	HCM, PD UI Visualization 01 Technical	HCM_PD_UI_1

Table A.1 Business Functions Relevant for Self-Service (Cont.)

Web Dynpro for ABAP Application	Description	Required Business Function
HRESS_A_CATS_1	Record Working Time	HCM_ESS_WDA_1
HRESS_A_PTARQ_LEAVREQ_APPL	Create Leave Request	HCM_ESS_WDA_1
HRESS_A_PTARQ_LEAVREQ_APPL	Leave Overview	HCM_ESS_WDA_1
HRESS_A_PTARQ_TIMEACC	View Time Account Balances	HCM_ESS_WDA_1
HRESS_A_CORRECTIONS	Clock In/Out Corrections	HCM_ESS_WDA_1
HRESS_A_TIME_DATESEL	Time Statement with Date Selection	HCM_ESS_WDA_1
HRESS_A_TIME_PERSEL	Time Statement with Period Selection	HCM_ESS_WDA_1

Table A.2 Available Web Dynpro for ABAP Applications for ESS

Web Dynpro for ABAP Application	Description	Required Business Function
HRESS_A_PAYSLIP	Salary Statement	HCM_ESS_WDA_1
HRESS_A_TCS	Total Compensation Statement	HCM_ESS_WDA_1
HRESS_A_PERSINFO	Personal Profile	HCM_ESS_WDA_1
ASR_PERSONNEL_FILE	Personnel File	HCM_ASR_CI_3
HRESS_A_EICAUTH	EIC Authentication	HCM_ESS_WDA_1
HRTMC_EMPLOYEE_PROFILE	Talent Profile	HCM_TMC_CI_1
HRRCF_A_STARTPAGE_INT_CAND	My Career Cockpit	HCM_ERC_CI_4
HRRCF_A_EMP_JOB_SEARCH	Job Search	HCM_ERC_CI_4
HRRCF_A_CANDIDATE_PROFILE_INT	My Candidate Profile	HCM_ERC_CI_4
HRRCF_A_REFCODE_SRCH_INT	Apply Using Reference Code	HCM_ERC_CI_4
HRRCF_A_PSETT_INT	Personal Settings (SAP E-Recruiting)	HCM_ERC_CI_4
HRESS_A_W2_REPRINT	W-2/W-2C Reprint (US Only)	HCM_ESS_WDA_1
HRESS_A_PER_US_ONLINE_W2	Election for Online W-2 (US Only)	HCM_ESS_WDA_1, HCM_LOC_CI_29
HRESS_A_REP_US_ONLINE_W2	Reporting of Online W-2 (US Only)	HCM_ESS_WDA_1, HCM_LOC_CI_29
HRESS_A_W4	W-4 Tax Withholding (US Only)	HCM_ESS_WDA_1
HRESS_A_EMPLOYEE_VERIFICATION	Employment Verification (US Only)	HCM_ESS_WDA_1

Table A.2 Available Web Dynpro for ABAP Applications for ESS (Cont.)

Web Dynpro for ABAP Application	Description	Required Business Function
HRMSS_HOMEPAGE	Home Page, includes Birthdays/Anniversaries and Deadline Monitor	HCM_MSS_WDA_1
HRMSS_TEAM_DETAIL	Team View	HCM_MSS_WDA_1
HRMSS_COMPETENCY_LONG_VIEW	Competency Matchup	HCM_MSS_WDA_1

Table A.3 Available Web Dynpro for ABAP Applications for MSS

Web Dynpro for ABAP Application	Description	Required Business Function
HRMSS_A_CATS_APPR	Time Recording Status for My Team	HCM_MSS_WDA_1
ASR_PROCESS_EXECUTE_FPM	Inbox: Execute Process	HCM_ASR_CI_3
ASR_PROCESS_SELECT	Inbox: Select Process	HCM_ASR_CI_3
HRMSS_A_CATS_APPR	Approve Multiple Time Sheets	HCM_MSS_WDA_1
HRMSS_A_CATS_APPROVAL_1	Approve Individual Time Sheet	HCM_MSS_WDA_1
HRESS_A_PTARQ_LEAVREQ_APPL	Approve Leave Request	HCM_ESS_WDA, HCM_CE_PT
HRMSS_A_CICO_APPR	Approve Clock In/Out Corrections	HCM_MSS_WDA_1
IBO_WDA_INBOX	Time Approval and Task Reminder	HCM_MSS_WDA_1
HRMSS_TEAM_PAGE	Attendance Overview	HCM_MSS_WDA_1
HRESS_A_LEA_TEAM_CALENDAR	Team Calendar	HCM_ESS_WDA_1
HRMSS_EMP_OVERVIEW_PROFILE	Employee Profile	HCM_MSS_WDA_1
ASR_PROCESSES_DISPLAY	Employee-Related Process Overview	HCM_ASR_CI_3
ASR_PROCESS_EXECUTE_FPM	Start Process for Employees/OM	HCM_ASR_CI_3
ASR_MASS_START_PROCESS	Start Process for Multiple Employees	HCM_ASR_CI_3
ASR_FORM_DISPLAY	Display Form	HCM_ASR_CI_3
HRASR_CALL_TX_ATTCH	Display Attachments	HCM_ASR_CI_3
LSO_MANAGE_PARTICIPANTS	Manage Participation	n/a
LSO_MANAGE_MANDATORY_ASSIGN	Manage Mandatory Assignments	HCM_LSO_CI_2
HRRCF_A_REQUI_MONITOR	Requisition Monitor	HCM_ERC_CI_4
HRRCF_A_QA_MSS	Questionnaire	HCM_ERC_CI_4
HRRCF_A_TP_ASSESS	Candidate Assessment	HCM_ERC_CI_4
HRRCF_A_REQ_ASSESS	Candidacy Assessment	HCM_ERC_CI_4
HRRCF_A_DATAOVERVIEW	Data Overview	HCM_ERC_CI_4

Table A.3 Available Web Dynpro for ABAP Applications for MSS (Cont.)

Web Dynpro for ABAP Application	Description	Required Business Function
HRRCF_C_REQUEST_BROWSER	Overview of Requisition Requests	HCM_ERC_CI_4
HRRCF_A_SUBSTITUTION_MAN-AGER	Specify Substitute (E-Recruiting)	HCM_ERC_CI_4
HRMSS_TALENT_HOME_PAGE	Talent Management Page	HCM_MSS_WDA_1
HAP_A_PMP_PIE_CHART	Pie Chart (SAP Performance Management	HCM_OSA_CI_1
HRMSS_COMPETENCY_LONG_VIEW	Competency Matchup	HCM_MSS_WDA_1
HAP_A_PMP_GOALS	Team Goals	HCM_OSA_CI_1
HRTMC_TA_DASHBOARD	Talent Assessment	HCM_TMC_CI_1
HRTMC_TA_ASSESSMENT	Assessment Document	HCM_TMC_CI_1
HRTMC_TA_DEV_PLAN	Development Plan	HCM_TMC_CI_1
HRTMC_TEAMVIEWER	Talent Information	HCM_TMC_CI_1
HRTMC_LONG_PROFILE	Talent Profile	HCM_TMC_CI_1
HRTMC_SIDE_BY_SIDE	Side-By-Side Comparison	HCM_TMC_CI_1
HRTMC_EMPLOYEE_PROFILE	Employee's Self-Description	HCM_TMC_CI_1
HAP_A_PMP_OVERVIEW	Performance Management (Predefined)	HCM_OSA_CI_1
HAP_A_PMP_MAIN	Appraisal Document (Predefined)	HCM_OSA_CI_1
HAP_START_PAGE_POWL_UI_MSS	Performance Management (Flexible)	HCM_OSA_CI_1
HAP_MAIN_DOCUMENT	Appraisal Document (Flexible)	HCM_OSA_CI_1
HAP_QUALIFICATION_PROFILE	Qualification Profile	HCM_OSA_CI_1
HAP_DOCUMENT_LINK	Additional Appraisal Documents in the Validity Period	HCM_OSA_CI_1
HCM_ECM_PLANNING_UI_GAF	Compensation Planning/ Approval	HCM_ECM_CI_2
HCM_ECM_PLANNING_OVERVIEW_OIF	Planning Overview	HCM_ECM_CI_2
HCM_ECM_TEAMVIEWER_OIF	Compensation Information	HCM_ECM_CI_2

Table A.3 Available Web Dynpro for ABAP Applications for MSS (Cont.)

Web Dynpro for ABAP Application	Description	Required Business Function
HCM_ECM_SIDEBYSIDE_OIF	Compensation Comparison	HCM_ECM_CI_2
HCM_ECM_PROFILE_OIF	Compensation Profile	HCM_ECM_CI_2
HRMSS_ORGPROFILE_TEAM-VIEWER	Organizational Information	HCM_MSS_WDA_1
HRMSS_ORGANIZATIONAL_PRO-FILE	Organization Profile	HCM_MSS_WDA_1
ASR_PA_PD_PROCESSES_DIS-PLAY	Organization-Related Process Overview	HCM_ASR_CI_3
HRMSS_POSPROFILE_TEAM-VIEWER	Position Information	HCM_MSS_WDA_1
HRMSS_POSITION_PROFILE	Position Profile	HCM_MSS_WDA_1
ASR_SRCH_PD_PROCESS	Search Processes (OM/PD)	HCM_ASR_CI_3
MAINTAIN_POSITION_REQ	Edit Position Details	n/a
HRMSS_REPORTING_LAUNCHPAD	Reports Launchpad	HCM_MSS_WDA_1
HRMSS_EMP_OVERVIEW_PROFILE	Generic UIBBs (User Interface Building Blocks) for Lists and Forms	n/a
HRMSS_TEAM	Reminder of Dates	HCM_MSS_WDA_1

Table A.3 Available Web Dynpro for ABAP Applications for MSS (Cont.)

Web Dynpro for ABAP Application	Description	Required Business Functions
HRPAO_PAOM_MASTERDATA	All services related to organization structure, position, organizational unit display, and maintenance as well as country-specific information	▸ HCM_PAO_CI_1 ▸ HCM_PAO_CI_2 ▸ HCM_PAO_CI_3 ▸ HCM_PAO_CI_4 ▸ HCM_PAO_CI_5

Table A.4 Available Web Dynpro for ABAP Application for HR Professional

SAPUI5 Application	Description	Associated OData Services
HRESS_MY_INFO_G	My Information	▸ HRESS_EMP_LANE_PROF_SERVICE ▸ /UI2/LAUNCHPAD
HRESS_WRKFEED_G	Work Feeds	▸ HRESS_EMP_WORK_FEEDS_SERVICE ▸ HRESS_WRK_FEED_SUB_OVERVIEW_SERVICE ▸ /IWFND/NOTIFICATIONSTORE
HRESS_MYSRV_G	My Services	▸ /UI2/LAUNCHPAD ▸ HRXSS_PERS_KEY
HRESS_LRNSOLN_G	My Learnings	▸ HRESS_EMP_LSO_SERVICE ▸ /UI2/LAUNCHPAD
HRPAO_SEARCH_C	Search	▸ PAO_SEARCH_SERVICE
HRMSS_MY_TEAM_G	My Team	▸ HROVIS_ORGCHART_SERVICE ▸ HRXSS_PERNR_MEMID_SERVICE
HRMSS_TEAMSRV_G	My Team Services	▸ /UI2/LAUNCHPAD ▸ HRXSS_PERS_KEY
HRMSS_TASKS_G	Approvals	▸ /UI2/LAUNCHPAD ▸ HRMSS_OTHER_APPROVALS_SERVICE ▸ /IWPGW/TASKPROCESSING
HRMSS_MGRANA_G	My KPIs/Status of All KPIs	▸ HRXSS_PERS_KEY ▸ /UI2/LAUNCHPAD
HRMSS_LPD_C	My Reports	▸ HRXSS_PERS_KEY ▸ /UI2/LAUNCHPAD
HRMSS_SUBS_G	Substitutions	▸ HRMSS_SUBS_ACTION_MENU ▸ HRMSS_SUBSTITUTION_SERVICE
HRESS_PAYSLIP_G	Salary Statement	▸ HRESS_PAYSLIP_SERVICE ▸ /UI2/LAUNCHPAD
HRESS_LEAVREQ_G	Leave Request	▸ HRESS_LEAVE_REQUEST_SERVICE
HRESS_TEAMCDR_G	Team Calendar	▸ HRESS_TEAM_CALENDAR_SERVICE
HRMSS_LR_APPR_G	Leave Request Approval	▸ HRMSS_LEAVE_APPROVAL_SERVICE
HRMSS_CATSAPR_G	CATS Approval	▸ HRMSS_CATS_APPROVAL_SERVICE

Table A.5 Available OData and SAPUI5 Services for HR Renewal

SAPUI5 Application	Description	Associated OData Services
HRESS_EMP_PRO_G	Employee Profile	▸ HRESS_EMP_PROFILE_SERVICE ▸ /UI2/LAUNCHPAD ▸ HRMSS_EMPLOYEE_NOTES_SERVICE
HCM_PD_ORGVIS_1	Workforce Viewer	▸ HROVIS_ORGCHART_SERVICE ▸ HRGEN_QUICK_VIEW_SERVICE ▸ /UI2/QUICKVIEW ▸ PAO_ACTIONMENU ▸ /UI2/LAUNCHPAD
HRPAO_SWFDUPD_G	Discussions	▸ PAO_STREAMWORK ▸ PAO_ACTIONMENU ▸ /UI2/QUICKVIEW
HRPAO_ORGFAVS_G	Organization	▸ PAO_ORGANIZATION_FAVORITES ▸ PAO_ACTIONMENU ▸ /UI2/QUICKVIEW
HRPAO_PROCESS_G	Processes	▸ PAO_PROCESSES ▸ /UI2/QUICKVIEW ▸ PAO_ACTIONMENU ▸ PAO_USERCONTEXT
HRPAO_SEARCH_G	Search	▸ PAO_SEARCH_SERVICE ▸ PAO_ACTIONMENU ▸ HRGEN_QUICK_VIEW_SERVICE ▸ /UI2/QUICKVIEW
HRPAO_TASKS_G	Tasks By Draft, Tasks By Time, Tasks By Priority	▸ /IWPGW/TASKPROCESSING ▸ PAO_USERCONTEXT
n/a	Time Account	▸ HRESS_TIME_ACCOUNTS_SERVICE
n/a	Quick View	▸ HRGEN_QUICK_VIEW_SERVICE
n/a	Employee Notes	▸ HRMSS_EMPLOYEE_NOTES_SERVICE
n/a	Navigation Rule	▸ HRMSS_NAV_URL_SERVICE
n/a	Action Menu	▸ PAO_ACTIONMENU

Table A.5 Available OData and SAPUI5 Services for HR Renewal (Cont.)

SAPUI5 Application	Description	Associated OData Services
HCM_LR_APV	Approve Leave Requests	/GBHCM/LEAVEAPPROVAL
HCM_TS_APV	Approve Time Sheet	SRA010_TIMESHEET_APPROVAL_SRV
HCM_BEN_MON	My Benefits	SRA007_BENEFITS_SRV
HCM_LR_CRE	My Leave Request	/GBHCM/LEAVEREQUEST
HCM_PS_MON	My Paystubs	SRA006_SRV
HCM_TS_CRE	My Timesheet	SRA002_TIMESHEET_SRV
CA_ALL_APV	My Approvals	/IWPGW/TASKPROCESSING

Table A.6 Available OData and SAPUI5 Services for SAP Fiori Apps

Role Name	Description	Single Roles Included
SAP_EMPLOYEE_ESS_UI5_1	Employee Self-Service composite role, consisting of employee-specific lanes	▸ SAP_EMPLOYEE_ESS_XX_UI5_1 ▸ SAP_EMPLOYEE_OTH_ESS_WDA_1 ▸ SAP_EMPLOYEE_OTH_ESS_WDA_2 ▸ SAP_HR_HAP_PMG_EMPLOYEE_SR ▸ SAP_HR_HAP_PMP_EMPLOYEE_SR
SAP_MANAGER_MSS_CR_UI5_1	PFCG role for the Manager	▸ SAP_ASR_MANAGER ▸ SAP_FI_TV_WEB_APPROVER_2 ▸ SAP_HR_CPS_DET_PLAN_L_SR_NWBC ▸ SAP_HR_LSO_HR-MANAGER ▸ SAP_HR_LSO_MANAGER ▸ SAP_MANAGER_MSS_OTH_NWBC ▸ SAP_MANAGER_MSS_SR_ANA_1 ▸ SAP_MANAGER_MSS_SR_NWBC_3 ▸ SAP_MANAGER_MSS_SR_UI5_1 ▸ SAP_RCF_MANAGER ▸ SAP_SR_TMC_MANAGER_6 ▸ SAP_TIME_MGR_XX_ESS_WDA_1

Table A.7 Available Standard Composite SAP Roles within Included Standard Single SAP Roles

Role Name	Description	Single Roles Included
SAP_NBPR_ESS_WDA_3_S	Employee Self-Service composite role (Web Dynpro for ABAP)	▸ SAP_NBPR_ASR_ESS_SR_HCM_CI_3-S ▸ SAP_NBPR_FI_TV_WEB_ESS_TRA_2-S ▸ SAP_NBPR_HR_HAP_PMG_ESS_SR-S ▸ SAP_NBPR_HR_HAP_PMP_ESS_SR-S ▸ SAP_NBPR_OTH_ESS_WDA_1-S ▸ SAP_NBPR_OTH_ESS_WDA_2-S ▸ SAP_NBPR_OTH_ESS_WDA_3-S ▸ SAP_NBPR_SR_TMC_ESS_6-S ▸ SAP_NBPR_XX_ESS_WDA_3-S
SAP_NBPR_MSS_NWBC_3_M	Manager Self-Service composite role (Web Dynpro for ABAP)	▸ SAP_NBPR_ASR_MSS-M ▸ SAP_NBPR_FI_TV_WEB_APPR_2-M ▸ SAP_NBPR_HR_CPS_DP_L_SR_NWBC-M ▸ SAP_NBPR_HR_LSO_HR-MANAGER-M ▸ SAP_NBPR_HR_LSO_MANAGER-M ▸ SAP_NBPR_MSS_OTH_NWBC-M ▸ SAP_NBPR_MSS_SR_NWBC_3-M ▸ SAP_NBPR_RCF_MSS-M ▸ SAP_NBPR_SR_TMC_MSS_6-M ▸ SAP_NBPR_TM_XX_ESS_WDA_1-M
SAP_PAO_HRPROFES-SIONAL_3	HR Professional composite role	▸ SAP_PAO_SR_HRLANE_LPD ▸ SAP_PAO_SR_HRLANE_ORGFAV ▸ SAP_PAO_SR_HRLANE_PROCESSES ▸ SAP_PAO_SR_HRLANE_SEARCH ▸ SAP_PAO_SR_HRLANE_SWFD ▸ SAP_PAO_SR_HRLANE_TASKS ▸ SAP_PAO_SR_HRPROF_EMPHIRE ▸ SAP_PAO_SR_HRPROF_EMPMAINT ▸ SAP_PAO_SR_HRPROF_SPBPERS ▸ SAP_PAO_SR_HRPROF_ORGUNIT ▸ SAP_PAO_SR_HRPROF_POSITION

Table A.7 Available Standard Composite SAP Roles within Included Standard Single SAP Roles (Cont.)

Vendor	Application(s)	Description
SAP	SAP Employee Lookup	Search a directory of coworkers and their organizational details.
SAP	SAP Timesheet and SAP Timesheet Lite	Allows employees to create, review, submit, and manage time entries.
SAP	SAP Leave Request and SAP Leave Request Lite	Give employees a quick and easy way to create and review leave requests on the go.
SAP	SAP Learning Assistant	Makes on-demand, online training available anytime and anywhere so that workers can access required classes to address compliance and job requirements.

Table A.8 SAP Mobile Platform Apps for ESS On-Premise or in the Cloud

Vendor	Application(s)	Description
SAP	SAP Manager Insight	Manage your people more effectively with secure iPad access to employee profiles and KPI reports—including headcount, diversity, and talent by location.
SAP	SAP HR Approvals	View and respond to leave requests and timesheet entries. Check for incomplete timesheets, overbooking, and overlapping leave requests. Review team calendars and employees' time account balances to evaluate requests.
SAP	SAP Interview Assistant	Display open requisitions, candidates, applications, and résumés or CVs, review candidates, schedule interviews, and evaluate candidates before, during, and after interviews.
EPI-USE	Skill Scanner	Provides a line manager with a single view of his or her employee's mandatory certifications and the compliance thereof.
sovanta	iPeople	Provides leadership-relevant HR information and KPIs for better decision making.
Worklogix	Manager Desktop	Provides managers with the ability to view, process, and approve eForms (personnel change requests).

Table A.9 SAP Mobile Platform Apps for MSS On-Premise or in the Cloud

B   The Authors

Jeremy Masters is an author, speaker, and SAP ERP HCM subject matter expert. He is also the co-founder and managing partner of Worklogix, which provides SAP ERP HCM professional services and software solutions to Fortune-500 companies. Mr. Masters has been an SAP ERP HCM practitioner for over 16 years, and spent his early years with Pricewaterhouse, PwC Consulting, and IBM Global Business Services. He has been involved in over 40 projects, many of them global in scope. Mr. Masters enjoys helping clients with architecting and implementing HR self-service and talent management solutions. Besides implementing HR Renewal and the new Employee and Manager Self-Services, he has worked with much of the latest talent management functionality, including Performance Management, Compensation Management, Succession Planning, and E-Recruiting.

You can reach him via email at *jmasters@worklogix.com*, on Twitter *@jeremymasters*, and on his website at *www.jeremymasters.com*.

Brandon Toombs is an independent consultant who has helped clients achieve results using SAP ERP HCM and SuccessFactors technology for over 15 years. He has served projects in every conceivable role: functional, technical, and project management. Mr. Toombs is a frequent speaker at SAP/SuccessFactors conferences and is also a founding member of the popular SAP HCM Insight Podcasts. He began his career as a CPA with Arthur Andersen before transitioning into HR technology while at PricewaterhouseCoopers.

You can reach him via email at *btoombs@toombsconsulting.com* or on Twitter *@brandontoombs*.

Kris Bland is a ramp-up coach for HR Renewal 1.0 (Phase II), EHP 6 (Phase II), and SAP ERP 6.0 EHP 5 upgrade and MSS 1.0 Add-on. She has completed SAP internal testing for EHP 6 ESS enhancements and was the CUV lead for HR Renewal 1.0. Ms. Bland's specialties include ESS, MSS, and Portals configuration with all enhancement packs. Part of the SAP internal test team for EHP 5 and EHP 6, she has completed internal acceptance testing for MSS Add-On 1.0 and validation testing of MSS Add-On 1.0 and HR Renewal 1.0.

Justin Morgalis has been helping clients implement SAP ERP HCM self-services since 2007. He comes from a consulting and development background, so he understands both the technical and functional aspects of SAP ERP HCM and can communicate them clearly to any audience. In the past three years, he has focused almost exclusively on projects with SAP ERP HCM Processes and Forms components, leading teams of both functional and technical resources to successful implementations. He earned his degree in psychology from the Georgia Institute of Technology in Atlanta, Georgia, where he lives with his wife and two sons.

Index

- ▶ Learn about every configuration step and find all relevant transactions easily

- ▶ Explore options for customizing ESS and MSS to meet specific business needs

- ▶ Benefit from hands-on tips and expert advice

Martin Gillet

Configuring and Customizing Employee and Manager Self-Services in SAP ERP HCM

With this detailed guide, you'll find all of the information you need for customizing Employee Self-Services, Manager Self-Services, and the Shared Services Center. You'll learn everything about the standard "out of the box" configuration, from the early release with ITS services to the latest Web Dynpro offering in ERP 6.0—and then you'll be ready to set up and customize these services to meet your specific business needs.

580 pages, 2011, $69.95/€69.95
ISBN 978-1-59229-356-8
www.sap-press.com/2430

Galileo Press

► Learn how to set up an effective forms workflow with HCM Processes and Forms

► Master cutting-edge form functionality and configuration with details on FPM non-Adobe forms

► Streamline your most common organizational data processes into one discrete process for optimal HR workflows

Justin Morgalis, Brandon Toombs

SAP ERP HCM Processes and Forms

Cut through the HR red tape with this comprehensive guide to customizing and implementing ERP HCM P&F. Streamline your most common organizational data processes into one discrete process for optimal HR workflows. Configure and optimize HCM P&F with ease through real-world examples, step-by-step instructions and tips and tricks. This title will teach you to maximize the powerful combination of web based forms, online document storage, and support structural based decision making. Perfect for busy consultants, managers and super users, this is an end-to-end solution that includes configuration steps, overall business scenarios, and the dos and donts of mapping business processes.

344 pages, 2013, $84.95/€69.95
ISBN 978-1-59229-425-1
www.sap-press.com/3124

- ▶ SuccessFactors: what it is, how it works, and what it can do for you

- ▶ Explore the SuccessFactors suite for your entire HR workflow

- ▶ Simplify business processes in Employee Central and other SuccessFactors modules

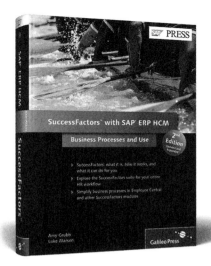

Amy Grubb, Luke Marson

SuccessFactors with SAP ERP HCM

Business Processes and Use

Looking to better your HR workflow? Discover the potential of SuccessFactors, SAP's HR cloud solution, with this introductory guide. Updated and revised, this edition covers new integration packages, additional SAP HANA Cloud Platform information, details on the Metadata Framework, and a look into the new Job Profile Builder. Discover what SucessFactors is, how it works, and what it can do for you.

644 pages, 2nd edition, 2015, $69.95/€69.95
ISBN 978-1-4932-1173-9
www.sap-press.com/3702

▶ Learn how the Cross-Application Time Sheet integrates with other SAP components

▶ Explore manager and end-user steps for time entry, release, and approval

▶ Get the information you need to configure and enhance CATS functionality

Manuel Gallardo, Martin Gillet

SAP CATS

Configuration, Use, and Processes

Whether you're looking to get data set up in your CATS system, better manage employees' activities, or add enhanced functionality, this is the book you need. Explore the different core functions of CATS, such as approval and transfer processes. Then find what you need to make SAP CATS specific to different business requirements and scenarios, such as integration with other SAP components.

464 pages, 2015, $79.95/€79.95
ISBN 978-1-59229-978-2
www.sap-press.com/3568

► Little-known tips and tricks from the SAP experts

► Save time and increase productivity with these easy-to-use tips and workarounds!

Ajay Jain Bhutoria, Cameron Lewis

100 Things You Should Know About

HR Management with SAP

Have you ever spent days trying to figure out how to generate a personnel report in SAP ERP HCM only to find out you just needed to click a few buttons. If so, you'll be delighted with this book—it unlocks the secrets of SAP ERP HCM. It provides users and super-users with 100 tips and workarounds you can use to increase productivity, save time, and improve the overall ease-of-use of SAP ERP HCM. The tips have been carefully selected to provide a collection of the best, most useful, and rarest information.

298 pages, 2011, $49.95/€49.95
ISBN 978-1-59229-361-2
www.sap-press.com/2437

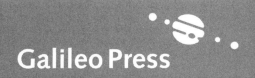

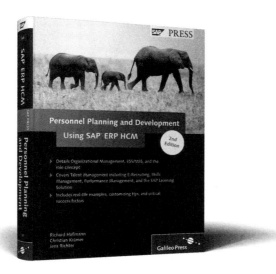

▶ Strategy, conception, and implementation made easy

▶ With numerous real-world examples, customization tips and critical success factors

▶ 2nd, updated and completely revised edition for SAP ERP 6.0

Haßmann, Krämer, Richter

Personnel Planning and Development Using SAP ERP HCM

Get a detailed overview of the SAP ERP HCM functions for personnel planning and development processes. Based on real-world technical requirements, you'll be introduced to strategies, concepts, and mapping of processes in HCM systems. Everything, from organizational management to skill management and development planning to e-recruiting and personnel cost planning is covered. And, you'll find valuable ideas for structuring your own processes efficiently, and learn how to implement, optimize, and customize SAP ERP HCM effectively. Numerous real-life examples and critical success factors are used throughout. This edition for SAP ERP 6.0 also includes coverage of Portal and BW.

564 pages, 2nd edition, 2010, $69.95/€69.95
ISBN 978-1-59229-187-8
www.sap-press.com/1681